ON PARTIES:
Essays Honoring Austin Ranney

ON PARTIES:
Essays Honoring Austin Ranney

Edited by
Nelson W. Polsby and
Raymond E. Wolfinger

with an introduction by
Douglas Rae

Institute of Governmental Studies Press
University of California, Berkeley
1999

Library of Congress Cataloging-in-Publication Data

On parties : essays honoring Austin Ranney / edited by Nelson W. Polsby and
Raymond Wolfinger : with an introduction by Douglas Rae.
       p. cm.
       Includes bibliographical references and index.
       ISBN 0-87772-388-5
       1. Political parties—United States. I. Polsby, Nelson W.   II.
    Wolfinger, Raymond E.
JK2261.058 1999
324.273—DC21   99-22656
                                           CIP

CONTENTS

FOREWORD

A half century ago Austin Ranney, freshly minted Ph.D. in hand from Yale, began his postdoctoral teaching career at the University of Illinois and published his doctoral dissertation, *The Doctrine of Responsible Party Government* (Champaign, Illinois: University of Illinois Press, 1948). He had been an instructor at Yale while he was a graduate student and also did some pick-up teaching at Wesleyan where he made the acquaintance of E. E. Schattschneider, the leading student of parties in the generation senior to his. In the ensuing 50 years, Ranney has contributed in a great many ways to the development of the professional study of politics, as managing editor and book review editor of the *American Political Science Review*, as president of the American Political Science Association, as a loyal member of three first-class political science departments (Illinois, Wisconsin, California) and a notably successful chairman at Berkeley, and as a cheerful, resourceful presence nearly everywhere two or more political scientists have gathered. His work has time and again provided inspiration to students and colleagues, especially in the study of political parties where his work has embraced theory and practice, field work and contemplation, and contributions to issues of measurement and to issues of institutional design and public policy.

A group of his friends and colleagues, to whom Ranney has been the kindliest of mentors, thought that in honor of his exemplary contributions to the discipline and the profession of political science it would be appropriate to gather a few essays surveying aspects of the field, 50 years on, and it seemed natural to pick political parties as the theme closest to Austin's heart. What we did not fully anticipate was the enthusiasm with which so many scholars would greet the opportunity to contribute to this volume and to offer appreciation in a concrete way for Austin's benign and constructive influence. The editors believe we have assembled a bumper crop of papers that collectively go a long way toward defining the field of political parties as they are studied today.

In particular, we might note the increasing entanglement of American parties in the legal system, a trend that not all of our textbooks have yet fully assimilated. Three of our contributors, one of them author of a notable text, focus on this topic. Classic party functions such as recruitment to public office, voter mobilization, policy deliberation, and the coordination of government receive attention, as does the perennial issue of party decline. Taking Ranney's stimulating work on all these topics as our inspiration, we asked contributors to reflect on recent trends in the development of party institutions and practices.

Assembling this book was a labor of love. In particular we thank Douglas Rae, one of Austin's most eminent students, for his encouragement of the project early on, and Thaddeus Kousser and Kathryn Pearson for assistance in putting the pieces together as they flowed into the office. Many of Austin's friends and neighbors, in the U.S. and abroad, who in the end did not write for this volume wanted to do so and to be affectionately remembered to him. Indeed this might easily have been a very long book. It is, however, perhaps long enough to give a reader a good overview of contemporary issues that animate current scholarly thinking about political parties.

—Nelson W. Polsby

Introduction

AUSTIN RANNEY AS MENTOR:
GETTING BEYOND THE TWO CULTURES IN 1963

I spent the winter of 1962-63 largely in North Hall near the crest of Bascom Hill, itself more or less the peak of Wisconsin's windswept Madison campus. Hideously cold by October outside, the place was ablaze indoors with something known then as the "behavioral revolution," an insurrection far better loved in some parts of the building than in others. This was on its face a dispute about the importation of empirical methods from nearby disciplines like statistics, econometrics, and social psychology—methods in which a Midwestern boy could see some good and little obvious harm.

Mind you, it wasn't as if the denizens of North Hall were absorbing the mathematics of rocket science, or putting them very rapidly into effect. Card sorters were to be seen and used only in the university's central computing lab, and every self-respecting "behaviorist" on the faculty boasted a few boxes of their output, often propped awkwardly on a shelf designed for books. The fanciest piece of equipment actually within the walls of North Hall was something known as a "rotary calculator." It weighed perhaps 40 pounds. You pushed or pulled levers up and down to enter each number, one lever for each digit, picked an operation (+, -, x, /) and then turned a big crank on the side of the thing so as to rotate the clanking metal disks within. If all went well, out came the result on the number-bearing dials at the top—so long as it didn't require anything so complex as a square root, which was beyond the contraption's capacity.

1

The larger world was of course in the midst of similar struggles and transformations under different labels. Western economies were coming under the command of professional corporate management as never before, some of it inspired by "scientific management" trained in imitation of engineering efficiency;[1] eastern economies labored under the weight of "scientific" socialism and the impossible complexities of centralized production planning. University disciplines dealing with the softest materials of all—psychology, sociology—found themselves increasingly subjected to the rigors of quantitative research. C. P. Snow's 1959 lecture titled "The Two Cultures," captured the spirit of the time for many of us, portraying literary intellectuals pitted against hard scientists as two mutually antagonistic tribes comprehending one another only with the greatest pain and difficulty. Thus, for example, Snow writes of having:

> . . . been present at gatherings of people who, by the standards of the traditional culture, are thought highly educated and who have with considerable gusto been expressing their incredulity at the illiteracy of scientists. Once or twice I have been provoked and have asked the company how many of them could describe the Second Law of Thermodynamics. The response was cold: it was also negative. Yet I was asking something which is the scientific equivalent of: *Have you read a work of Shakespeare's?*[2]

Local differences of opinion in political science at North Hall in 1963 were almost uniformly better humored than the conversation Snow recounts, but seldom much more enlightening. On the one side stood the enduring oppositions that place politics near the center of any advanced civilization: the threats of violence, coercion, tribalism, and poverty set against the promises of order, liberty, democracy, and prosperity. The serious work of political discourse was about the best achievable solution to very complex human problems, linking a subtle commitment to values

---

[1]See, for instance, Alfred Chandler, *Scale & Scope: The Dynamic of Industrial Capitalism* (Cambridge: Harvard University Press, 1959). See also Robert Kanigel, *The One Best Way* (New York: Viking, 1997).

[2]C. P. Snow, the Rede Lecture at Cambridge University, "The Two Cultures" (1959) as reprinted in *The Two Cultures* with an introduction by Stefan Collini (Cambridge: Cambridge University Press, 1993), 14.

with a complex calculus about ends and means. On the other side stood a menu of methodological oppositions. What was called "institutionalism" embraced textual exegesis, institutional exposition, case law, narrative history and the soft tools of premodernist humanism. "Behaviorism" (a.k.a. "behavioralism") embraced systematic quantification, factor analysis, causal modeling, and regression. The issue, it seemed, was not *whether* to admit the utility of these more science-like methods: No sane person could doubt the power of quantitative reason, so long as it was usefully related to the issues that brought us together in the study of politics. It was, in retrospect, hard to see how or why one would elect to chose between the two approaches. Yet, as I recall 1962-63, the Madison faculty were largely divided between: (1) people doing political research by textual and institutional methods with a little sneer toward empirical methods, and (2) people applying quantitative methods to whatever empirical questions they could answer, but failing too often to advance understanding of politics. Failures of the latter type were caused not by the use of good empirical tools, but by letting those tools determine the questions being asked. It was almost enough to make me imagine that even law school could be more interesting.

Austin Ranney arrived at North Hall in 1963, awarded a corner office facing Bascom Plaza (as I imagined) in recognition of his distinction. Whatever may have explained the quality of his office, North Hall was changed beyond recognition by his coming. Here, to begin with, was a balding 43-year-old professor *looking* something like a younger brother of C. P. Snow. Moreover, the new man's mastery of the English language was no less measured or precise than Snow's. I remember a discussion in which Austin used the terms "accurate" and "precise" in a way that suggested he thought they were logically independent of one another: one could achieve either without even coming close to the other. I would like to believe I repressed my objection without making an immediate fool of myself, but I may be mistaken in this. Here, more remarkably, was an intellectual who doubtless knew both the important consequence of the Second Law of Thermodynamics and the intricacies of Hamlet, yet felt very little compulsion to show off either. I don't actually remember Austin reciting any physics, but I do remember him laying on entertaining and appropriate "squibs" from Shakespeare ("squibs" was Austin's actual term, as I recall).

Here was a scholar whose work was wholly loyal to the big questions of politics, the "eternal verities" as he called them with a twinkle of irony. He and Willmoore Kendall began their justly famed 1956 text by asking "Is the American party system *a valuable agency of democratic government?*"[3] This was at once a normative and an empirical question about the relationship between a complex idea and a still more complex set of practices and institutions, made real by the very much more complex interplay of decisions taken by thousands of players in the game of party politics over the decades. Here was a mind accomplished beyond ordinary standards in the analysis of a text, the unfolding of a narrative, the nuanced shaping of an idea. More than anyone else in that era, with the possible exception of V. O. Key, Austin understood the interface between ideas and empirics.

Ranney knew, for example, that one could never begin to evaluate the landscape of American party politics without the power of elementary data analysis. His table-making was brilliant and simple: decide what's worth counting, count it, find the right cut points, create a table that speaks to the issue in hand. The text with Kendall quickly became a model for us all in this respect. He also knew how to use diagrams of the sorts that did not come naturally to old-time political science in illuminating old-time political ideas. One instance concerned the notion of "limited majority rule." He drew a circle to represent all the things a government could imaginably do, then sliced off a chord within it to represent things a bare majority could not do under this doctrine.[4] Elegant, simple, and exactly on point.

Writing a dissertation under Austin's direction was a privilege, for me and for others represented in this volume. He would typically supply a surgical dissection of the chapter in question in advance of the meeting. After brief pleasantries, sometimes having to do with his beloved Packers, one was expected to arrive ready to respond to his inquiries. His mark-up—composed of tiny lettering, rounded with great precision so that every figure was distinct from those before and after it—left little room for doubt about his intent. I remember his particular intolerance for my all too numerous "weasel words"—words that allowed a young author to have it both ways at the expense of his reader's understanding (e.g., "usually," "tend," "trend," and "all else equal"). He was likewise impatient with localist and

---

[3]*Democracy & the American Party System* (New York: Harcourt, Brace & Co., 1956), 1.

[4]This appears in Ranney & Kendall, 33. I think I recall it from live action in the North Hall seminar room.

antiquarian embellishment, things falling under his "How's by us in Wisconsin" heading. After a while, one tried to anticipate his objections, but it was perhaps better to blunder into them in order to gain his insight about a way around or through the problem. He was never a dogmatist, since he always posed queries requiring answers he did not propose to supply. What he did insist upon invariably was that the response be loyal to the questions that drove an investigation. I can remember more than once wandering off on some hopeless speculation, only to be brought up short by Austin's conspicuous examination of the face of his watch.

What made—and to this day makes—Austin Ranney a master-scholar is his sure sense for the priority of question over hypothesis and hypothesis over datum. Not just any question, and not just any hypothesis. He has always and invariably insisted on questions that illuminate the big oppositions, the "hows" and "whys" of politics in its largest sense. Think of the corpus stretching from his Yale dissertation on responsible party government, through his work on the McGovern-Fraser Commission, across his work on the recruitment of British MPs, or his more recent work on press and media. Loyalty to the big question, and a clear sense of its governing relationship to all else, is the constant. Method is the variable, chosen with a craftsman's judgment of the tool best fitted to the chore in hand. I suspect that he has always taken some private pleasure in his own skills in marshalling evidence, even perhaps in a trick of inference here or there. But I am equally sure that he has never allowed even the most brilliant stroke of method to blind his gaze in a way that obscures the anchoring issue under investigation. His influence on the contributors to this volume in this respect is apparent. Whether by imitation or indoctrination at Ranney's hand, we are all methodological eclectics, ready to use whatever scrap of information will advance an inquiry into politics in its largest sense.

—Douglas Rae
Richard Ely Professor of Management and Political Science
Yale University

I. Parties in American Law

CHAPTER 1

Constitutional Law for Political Parties

Jack W. Peltason
University of California, Irvine

It is hard to believe the Founding Fathers thought they could create a system of governance in which political parties—factions as they called them—would have a limited or no role. They had experienced parties in the colonies and were fully aware of them in England. They did not ignore the subject entirely. James Madison, who had as much to do with the writing of the Constitution as anyone, penned what remains the most important treatise on political parties (political parties were but one form of factions). In *Federalist* No. 10 he promoted the Constitution for its cure for the "violence of factions" but he did not suggest they had been abolished. On the contrary as he wrote, "Liberty is to faction what air is to fire" and the latent causes of faction are . . . sown in the nature of man."

Yet the founders, practical politicians all, made no direct provision in the Constitution for the role of parties either in the operation of the national government or in the regulation of parties among the enumerated powers granted to Congress. In fact there is no mention of political parties in the original Constitution or in its subsequent amendments.

The constitutional law of political parties has developed, as we say in the textbooks, primarily as a result of custom and usage. Nonetheless the Supreme Court, most especially since World War II, has been called on to umpire a variety of disputes about these "unwritten constitutional features." The Court has had to develop this constitutional law and to elaborate on the constitutional role of political parties without any textual guidance from the Constitution itself. In fact the only hint in the entire Constitution that political parties exist is in the Twenty-Fourth Amendment that stipulates that the right of citizens of the United States to vote in any *primary* or other election for president or vice president, for electors for president or vice president, or for senator or representative in Congress, "shall not be denied or abridged by the United States or any State by reason of failure to pay any poll tax or other tax."

Among the enduring issues that underlie much of the constitutional law of political parties is to determine their constitutional status. Since they are not mentioned in the Constitution for any special status, are they merely private associations no different from other private associations such as labor unions, the chamber of commerce, or the Sierra Club and thus entitled to no more or no less protection than these associations? Or because of their critical role in the holding of elections, in selecting candidates, in running campaigns and in the operation of the government, are parties quasi-public organizations entitled to special status? If so, does that special status give them more protection from governmental regulation or does it legitimate state regulation of parties in ways that would be inappropriate for other private associations? Are parties, as the framers seem to believe, dangerous institutions, a belief also prompted by populist concerns that parties are instruments used by elites to dominate government that may legitimately be regulated to insure that they do not corrupt the democratic process? What about our two-party system? Is protection for such a system a legitimate governmental goal?

The Court, through numerous decisions, has established that political parties are entitled to considerable constitutional protection. The Court has shown even more concern for the right of individuals "to associate with the political party of one's choice" and "to associate with others for the common advancement of political beliefs and ideas."[1] The Supreme Court has pointed out that although states have broad powers to regulate elections and to provide for access to ballots, if a state law "burdens the rights of political parties and their members, it can survive constitutional scrutiny only if the State shows that the law advances a compelling state interest."[2] The compelling state interest test, although hard to define, nonetheless places the burden on governments to make the case for restricting the way parties go about their business. However, the Court has substantially modified the compelling interest test by limiting its application to

---

[1]Kusper v. Pointikes, 414 U.S. 51 (1973).
[2]Eu v. San Francisco Democratic Comm., 489 U.S. 214 (1989).

"regulations imposing severe burdens," whereas "lesser burdens . . . trigger less exacting review."[3]

A comprehensive coverage of the Supreme Court decisions relating to political parties would take a book. This essay, most appropriately in recognition of the contributions of one of our great scholars of party government both in the United states and the United Kingdom, focuses on only some of the Supreme Court decisions of the last several decades as they have dealt with *some* aspects of national and state regulation of political parties. Other questions such as partisan reapportionment and a comprehensive discussion of party finance have to be left to other times and places. The constitutional law relating to party primaries is the focus of Leon Epstein's companion essay.

NATIONAL PARTIES:
PRESIDENTIAL ELECTORS AS PARTY AGENTS

American parties have been notoriously unable to impose any kind of discipline upon those who speak in their name. The one conspicuous exception relates to the electoral college where throughout two centuries electors have acted as party-instructed delegates.

The framers delegated to the state legislatures the power to provide for the selection of presidential and vice presidential electors. During the early decades of the Republic, the states chose electors in a variety of ways: by the legislature itself in joint ballot, by the legislature through concurrent vote of the two houses, on a district basis, partly by the legislature and partly by the voters, and by the legislature from a list of candidates.[4]

However electors are chosen, the framers clearly intended for them to be free of any party discipline and to be able to exercise their own judgments. Yet in the very first contested election, that of 1796, most electors were already informally pledged to party candidates. In the 50 presidential elections since then, there have been only a handful of faithless electors and none ever threatened to upset the outcome of any election. By and large parties have imposed this discipline by taking care to select electors who would not be inclined to ignore their pledge. Only about half

---

[3]Timmons v. Twin Cities Area New Party, 137 L Ed 2d 589 (1997).
[4]McPherson v. Blacker, 146 U.S. 1 (1892).

of the states make any attempt legally to bind electors and even fewer impose any penalty upon those who ignore party discipline.

By the 1800 elections it was clear that the framers' failure to anticipate that presidential electors would be political party agents made unworkable the procedures for choosing the president and vice president. The Twelfth Amendment was necessary to adjust for party-instructed electors. It did so by calling on electors to cast separate ballots for president and vice president. The amendment itself did nothing, however, to limit electors' freedom to vote for anybody they wish other than to insist that at least one of the persons be from a state other than their own.

It was not until 1952 that the Supreme Court decided whether or not a political party could try to constrain its electors' freedom of choice. Electors chosen on the Democratic slate in the 1948 Alabama elections instead of voting for the candidates nominated by the Democratic National Convention—Harry Truman and Alben Barkley—voted for the States Rights Candidates, Strom Thurmond and Fielding Wright. In 1952, in order to foreclose a repetition of similar events, Alabama's Democratic Executive Committee, acting under general authority granted by Alabama laws, imposed a rule that no one could be certified as a candidate for presidential elector who had not pledged to support the nominees of the Democratic national convention.

The Alabama Supreme Court, upon petition of Edmund Blair, issued a writ of mandamus to the secretary of state to compel him to certify Blair as a Democratic candidate for elector. Blair had refused to take an oath to vote for the candidates of the national convention on the grounds that no state could restrict the freedom of a federal elector granted to such electors by the Twelfth Amendment. Said the Alabama Court;

> We appreciate the argument that from time immemorial, the electors selected to vote in the college have voted in accordance with the wishes of the party to which they belong. But in doing so, the effective compulsion has been party loyalty. But the Twelfth Amendment does not make it so. The nominees of the party for president and vice president may have become disqualified or peculiarly offensive not only to the electors but their constituents also. They should be free to vote for another, as contemplated by the Twelfth Amendment.[5]

---

[5]Ray v. Blair, 343 U.S. 214 (1952).

If one takes the "orginalist" line, the Alabama Supreme Court had the best argument. Nonetheless, the United States Supreme Court reversed the decision of the Alabama Supreme Court. Note the Supreme Court did not decide that a state or a political party could compel electors to comply with their pledge or punish those who fail to do so. Rather, speaking through Justice Stanley Reed, the Court contended that the Twelfth Amendment does not prevent electors from pledging themselves to the candidates of particular parties and from allowing states to authorize political parties to refuse to certify as candidates of their party persons who refused to take such a pledge. Justice Reed rejected as "impossible to accept" the suggestion that in the first elections under the Constitution that candidates for electors—contemporaries of the founders—"would have hesitated, because of constitutional limitation, to pledge themselves to support party nominees in the event of their election for electors." On the contrary, the Court endorsed, "the long-continued practical interpretation of the constitutional propriety of an implied or oral pledge."

Justice Robert H. Jackson, joined by Justice William O. Douglas, dissented. Citing *Federalist* No. 68 he concluded, "the Framers intended for electors to be free agents, to exercise their independent and nonpartisan judgment and that no state should be allowed to control how electors perform their federal duty." Jackson admitted Alabama's law did no more than to make legal what has become a constitutional custom, but although custom and usage may "impart changed content to constitutional generalities," such as "due process of law," or "equal protection," or "commerce among the states," a political practice, "which has its origin in custom must rely upon custom for its sanctions."

Justices Jackson and Douglas were unwilling "to seek an enhancement of national party influence." Justice Jackson specifically stated that although he would not object to the demise of the electoral college system, he did object to the Court's "sanctioning a new instrument that centralizes party control and secures the central management in dominance of the local vote." *Ray v. Blair* was a victory for those who favor a strong party system and for those who would allow custom and usage to override original intent. It is also another illustration of the Supreme Court's general bias in favor of supporting the national party as against state or local party action. Although in this case the Court was sustaining a state law, it was a state law reinforcing the control of the national party.

THE NATIONAL CONVENTION VERSUS
STATE LEGISLATURES AND STATE PARTIES

The Supreme Court has been consistently "pro national party convention." It has invariably upheld the right of a political party to determine how it will operate its national conventions including how to select delegates despite conflicting state laws or state party practices. The demise of the national convention as the site where the party really chooses its presidential candidates makes these decisions of less significance. These rulings do, however, reflect the Court's general bias in favor of national parties over state parties and state laws, although it could be that this bias reflects a "liberal court's" hostility toward attempts by conservatives to use state laws to affect presidential nominations.

The leading case, *Cousins v. Wigoda,* stemmed from the 1972 Democratic Convention's Credential Committee's refusal to seat delegates chosen by the Cook County Democratic Organization because of lack of compliance with guidelines calling for delegations consisting of women, minorities, and young people, and because of the Cook County organization's use of slate-making practices. Delegates denied seating sought by a variety of legal maneuvers to have the Illinois and federal courts hold that state law rather than the rules of the national convention should determine who were the appropriate delegates to the convention.

The guidelines in dispute were the product of the 1968 Democratic Convention's response to the pressures of the McCarthy delegates to create a Reform Commission on Delegate Selection. This commission, which came to be known as the McGovern-Fraser Commission, on which Austin Ranney served, among other things, adopted rules calling for abolition of the unit rule, prohibited slate making, and called for delegations from each state reflecting a proportional representation of women, minorities, and young people. These requirements came in direct conflict with many state laws and state party practices.

In a sweeping holding, the Court, speaking through Justice William J. Brennan declared, "In the selection of candidates for national office a national party convention serves the pervasive national interest, which is paramount to any interest of a state in protecting the integrity its electoral process."[6] The Court then modified this declaration, by noting that it did not decide whether the decision of a national political party about delegate selection constitutes state or national governmental action, whether national political parties are subject to the principles of the reapportionment decisions or other constitutional restraints on their methods of delegate selection and allocation, or whether national political parties and their nominating conventions are subject to regulation by, or only by Congress. Nonetheless the language of the Court's decision gave considerable latitude to national conventions in structuring party governance.

The Court followed *Cousins v. Wigoda* eight years later when it sustained the 1980 Democratic National Convention's rule that delegates had to affiliate publicly with the Democratic party. This rule, the National Democrats insisted, took precedence over Wisconsin's law requiring delegates, who themselves were chosen in party caucuses and had openly affiliated with the Democratic party, to pledge they would support the winning presidential candidate in their district of a preceding open presidential preference primary in which there was no assurance that all those who voted were Democrats.[7] The national Democrats argued that they had a constitutionally protected right not to be compelled to seat delegations chosen in violation of party rules.

Justice Potter Stewart speaking for Chief Justice Warren Burger, and Justices William Brennan, Byron R. White, Thurgood Marshall, and John Paul Stevens, reaffirmed that a political party's constitutionally protected right of political association includes the right to exclude from its membership persons who do not share the beliefs of or indicate their willingness to support the party and its candidates. To Justice Potter Stewart the issues were simple: "A political party's choice among the various ways of determining the makeup of a State's delegation to the party's national convention is protected by the Constitution."[8]

---

[6]Cousins v. Wigoda, 419 U.S. 477 (1975).

[7]This rule was based on a study of David Adamany, which found that crossover voters comprised from 26 percent to 34 percent of the primary voters in the Democratic primaries and that these voters differed significantly from those who called themselves Democrats.

[8]Democratic Party of U.S. v. Wisconsin, 450 U.S. 107 (1981).

Justice Lewis F. Powell in a dissent joined by Justice Harry A. Blackmun and William H. Rehnquist conceded that the nomination of a candidate for president is a principal function of a national political party and that Wisconsin had attempted to regulate the terms on which individuals can become a member of the party. But adopting Austin Ranney's description of major political parties as being "characterized by a fluidity and overlap of philosophy and membership," he concluded that they suffer little damage by being forced to admit to their membership "persons who might be less than one hundred percent committed to them."

Justice Lewis F. Powell suggested that if a national major party "were an organization with a particular ideological orientation or political mission" then perhaps he would favor a different result. "In such a case, the state law might well open the organization to participation by persons with incompatible beliefs and interfere with the association rights of its founders." If however, as Justice Powell further elaborated in a footnote, a national party decided that it no longer wished to be a nonideological party, "it would call into question the institutional status achieved by the two major parties in state and federal law." He did not elaborate what the consequences would be, but hinted that an ideologically cohesive major party might be entitled to great constitutional freedom to exclude from its membership persons for ideological reasons. On the other hand, such a party could lose its special status as a major party with all the privileges that flow from that status. It would also seem to follow according to Justice Powell's reasoning that a minor party that took a strong ideological line, as say a Socialist party, or a White Supremacist party, or a Black Power party, might not be subject to governmental regulations affecting its membership nor might such a party even be constrained by the Fourteenth, Fifteenth, or Nineteenth Amendments.

STATE POLITICAL PARTIES

State Regulation of the Internal Party Affairs

States extensively regulate how parties operate and have an interest in ensuring that there are "fair and honest elections, that factionalism is minimized, and voters are presented with coherent and understandable choices."[9] Because the two major parties control the state legislatures, they have seldom needed the courts to protect their interests. In the few cases in which they have done so, the Court has generally sided with the party and struck down the offending state regulation.

The leading case is *Eu v. San Francisco Democratic Committee* in which the California Democratic, Republican, and Libertarian parties, joined by "prominent political scientists," and election officials not only from California but from around the nation, challenged provisions of the California Elections Code forbidding official governing bodies of political parties from endorsing or opposing candidates in primary elections and making it a misdemeanor for any candidate in a primary to claim official party endorsement. Other sections of the code limited party officials' terms of office, required that chairs of the party central committee be rotated between residents of northern and southern California, and required parties to establish official governing bodies at the county level.

The Court, speaking through Justice Thurgood Marshall, tacitly had little difficulty in holding these provisions unconstitutional. Thurgood Marshall pointed out that the constitutional right of association means not only that an individual has a right to associate with the political party of her choice, but also that the party as an organization has a right to identify the people who constitute that association and by implication those who do not. In a footnote he pointed to the example of Tom Metzger who won the Democratic party primary for the United States House of Representatives from the San Diego area in 1980 even though he was a Grand Dragon of the Ku Klux Klan and held views opposed to those of the Democratic party.

Marshall was not persuaded by California's contention that its ban on party endorsements was justified in order to promote stable government and protect voters from confusion and undue influence. California had not shown that its political system was any more stable as a result of this ban than it had been prior to its enactment nor did the state explain why California is so peculiar that it unlike any other state felt the need for such a ban. Nor did the fact that a party that makes primary endorsements risks intraparty friction seem to justify such a ban.

Nor was California any more successful in explaining why it should have the constitutional authority to tell political parties how to organize and

---

[9]Marchiro v. Chaney, 442 U.S. 191 (1979).

specify terms and requirements for party officials. Restrictions that limit a political party's discretion in how to organize itself, conduct its affairs, and select its leaders can only be justified by compelling state interests, and California failed to show that these regulations were necessary to ensure than an election is orderly and fair.

The issue was not unique to California. Other states, for example Utah, called for the chair and vice chairs of political parties to be of different gender. Following the *Eu* decision these provisions were no longer enforceable and in most instances were revised.

Despite these resounding words in defense of a party's freedom to endorse candidates in primaries, a year later the Court refused to hold facially unconstitutional Article II, #6 B of the California Constitution that provides that all judicial, school, county, and city offices shall be nonpartisan and prohibits political parties and party central committee from endorsing, supporting, or opposing candidates for these offices. The majority held that the issues as presented were not ripe for decision and did not present concrete cases. Justices Thurgood Marshall and Harry A. Blackmun would have held the California constitutional provision a violation of the First Amendment whereas Justice Byron White took the opposite view, at least so far as allowing California to exclude party designations from the ballot and exclude any party endorsements from being noted on the state-prepared and distributed voter pamphlet.

It is highly probable that the issue will be before the Court again. Unless there is a substantial change in views, when the Court gets to the merits it seems likely it will sustain prohibitions against party labels on ballots but declare unconstitutional prohibitions against party endorsement of candidates, even those running in a nonpartisan elections.

Raiding, the Sore Loser, and Protecting the Primary System

In *Rosario v Rockefeller* (1973)[10] the Court upheld a New York law that required voters to enroll in the party of their choice at least 30 days before the general election, that is eight months before a presidential and 11 months before a nonpresidential primary. Justice Potter Stewart speaking for the Court found New York's law a reasonable way to prevent primary

---

[10]Rosario v. Rockefeller, 410 U.S. 752 (1973).

raiding. Justice Lewis F. Powell, one of the justices who in other contexts has been one of the most eloquent champions of the party system, in a dissent joined by Justices William O. Douglas, William J. Brennan, and Thurgood Marshall indicated that he would have supported a shorter cutoff date, but found New York's law an unconstitutional infringement both on the right to vote and on the "closely related right to associate with the party of one's choice." Said Justice Lewis F. Powell, "Partisan political activities do not constantly engage the attention of large numbers of Americans, especially as party labels and loyalties tend to be less persuasive than issues and the qualities of individual candidates." The right, he argued, to cross over in registration from one major nonideological party to another such party deserves constitutional protection, especially if the motives are "quite unrelated to a desire to raid or distort a party's primary."[11]

Less than a year after sustaining New York's law the Court struck down an Illinois requirement that prohibited a person from voting in the primary of one political party if the voter had voted in the primary of any other party within the preceding 23 months. Whereas New York's rules only required one to meet a deadline, Illinois's rules precluded party switchers from voting in the next primary of another party. The Illinois rules thus kept voters from having a voice in the party of their most recent choice. Justice Harry A. Blackmun, who subsequently moved to the "antiparty" side on most issues, in this instance dissented along with Chief Justice Warren Burger, in behalf of allowing states to minimize party switching. He displayed considerable sympathy for Illinois's attempt to prevent organized party raiding, which could disrupt the orderly process of party primary balloting, most especially, "With respect to a State like Illinois, where party regimentation on an extensive scale is legendary."[12]

In 1974 in *Storer v. Brown* the Court supported the interests of party stability when California was allowed to prevent candidates from running as independents if they had been defeated in a party primary that year or if they had been affiliated with or voted in a party primary within the year." A state has a legitimate interest in preventing "splintered parties and unrestrained factionalism" especially with respect to elections wholly within its own boundaries. Justice White speaking for the Court attributed to

---

[11]*Ibid.*

[12]Kusper v. Pontikes, 414 U.S 51 (1973).

Californians a concern for avoiding party factionalism that is not so apparent to other observers of California's rather notorious antiparty history. He wrote, "A State need not take the course California has, but California apparently believes with the founding fathers that splintered parties and unrestrained factionalism may do significant damage to the practice of government."[13]

Promoting a Two-Party System

There is nothing in the formal constitutional structure that guarantees that we have a two rather than multiparty system. On the other hand, there is nothing in the Constitution that forbids legislatures dominated by the two parties from adopting structures that promote the two-party system such as the "first-past-the-post" single-member election district system for legislators and winner-take-all presidential elections.

The Court has acknowledged that Congress and the state legislatures have a legitimate interest in trying to maintain a two-party system. It has reaffirmed, over the dissent on this specific point of Justices John Paul Stevens and Ruth Bader Ginsburg, that the Constitution permits state legislatures "to decide that political stability is best served through a healthy two-party system."[14] It does not follow, however, "that the Democrats or the Republicans be one of those two parties."[15] As Justice Stevens has pointed out, "the particular interests of the major parties can[not] automatically be characterized as legitimate state interest."[16] Neither the Democratic nor Republican parties are entitled to constitutional protection to guarantee their existence.

Perhaps the major congressional act that singles out the two major parties for special protection is the Presidential Election Campaign Fund Act of 1971, part of the Federal Election Campaign Act (FECA). It, along with major amendments in 1974, provides considerably more funding for the major parties, and for their candidates than for minor or new parties.

---

[13]Storer v. Brown, 415 U.S. 737 (1974).
[14]Timmons v. Twin Cities Area New Party, 137 L Ed 2d 589 (1997).
[15]Anderson v. Celebrezze, 460 U.S. 780 (1983).
[16]*Ibid.*

The act provides funds to cover the costs for national nominating conventions for parties whose candidate for president in the most recent elections received 25 percent of the popular vote. Money is also provided to the candidates of major parties to be used in general presidential elections if candidates pledge not to take additional *direct* contributions or incur additional *direct* expenses. Federal funds are also available for candidates who seek presidential nominations via presidential primaries, including primaries of minor parties, if the candidate raises a threshold amount in each of 20 states.

Depending on the percentage of votes its presidential candidate received in the *last* presidential election, lesser amounts are provided for minor parties and their candidates. Candidates of new political parties receive partial funding *after* the election if the candidate receives five percent or more of the popular vote.[17] Minor and new party candidates may continue to receive private contributions.[18] The Supreme Court majority had no difficulty in sustaining the congressional distinction between major and minor party funding.[19] In addition to recognizing Congress's interest in not squandering public money by funding hopeless candidates, the Court accepted the legitimacy of the "important interest against providing artificial incentives to 'splintered parties and unrestrained factionalism'." The Court took judicial notice of the fact that throughout our history, except for the presidential elections of 1856 and 1860 when the Whigs were replaced by the Republicans, "no third party has posed a credible threat to the two major parties in presidential elections." Said the Court, "Congress was, of course, aware of this fact of American life, and thus was justified in

---

[17]John Anderson based on his 1980 showing qualified for 1984 funds if he had chosen to run again. In 1996 Perot's Reform party based on its showing in the 1992 elections qualified for $30 million of federal funding and as a result of its 1996 showing retained that status for the elections of 2000.

[18]See the Federal Election Commissions home page:http://www.fed.gov/pages/publfund.

[19]In FECA Congress defined a majority party as a party whose candidate for president in the most recent election received 25 percent or more of the popular vote, a minor party is a party whose candidate received at least five percent but less than 25 percent of the vote, and all other parties as those receiving less than five percent of the vote.

providing both major parties full funding and all other parties only a percentage of the major-party entitlement."[20]

Chief Justice Burger and Justice William H. Rehnquist dissented not only from the proposition that Congress could fund major party primary campaigns and provide financial support to a major party but not to minor party candidates, but also from the Court's failure to meet "head on the issue of whether public financial assistance to the private political activity of individual citizens and parties is a legitimate expenditure of public funds." "In my view," Chief Justice Burger wrote, "the inappropriateness of subsidizing, from general revenues, the actual political dialogue of the people—the process which begets the Government itself—is as basic to our national tradition as the separation of church and state also deriving from the First Amendment. Or the separation of civilian and military authority, neither of which is explicit in the Constitution both of which have developed through case-by-case adjudication in express provisions of the Constitution. . . . Delegate selection and the management of political conventions is a strictly private political matter, not the business of Government inspectors."

But even if Congress could finance party activity, Chief Justice Burger objected to what he charged was a law that "invidiously discriminates against minor parties." "The fact that there have been few drastic realignments in our basic two-party structure in 200 years is no constitutional justification for freezing the status quo of the present major parties at the expense of such future political moments. In short, I see grave risks in legislation enacted by incumbents of the major political parties which distinctly disadvantages minor parties or independent candidates."

Justice Rehnquist made the same point. Conceding that Congress has an interest in not "funding hopeless candidacies," and could legitimately require "some preliminary showing of a significant modicum of support" to be eligible for public funds, he contended that Congress had done a good deal more than that. "It has enshrined the Republican and Democratic Parties in a permanently preferred position." "I find it impossible," he continued, "to subscribe to the Court's reasoning that because no third party has posed a credible threat to the two major parties in presidential elections

---

[20]Buckley v. Valeo.

since 1860, Congress may by law attempt to assure that this pattern will endure forever."

The Court has also approved the practice of most states of paying for the costs connected with primary elections of major but not minor parties. The test case involved Texas's practice of funding only the primaries of parties whose gubernatorial candidate polled more than 20 percent of the votes in the last general election.[21]

Speaking for the Court Justice White sustained the Texas practice.[22] Justice White wrote, "We cannot agree that the State, simply because it defrays the expenses of party primary elections, must also finance the efforts of every nascent political group seeking to organize itself and unsuccessfully attempting to win a place on the general election ballot."[23] The Court again reemphasized that the Constitution permits states to "decide that political stability is best served through a healthy two-party system," and while the interest in preserving a stable two-party system "will not justify unreasonable exclusionary restrictions. . . . States need not remove all of the many hurdles third parties face in the American political arena today." The Court did, however, strike down the Texas practice of printing on the absentee ballot only the names of the two major political parties. Texas failed to give any reason for this practice.

When Minnesota banned "fusion candidates," that is allowing a political party to nominate a person nominated by another party, it did so in part to promote and protect the two-party system. Chief Justice Rehnquist for the Court sustained the ban. Although noting that a state may not "completely insulate the two-party system from minor parities or independent candidates' competition and influence, he wrote, "states may enact

---

[21]Parties that polled less than this, but more than two percent of the total vote could nominate either by primary or by convention but with no state subvention. Parties that polled less than two percent of the total gubernatorial vote in the preceding general election or did not nominate a candidate for governor were required to nominate by convention and if there were not at the convention voters equal to at least one percent of the total vote for governor at the last election, the only way their candidates could get on the ballot would be to circulate petitions.

[22]American Party of Texas v. White, 415 U.S. 767 (1974).

[23]American Party of Texas v. White, 415 U.S. 767 (1974).

reasonable election regulations that favor the traditional two-party system."[24]

Chief Justice Rehnquist had pointed out that the ban on endorsing candidates nominated by another party applied to major as well as minor parties. Justice Stevens, with whom Justice Ginsburg joined in dissent, responded that the ban in fact is only a constraint on minor parties. For it is only minor parties that use fusion politics to build strength. He wrote, "In my opinion legislation that would otherwise be unconstitutional because it burdens First Amendment interest and discriminates against minor political parties cannot survive simply because it benefits the two major parties."

Justice David H. Souter also dissented, but he did not reject the contention that states have the right to attempt to preserve the two-party system. Based on evidence that the two-party system is in some jeopardy, and "if it could be shown that the two-party system would be undermined by fusion candidates, then it might furnish the basis to recognize the constitutionality of Minnesota's action." However, he felt that the case had not yet been made.[25]

Thus the Court has developed a constitutional law that recognizes the power of the states, provided they do not go too far as to choke off the role of minor parties, to protect and promote the two-party system. What is "too far?"

Protecting Minor Parties

The two major parties have sufficient political clout to protect their interests, in fact so much political clout the danger is they will make it difficult if not impossible for minor parties to operate. To this point Justice John Paul Stevens, citing Justice Harlan Fiske Stone's celebrated footnote number 4 in *United States v. Carolene Products Co.*[26] in a footnote of his own wrote, "[B]ecause the interests of minor parties and independent candidates are not well represented in state legislatures, the risk that the

---

[24]Timmons v. Twin Cities Area New Party, 137 L Ed 2d 589 (1997).
[25]*Ibid.*
[26]304 U.S. 144 (1938).

First Amendment rights of those groups will be ignored in legislative decision making may warrant more careful judicial scrutiny."[27]

"For more than two decades, this Court has recognized the constitutional right of citizens to create and develop new political parties."[28] The Court has been especially concerned to protect the rights of new and third parties to have their candidates' names placed on general election ballots. Any state legislation or regulation that threatens this right must be justified by weighty reasons, and any restriction must be narrowly drawn to advance a state interest of compelling importance.[29]

The foundation case is *Williams v. Rhodes*,[30] in which the Court set aside Ohio's requirement that in order for new parties to have a place on the ballot for their candidates for presidential electors, 90 days before the election they must present petitions with signatures equal to 15 percent of those who voted in the most recent gubernatorial election. (Established parties retained their places on ballots as long as they polled 10 percent of the votes in the last gubernatorial election.) This requirement for new parties was contested by George Wallace's Independent party, which had gathered the required number but failed to meet the 90-day deadline and by the Socialist Workers party, which did not even try to meet that requirement since it had only 108 members.

Ohio argued that under Article II its legislature had complete power to decide how electors should be appointed, even to the extent of not giving the choice to the electorate at all. It had exercised this discretion with the aim of putting into place a system designed to prevent candidates from getting elected with less than a majority of the popular vote.

Justice Hugo Black, for the Court, conceded that Ohio had a legitimate interest in maintaining a two-party system as a means to encourage compromise and to discourage fractionalizing among political parties. However, he concluded, "The Ohio System does not merely favor a 'two-party system'; it favors two particular parties—the Republicans and the Democrats—and in effect tends to give them a complete monopoly. . . .

---

[27] Anderson v. Celebrezze, 460 U.S. 780 (1983).
[28] Norman v. Reed, 502 U.S. 267 (1992).
[29] Norman v. Reed, 502 U.S. 279 (1992).
[30] 393 U.S. 23 (1968).

There is, of course, no reason why two parties should retain a permanent monopoly on the right to have people vote for or against them."

Justice Potter Stewart and Byron White, and surprisingly Chief Justice Earl Warren dissented. Stewart and White based their dissents on the grounds that "the appointment and mode of appointment of electors belong exclusively to the states under the Constitution of the United States," including if it so wished, having the "state Legislature . . . nominate two slates of electors, and allow all eligible voters of the state to choose between them" so long as it did not violate the Fifteenth, Nineteenth, or Twenty-Fourth Amendments. The fact that Ohio chose to give the two major parties an advantage in presidential elections was well within the legislature's discretion.

Chief Justice Warren dissented on procedural grounds that both Wallace's Independent party and the Socialist Labor party had delayed until too long to seek equitable relief and that the Supreme Court should not be forced in such a short time, seven days, to consider "the important constitutional questions presented by these cases. I think it fair to say that the ramifications of our decision today may be comparable to those of *Baker v. Carr*." And it will be remembered that Warren felt that *Baker v. Carr* was the most important case during his tenure.

Four years later the Court upheld Georgia's requirement that in order for a new political party to hold a primary election and have its candidate placed on the general election ballot it had to file a petition signed by at least five percent of those eligible to vote at the last general election for the office in question. Parties exempted from the petition requirement were those whose candidate received 20 percent or more of the vote at the most recent gubernatorial or presidential election.

Whereas the complexity and totality of Ohio's regulations in effect had given the Republicans and the Democrats a complete monopoly, Georgia's rules did not "freeze the political status quo."[31] A state does not violate the equal protection clause by taking into account "obvious differences in kind between the needs and potentials of a political party with historically established broad support, on the one hand, and a new or small political organization on the other." A state has a legitimate interest in requiring some modest showing of support before listing a new political party on the

---

[31]Jenness v. Fortson, 403 U.S. 431 (1971).

ballot in order to avoid "confusion, deception, and even frustration of the democratic process at the general election."

These two cases bracket the issues: Ohio's requirement of 15 percent of the vote had made it practically impossible for new parties to get a place on a ballot, Georgia's five percent had given a new party a reasonable chance to place its candidates before the electorate. In cases since then the Court has threaded its way between these two extremes.

Illinois has had a number of encounters with the Supreme Court as the result of its attempt to make as a prerequisite for a new party to be given a place on the ballot that the new party demonstrate strength spread throughout the electoral districts in which it wishes to operate. These requirements should be seen in the context of Illinois politics, the battle between the Cook County upstate Democrats and the downstate Republicans as well as the division between the Chicago Democrats and the Cook County Republican suburbs.

On the eve of the 1948 elections, pre *Baker v. Carr*, when the Court was unwilling to review most issues relating to state regulation of political parties, the Supreme Court refused to set aside an Illinois law that was keeping Henry Wallace's Progressive party off the ballot. That law, which had been in effect since 1935, required a new political party to secure the signatures of at least 25,000 qualified voters and that within that aggregate there be signatures of two hundred qualified voters from each of at least 50 of the state's 102 counties. In a *per curiam* decision, *MacDougall v. Green*, the Court held, "it is allowable State policy to require that candidates for state-wide office should have support not limited to a concentrated locality."[32] Justices William Douglas, Hugo Black, and Frank Murphy dissented on equal protection grounds since Illinois made no attempt to make the required signatures even approximately proportionate to the distribution of voters among the various counties of the state.

By 1969 the political balance had turned in favor of those justices who were not reluctant to set aside state election laws they felt unfairly deprived persons of equal protection of the laws. Justice William Douglas speaking

---

[32]MacDougall v. Green, 335 U.S. 281 (1948).

for the Court reversed *MacDougall v. Green* and declared the Illinois requirement unconstitutional.[33]

Illinois then amended its laws so that it would continue to take at least 25,000 signatures to get on a statewide ballot, and for getting on the ballot of a political subdivision such as a county or a city, it would take signatures equal to five percent of those who voted in that political subdivision in the most recent general election. As a consequence of the concentration of people in Cook County, it took more signatures for a new political party to operate in Cook County elections than to get on a statewide ballot.[34]

Again the Court held this requirement to be unconstitutional. Justice Thurgood Marshall, speaking for the Court, used the occasion to defend the role of third parties as means of political protest.[35] Although a state has a right to try to screen out frivolous candidates, that right must be balanced "in light of the significant role that third parties have played in the political development of the Nation." "Abolitionists, Progressives, and Populists," he continued, "have undeniably had influence, if not always electoral success." He pointed out that third parties play a role as "a means of disseminating ideas as well as attaining political office" and "overbroad restrictions on ballot access jeopardize this form of political expression."

Illinois then amended its laws to require new political parties to have their nominating petitions signed by 25,000 voters, statewide, and if they wish to run candidates solely for offices within a large political subdivision like Cook County, they need 25,000 signatures from that subdivision. If, however, the subdivision itself compromises separate districts from which some of its officers are elected, party organizers must seek 25,000 signatures from each district. A party successful in gathering five percent of the vote in the next election becomes an established political party freed from signature requirements. A party becomes established, however, only in the political subdivision where it has fielded candidates. Thus a party that ran well in Chicago's elections but not in Cook County suburbs would not be established in Cook County. When the Harold Washington party, which was established in Chicago in 1989, sought in 1990 to expand into

---

[33]Moore v. Oglivie, 384 U.S. 81 (1969). Justice Thurgood Marshall in Illinois Elections Bd. v. Socialists Workers Party, 440 U.S. 173.

[34]*Ibid.*

[35]Illinois Elections Bd. v. Socialist Workers Party, 440 U.S. 173 (1979).

Cook County, it challenged the requirement that it had to collect 25,000 signatures from both the city district and the suburban district.

Justice David H. Souter speaking for the Court recognized the state's legitimate interest in ensuring that new parties have support in every subdivision, but he concluded Illinois could have done so "without raising the overall quantum of needed support above what the State expects of new parties fielding candidates only for statewide office."[36]

Justice Antonin Scalia, who has become the Court's leading champion of the right of states to promote a two-party system, dissented. Citing Madison that the dangers of factionalism decrease as the political unit becomes larger, he argued, "It is reasonable to require a purported 'party,' which presumably has policy plans for the political subdivision, to run candidates in all the districts that elect the multimember board governing the subdivision. Otherwise, it is less a 'party' than an election committee for one member of the board." He continued, "There is not much chance the State as a whole will be hamstrung by a multitude of so-called 'parties,' each of which represents the sectional interest of only one or a few districts; there is a real possibility that the Cook County Board will be stalemated by an equal division between 'City Party' and 'County Party' members."[37]

In the spring of 1980 the Court again struck a blow in behalf of emerging political parties, or at least independent presidential candidates, when John Anderson challenged Ohio's requirement that an independent candidate for president must file nominating petitions in March in order to appear on the general election ballot the following November. In March Anderson was still contending for the Republican nomination. Justice Stevens speaking for the Court struck down this early filing date and significantly asserted, "the State has a less important interest in regulating presidential elections than statewide or local elections."[38] Justice Stevens found little to support Ohio's contention that voter education is served by an early filing deadline. Nor was he persuaded by the major thrust of Ohio's argument that it wished to protect the two major political parties from "damaging intraparty feuding," and to make it difficult for persons

---

[36]Norman v. Reed, 502 U.S. 279 (1992).
[37]*Ibid.*
[38]Anderson v. Celebrezze, 460 U.S. 780 (1983).

such as Anderson to abandon efforts to win a party primary and then to run as an independent and thus splinter the Ohio Republican party.

Ohio had boldly asserted an interest in political stability by protecting existing political parties from competition for workers, for voter support, and for finances. The Court was unsympathetic. "Protecting the Republican and Democratic Parties from external competition cannot justify the virtual exclusion of other political aspirants from the political arena." First Amendment values "outweigh the State's interest in protecting the two major political parties." A state may have a legitimate interest in preventing splintered parties and unrestrained factionalism, but not at the price of keeping sore losers from running for president.

Justices William H. Rehnquist in a dissent joined by Justices Byron White, Lewis F. Powell, and Sandra Day O'Connor responded to Steven's assertion that a state has less of an interest in regulating presidential than state elections by insisting, "While the Presidential electors may serve a short term and may speak only one time on behalf of the voters they represent, their role in casting Ohio's electoral votes for a President may be second to none in importance." Ohio had ample power to establish a system that would keep a presidential candidate who "after seeing his hopes turn to ashes, wants to try another route, bolting from the party to form an independent candidacy."

Despite its bias in favor of protecting emerging political parties, the Court nonetheless has upheld the right of a state to limit its ballot to candidates of parties who had given some indication of some modest level of public support. The leading case arose out of Washington, the pioneering blanket primary state. Washington makes it about as easy as possible for an independent or a new party candidate to get on the ballot. Prior to 1977 it allowed minor parties to nominate candidates in a convention and then have their name placed on the general election ballot if they could certify that at least 100 registered voters participated in the convention. Then in 1977 it imposed the additional requirement that a nominee of a minor party had to also run in the primary and receive at least one percent of all votes cast for that particular office. The Court had little difficulty in upholding this requirement of a modicum of voter support in order to reserve the general election ballot for major struggles.[39]

---

[39]Munro v. Socialist Workers Party, 479 U.S. 189 (1986).

Even this requirement was too much for Thurgood Marshall and William J. Brennan who dissented insisting that regulations designed to keep minor parties from the general election ballot had to be subject to strict scrutiny and a demonstration that they were "necessary to further a compelling state interest" and are "narrowly tailored to achieve that goal" because "major parties, which by definition are ordinarily in control of legislative institutions, may seek to perpetuate themselves at the expense of developing minor parties." Thurgood Marshall returned to his theme that minor parties are entitled to special protection because they contribute "to diversity and competition in the marketplace of ideas" even if they have no chance of winning an election.

A decade later the Court sustained Hawaii's right not to count write-in votes. Justice White speaking for the Court pointed out, "the function of the election process is 'to winnow out and finally reject all but the chosen candidates' not to provide a means of giving vent to 'short-range political goals, pique, or undermine the ability of States to operate elections fairly and efficiently'."[40]

Justice Anthony M. Kennedy, dissenting with Justice Harry A. Blackmun and John Paul Stevens, argued that because the Democratic party is predominant in Hawaii the Democratic candidates are often the only ones on the ballot so that the ban on write-in voting denied voters the right to cast a meaningful vote.

Minor Parties and Disclosure Requirements

As campaign financing becomes a more pressing matter of public concern, it seems likely that greater attention will focus on disclosure requirements. So far there are only two direct Supreme Court holdings relating to the power of governments to force parties to disclose their finances.

In *Buckley v. Valeo* the Court ruled Congress can compel the two major parties to disclose the names of contributors and receipts of expenditures, but First Amendment considerations may protect minor parties from these disclosure requirements if the party can show "reasonable probability" that

---

[40]Burdick v. Takushi, 504 U.S. 428 (1992).

the compelled disclosures will subject those identified to "threats, harassment, or reprisals."

True to its word, six years after its *Buckley* decision, the Court held that Ohio could not apply to the Socialist Workers party its requirement that every political party report the names and address of campaign contributors and receipts of campaign disbursements. Whereas in the case of major parties the government's interests in enhancement of voters' knowledge, deterrence of corruption, and enforcement of contribution limitations justify reporting and disclosure requirements, in the case of minor political parties the balance of interest for compelled disclosures is diminished. Minor party candidates' improbability of winning reduces the dangers of corruption and vote buying. At the same time, the potential for impairing First Amendment interests is substantially greater. Not all minor parties, however, are entitled to this constitutional exemption from reporting requirements. Only those that offer evidence of past or present harassment of members due to their ties to the organization are exempted.

The Court's writing of the constitutional law for minor political parties makes sense: a state has ample discretion to make reasonable distinctions between established parties and emerging ones as long as its regulations do not completely freeze out the emergence of new parties. Our constitutional system, rather sensibly I think, has a bias in favor of the maintenance of a two-party system without guaranteeing it or insuring that the Democrats and Republicans will always be one of these two parties.

Party Patronage

The most extended discussion by Supreme Court justices about the role of political parties in our constitutional system is to be found in a series of decisions relating to political patronage. Beginning in 1976 in *Elrod v. Burns*,[41] through *Branti v. Finkely*,[42] (1980) and *Rutan v. Republican Party of Illinois* (1990),[43] the Court has struck down the political patronage system. Senator William L. March is reputed to have said that President Andrew Jackson saw nothing wrong in the rule "To the victor belong the

---

[41]427 U.S. 347 (1976).
[42]445 U.S 507 (1980).
[43]497 U.S 62 (1990).

spoils." A century and a half later Justice William J. Brennan, delivering an opinion for the Court, said, "To the victor belong only those spoils that may be constitutionally obtained."[44]

These three cases feature a heated exchange among the justices reflecting differing views about the relative balance between the rights to a governmental job as against government's interest in promoting a strong and disciplined two-party system. The writings of political scientists are much in evidence in these opinions. Justice Brennan led the liberal justices in declaring party patronage to be unconstitutional. Justices White, Powell, and Scalia, most especially the last two, wrote sharp dissents on behalf of party government.

As a result of these three decisions, except for posts where party membership is demonstrably relevant, government employees or applicants for government jobs may not be discharged or denied a job, promotion, transfer, of any other benefit of public employment because of their failure to belong to the winning political party or for expressing views about public policies contrary to those of the winning party. Justice John Paul Stevens, providing examples of public employees constitutionally protected from discharge or other disadvantage for party reasons, cited a coach of a state university football team. Such a coach, he pointed out, formulates policy, but nonetheless, he argued, "no one could seriously claim that Republicans make better coaches than Democrats, or vice versa."[45] (Justice Stevens apparently does not know very many intense political parties, or coaches for that matter.) As examples of officials who could be discharged for political reasons, Justice Stevens mentioned election judges and assistants who help governors write speeches.

In *Elrod v. Burns*, the first of this trilogy, Brennan spoke only for a plurality since Stevens did not participate and Stewart and Blackmun, while concurring in the judgment, specifically refused to join in the general condemnation of patronage. Since this case involved nonpolicymaking, nonconfidential government employees, all that needed to be decided to dispose of this case was whether such employees could be dismissed solely for their political association.

---

[44]Rutan v. Republican Party of Illinois, 497 U.S. 62 (1990).
[45]Branti v. Finkely, 445 U.S. 507 (1980).

Democrat Richard Elrod, after defeating the Republican incumbent to become sheriff of Cook County, following a long-standing Cook County tradition, fired the Republican deputies. Justice Brennan, speaking for the plurality, held that preservation of the two-party system is a legitimate governmental interest, but it did not justify overriding the First Amendment right of persons to hold a government job while working for the party of their choice. He was not persuaded by the sheriff's contention that by replacing Republicans with Democrats, the sheriff had furthered Cook County and Illinois's interest in seeing to it that the wishes of the electorate are carried out.

Furthermore, Justice Brennan was skeptical that the elimination of patronage in fact would bring about the demise of party politics. Political parties, he contended, "are nurtured by other, less intrusive and equally effective methods." In short, his position seems to have been that even if a state has an interest in preserving the two-party system, patronage no longer helps it to do so.

Justice Powell, joined by Chief Justice Burger and Justice Rehnquist, wrote at length on the virtues of patronage, "a practice as old as the Republic, a practice which has contributed significantly to the democratization of American politics," a practice that strengthens parties and hence encourages "the development of institutional responsibility to the electorate on a permanent basis." He noted the special role of patronage as a way for minorities to access jobs and to participate in the political process. He responded to the plurality's contention that the elimination of patronage dismissals would not bring about the demise of parties, by writing, "one cannot avoid the impression, however, that even a threatened demise of parties would not trouble the plurality."

Justice Powell then wrote one of the strongest proparty statements ever penned by a Supreme Court justice. There is a strong governmental interest in encouraging stable political parties and avoiding excessive political fragmentation. In words that would warm the hearts of those political scientists who have argued on behalf of a strong party system he wrote, "It is difficult to overestimate the contributions to our system by the major political parties, fortunately limited in number compared to the fractionalization that has made the continued existence of democratic government doubtful in some other countries. Parties generally are stable, high profile, and permanent institutions. When the names on a long ballot are meaningless to the average voter, party affiliation affords a guidepost by which voters may rationalize a myriad of political choices. Voters can and do hold parties to long-term accountability, and it is not too much to say that, in their absence, responsive and responsible performance in low-profile offices, particularly, is difficult to maintain."

Four years later, in a case involving public defenders in New York's Rockland County, Justice Stevens, who had not participated in *Elrod*, speaking for Chief Justice Burger, who had voted for patronage in *Elrod*, turned the antipatronage plurality of Elrod into a solid majority. Justice Steven's opinion based on the premise that the "First Amendment prohibits the dismissal of a public employee solely because of his private political beliefs" was devoted to drawing the line between the few positions where political beliefs and associations might be a relevant criteria for getting or holding a public office and those in which it could not.[46]

Justice Powell in dissent renewed his defense of patronage and of the role of political parties. "Until today," he wrote, "I would have believed that the importance of political parties was self-evident." He once again contended, "patronage appointments help build stable political parties by offering rewards to persons who assume the tasks necessary to the continued functioning of political organizations." He contended that "patronage is especially important to candidates who are neither wealthy nor capable of attracting substantial contributions." He argued, "patronage also permits political parties to implement their electoral promises. The failure to sustain party discipline, at least at the national level, has been traced to the inability of successful political parties to offer patronage positions to their members or to the supporters of elected officials."

Justice Powell, again sounding like a political scientist, continued: "The breakdown of party discipline that handicaps elected officials also limits the ability of the electorate to choose wisely among candidates. Our national party system is predicated upon the assumption that political parties sponsor, and are responsible for, the performance of the persons they nominate for office. . . . Broad-based political parties supply an essential coherence and flexibility to the American political scene. . . . The decline of party strength inevitably will enhance the influence of special interest groups."

---

[46]Branti v. Finkely, 445 U.S. 507 (1980).

The third case involved Illinois Governor James Thompson's practice of limiting state employment to those who supported the Republican party. It featured a running argument between Justice Brennnan and Justice Scalia who on Powell's retirement has taken over as the Court's leading advocate for strong political parties. Justice Brennan who wrote for the Court in holding Thompson's dismissal of Democrats as unconstitutional did not question that governments have the constitutional right to promote party stability, but denied they could do so by means that discourage free political expression by public employees. Furthermore, citing the works of Frank Sorauf and Larry Sabato, he contended, "Political parties have already survived the substantial decline in patronage employment practices in this century."[47] Justice Stevens, concurring with Justice Brennan, argued that patronage did not foster the two-party system. In a sense he contended that the Court majority in these antipatronage decisions was not antiparty but recognized the realities of modern political parties.

Justice Scalia opened his dissent with George Washington Plunkitt of Tammany Hall's famous "sillygism,"

> First, this great and glorious county was built up by political parties; second, parties can't hold together if their workers don't get offices when they win; third, if the parties go to pieces, the government they built up must go to pieces, too; fourth, then there'll be hell to pay.

Scalia insisted that

> the whole point of my dissent is that the desirability of patronage is a policy question to be decided by the people's representatives. I do not mean, therefore, to endorse that system. But in order to demonstrate that a legislature could reasonably determine that its benefits outweigh its liabilities, I must describe those benefits as the proponents of patronage see them.
>
> It is self-evident that eliminating patronage will significantly undermine party discipline, and that as party discipline wanes, so will the strength of the two-party system. . . . The statement by Justice Brennnan that 'political parties have already survived' has a positively whistling-in-the graveyard character to it. Parties have assuredly survived—but as

---

[47]Rutan v. Republican Party of Illinois, 497 U.S. 62 (1990).

what? As the forges upon which many of the essential compromises of American political life are hammered out? Or merely as convenient vehicles for the conducting of national presidential elections?

The patronage system does not, of course, merely foster political parties in general; it fosters the two-party system in particular. Not only is the two-party system more likely to emerge, but the differences between those parties are more likely to be moderated. . . . Equally apparent is the relatively destabilizing nature of a system in which candidates cannot rely upon patronage-based party loyalty for their campaign support, but must attract workers and raise funds by appealing to various interest groups. . . . Our decision today will greatly accelerate the trend that prior decisions by contributing to the decline of party strength have contributed to the growth of interest-group politics in the last decade.

These debates between Justice Brennan with Justices Scalia, and Powell, take place over questions, some empirical others theoretical, that form the core of much of the literature of our discipline over the last several decades. What is the evidence that patronage sustains a two party system? Do parties mitigate the negative tendencies of special interests? Do we want a party system more like that of England or are we best served by our rather decentralized, loosely structured, nonideological parties? In addressing these questions the justices frequently cite the work of political scientists. It should also be noted that some of the justices have themselves been active in our political life and all of them came through a process in which their appointment was very much involved with party politics. The justices seem to me to be pretty good political scientists and are as divided on these questions as are we.

Financing Political Parties

The United States traditionally has had candidate-centered rather than party-centered campaigns, but for most of our history and for most elections candidates have run as party candidates. The Supreme Court has been willing to tolerate some but not comprehensive congressional and state regulation of political parties' ability to raise and spend funds. The leading case is *Buckley v. Valeo* with perhaps the longest *per curiam* opinion in the Court's history, 235 pages including appendix in the preliminary print. If not the longest *per*, it is certainly among the most criticized. The critics come from both the left and the right side of the political spectrum, but the predominant critics are those who believe that this decision effectively prevents congressional regulation of campaign and party finance and results in giving the wealthy a great advantage in our political contests.

The case stemmed from challenges to the Federal Election Campaign Act of 1971 (FECA) as extensively amended in 1974. Congress in the act sought both to remedy the appearance of a corrupt political process—one in which large contributors seem to buy legislative votes—and "to level the electoral playing field by reducing campaign costs."[48] FECA is complex, and the issues flowing from it do not directly relate to the constitutional law of political parties, but it did set limits on what can be contributed to political parties and what they could *directly* spend for the election of individual candidates.

The spending limitations other than those presidential candidates accept in return for public funding did not survive *Buckley*. The Court distinguished between spending and contributing and concluded that spending ceilings impose significantly more severe restrictions on protected First Amendment freedoms than do limits on financial contributions. Of especial significance, the Court concluded that the only constitutional justifications for regulating party finances are to prevent corruption and the appearance of corruption. It rejected as a legitimate congressional goal an attempt to redress the balance of political influence between the rich and the rest of the electorate. Said the Court: "[T]he concept that government may restrict the speech of some elements of our society in order to enhance the relative voice of others is wholly foreign to the First Amendment. . . . The First Amendment's protection against governmental abridgment of free expression cannot properly be made to depend on a person's financial ability to engage in public discussion."[49]

The Court acknowledged the troubling fact that contribution limitations discriminate against minor-party and independent candidates, "but the record provides no basis for concluding that the Act invidiously disadvantages such candidates." On the contrary, the $1,000 restriction on contributions would appear to benefit minor-party and independent

---

[48]Buckley v. Valeo, 424 U.S. 1 (1976).
[49]Buckley v. Valeo, 424 U.S. 1 (1976).

candidates because "major-party candidates receive far more money in large contributions."

The most important Supreme Court pronouncement since *Buckley* most directly related to the constitutional law of political parties is *Colorado Republican Campaign Comm v. FEC*. In the spring of 1986 before either the Democratic primary or the Republican convention had nominated their respective candidates, the Republican Campaign Committee of Colorado ran radio advertisements attacking Congressman Timothy Wirth, the leading prospective Democratic senatorial candidate. These announcements although clearly attacking Wirth's record carefully avoided any specific advocacy that listeners should vote against Wirth or for his potential Republican opponent.

On complaint by the Democratic party the FEC held that the Colorado Republican party had violated the act. It ruled that because of the very nature of a political party all of its spending should be presumed to be coordinated with that of its candidates. The Colorado Republican party did not dispute the FEC's contention that party spending should be presumed to be coordinated with that of its candidates. They argued that because the party and its candidates are identical, the First Amendment forbids Congress to impose any spending limitations on political parties, whether or not that spending by the political party is coordinated with its candidates.

The Supreme Court reversed the FEC and decided that the Colorado Republican party had not violated the act, but there was no consensus among the justices as to why this was so. Justice Stephen Breyer joined by Justice Sandra Day O'Connor and Justice David H. Souter were of the view that in this particular instance the Republican party had not coordinated its radio messages with any of the three potential Republican candidates. Thus, these expenditures were "independent" and could not be considered to be contributions to the campaigns of the eventual Republican nominees. They refused to discuss the question of whether the First Amendment forbids congressional efforts to limit expenditures "coordinated" with the candidates because they felt this to be an issue of such importance that it should be addressed more directly and was unnecessary to the disposition of this particular case.

Justices Anthony M. Kennedy, Chief Justice William H. Rehnquist, Justice Antonin Scalia, and Justice Clarence Thomas concluded that because of the special and unique role of political parties, Congress could not limit their expenditures, even if made "in cooperation, consultation, or concert with" a candidate. Said Justice Anthony M. Kennedy, "We have a constitutional tradition of political parties and their candidates engaging in joint First Amendment activity; we also have a practical identity of interests between the two entities during an election. . . . Political parties have a unique role in serving the First Amendment principle that debate on public issues should be uninhibited, robust, and wide-open."

Justice Clarence Thomas joined Antonin Scalia in his opinion advocating on behalf of the constitutionally protected right of political parties to raise and spend money proparty. Citing the work of political scientists, of

> the fact that major parties are so large and consist of diverse interests and ideologies, the anti-corruption rationale used to justify congressional limitations loses its force. . . . Parties and candidates have traditionally worked together to achieve their common goals, and when they engage in that work, there is no risk to the Republic. To the contrary, the danger to the Republic lies in government suppression of such activities.

Justices John Paul Stevens and Ruth Bader Ginsburg, sounding like Progressives of the early 1900s, found the close relationship between parties and candidates rather than justifying an extension of First Amendment protections to political parties creates "a special danger that the party—or the persons who control the party—will abuse the influence it has over the candidate by virtue of its power to spend." In addition Justices John Paul Stevens and Ruth Bader Ginsburg, unlike the majority, have consistently taken the view that Congress has an important interest "in leveling the electoral playing field by constraining the cost of federal campaigns."

CONCLUSION

During the last four decades the Supreme Court has been developing the constitutional law of political parties. In doing so the justices have practiced pretty good political science. They have cited our literature, explored data, and have taken sides on the continuing debates as to whether more cohesive and disciplined political parties are to be preferred over non-ideological, decentralized American parties. They have speculated on the role of patronage and the consequences of various kinds of nominating systems.

There has been somewhat less of a predictable division between conservative and liberal justices, or between judicial activists against judicial restraint advocates than we are accustomed to seeing in cases of the other great issues. Nonetheless there have been some consistent judicial line-ups. Justices Lewis F. Powell, Antonin Scalia, and Clarence Thomas have been the most explicit defenders of the right of governments to promote and protect the two-party system. They have relied heavily upon the works of political scientists including those of Austin Ranney in staking out that position. On the other side, the "liberal" justices—William J. Brennan, William Douglas, Thurgood Marshall, John Paul Stevens—also drawing upon the works of political scientists, have been more skeptical about state governmental regulations designed to make it difficult for new and third parties to get on ballots. They have also been less sympathetic to state claims that it needs to act to promote party stability and to reduce factionalism. In a somewhat similar line-up, the conservative justices have demonstrated a greater tendency to disapprove on First Amendment grounds of governmental constraints on the rights of political parties or any body else to raise, contribute, and spend funds on political campaigning than their more liberal brethren and sisters have shown. Whereas the liberal judges contend that Congress and the states have the constitutional power to try to reduce the influence of wealth as a factor in determining which parties and candidates win elections, the conservative justices, so far in the majority, have insisted that the First Amendment deprives governments of the power to do so.

And as is true of all phases of constitutional law, the constitutional law of political parties is always in the process of becoming. The next big issues are likely to revolve around issues of campaign financing. But no less pressing are questions about the power of states to force political parties to open their primaries and to constrain their right to endorse candidates. It is dangerous to speculate on where the Court will come out on these questions, but it is comforting to know that the justices—on both sides of these issues—will rely heavily on the works and writings of political scientists such as Austin Ranney.

CHAPTER 2

The American Party Primary

Leon D. Epstein
University of Wisconsin-Madison

I am not the first to note the distinctiveness of the American primary as a means of selecting party candidates for public office. Austin Ranney made the point clearly and effectively in his comparative study of candidate selection in democratic nations.[1] Nor is this the first time that I have followed Ranney and others in discussing the subject. Here, I shall try only to expound more sharply the distinctiveness of the American party primary and emphasize recent legal and political challenges to its institutional status.

As Ranney's comparative study shows, most other democratic nations leave candidate selection entirely to party organizations, and the few nations whose laws stipulate the involvement of party members in candidate selection do so with respect to organizational (ordinarily dues-paying) members of parties. These laws leave the process to be managed by party organizations; they do not impose state-run elections to choose party candidates. Parties that conduct primaries of their own to choose candidates, as Israeli parties have lately done, poll their own organizational members. Exceptionally, somewhere in the currently enlarged democratic universe, a broader and less well-defined portion of the electorate may participate.[2]

---

[1] Austin Ranney, "Candidate Selection," in *Democracy at the Polls*, ed. David Butler, Howard R. Penniman, and Austin Ranney (Washington, D.C.: American Enterprise Institute, 1981).

[2] An unusual popular involvement seems to have occurred in Bulgaria when 860,000 votes were cast in a 1996 party primary to choose a presidential nominee. John R. Lampe, "Bulgaria's Best and Worst of Times," *The Woodrow Wilson Center Report* 8 (June 1997): 4-5. Also recent reports of presidential primaries in Latin America suggest mass participation in party nominations that resembles

But unless I have missed an innovation since Ranney's study, in no nation apart from the United States are party nominees regularly selected by unorganized voters in legally mandated, state-conducted elections. It seems reasonable to treat our practice as "peculiar to America." So it is treated by Anthony King, who regards the primary as an especially significant element, along with the initiative, referendum, and recall, in a hyperdemocracy that he associates with an excessive vulnerability of American officeholders to popular opinion.[3]

In use for much of this century, the American party primary, in almost all states, legally provides for the selection of major party candidates by voters whose participation does not require organized party membership. The most that states ask is that voters enroll or register by party, in advance of a primary election, thus producing the familiar closed primary as distinguished from a nearly open primary in which voters need only make a public declaration of party choice at the polls, and from an open primary (including its blanket version) in which voters make no public disclosure of party. Differences between closed, nearly open, and open primaries, and within each broad category, are often so consequential that a more refined classification is useful. At this point, however, I want to stress characteristics that are common to almost all of our party primaries: Nonorganizational voters bestow the party label that candidates will bear on the general election ballot, and they do so in state-provided elections that are usually (though not always) legally mandated for the selection (nomination) of major-party candidates for most offices. Voter eligibility in these party primaries is generally determined by statutes, which, to be sure, have been enacted by legislators bearing party labels. Lately, particular party organizations have asserted a constitutional right to modify statutory eligibility rules in a manner whose possible consequences I shall explore.

A few distinctions are in order. The kind of primary I am discussing is crucially different not only from party candidate selection elsewhere including the candidate-selection polls that local American parties often conducted among their adherents during the nineteenth century. Those polls, following the early Crawford county "primary" in Pennsylvania, were

---

practices in the United States.

[3]Anthony King, *Running Scared: Why America's Politicians Campaign Too Much and Govern Too Little* (New York: The Free Press, 1997), 65.

obvious precursors of the modern primary insofar as they involved more voters than did caucuses, but the practice was established by party rule rather than by state law. It did not directly select candidates for statewide offices. Nor, of course, should the twentieth-century party primary be confused with the contemporaneous nonpartisan primary used in many American local and some statewide elections simply to determine which two candidates, among three or more in a first election, will contest a second, or run-off, election. Whether or not such candidates do in fact belong to parties, or have party support, they appear on the ballot only as individuals seeking office, not as candidates seeking to win a party label. Therefore, in a comparative perspective, the nonpartisan primary looks less strange than an American party primary since other nations have first elections and run-offs, though usually with party labels on the ballot and certainly with party sponsorship of candidates.

HOW DID WE GET IT?

One might well wonder how we happened to establish the party primary. It is more peculiarly American than the separation of powers to which we are so famously committed. Not only have some other nations established systems based in varying degrees on the separation of powers, but the separation doctrine had European intellectual and institutional origins. Indeed, the framers of our Constitution sought to improve what they believed to be Britain's failed version of the separation of powers. In contrast, the party primary of the twentieth century is an indigenous institution that developed in special circumstances at the beginning of the century. Those circumstances help explain the substantial intrusion of governmental authority in party affairs that characterizes our primary election system. It is hard to imagine that anything like it would now be invented for a newly created or newly reformed political democracy. To give voters a chance to choose candidates, the more likely system is one like France's in which candidates bearing party labels compete on a first ballot for the top two places on a second ballot. That system serves so simply the participatory principles of our early twentieth-century reformers that we might well ask why they did not propose it instead of the party primary. It would be compatible (as is the nonpartisan primary) with our candidate-centered political culture, in which voters both nominate and elect, and it would avoid the intrusion of state authority in a party's candidate selection.

45

Only recently has an American state, Louisiana, adopted something similar that I shall subsequently discuss.

Well-suited though the party primary is to our candidate-centered politics, it is not the only conceivable means to pursue them. Understandably, then, we attribute the development of the twentieth-century party primary to particular American circumstances around 1900 as well as to a general tendency toward candidate-centered politics. Having discussed those historical circumstances at some length a dozen years ago,[4] and realizing that they are familiar anyway, I shall merely summarize their relevance here. Our nineteenth-century parties, while the first large-scale democratic parties in the world and the dominant forces in elections and in government, were loosely bounded organizations. Typically, they did not have regularized dues-paying members in the modern European party pattern, and their candidate-selection practices varied greatly as long as those practices remained essentially private associational matters. Some parties in some places ran Crawford County-type primaries or relatively open caucuses in which large numbers of their voters might participate either to select local candidates or to select delegates to district and state conventions that would select candidates for higher level offices. Other parties, most notoriously in large cities, had caucuses consisting mostly of patronage-minded followers who routinely approved the choices of their leaders. By the later decades of the nineteenth century, these practices were widely perceived as corrupt. The very looseness of "membership" in the dominant Republican and Democratic parties was conducive to irregularities. As early as the 1870s and 1880s, several states tried, ineffectively, to regulate candidate-selection practices. More tried to do so between 1880 and 1890 after adopting the Australian, government-printed ballot instead of the party-printed strip ballots previously used in general elections. States now established regulatory standards for a party to meet in order to get its label and its candidates on the general-election ballot. Hence, during the 1890s and just afterward, many state laws specified party candidate-selection practices in considerable detail. But these laws were perceived as ineffective both in dealing with corruption and in democratizing candidate

---

[4]Leon D. Epstein, *Political Parties in the American Mold* (Madison: University of Wisconsin Press, 1986), 155-74.

selection—an especially important goal in one-party states where nomination tended to ensure election.

Against this background at the start of the twentieth century, the adoption of the state-mandated, state-provided primary can be understood as another step, though a large step, in the effort to reform candidate selection by organizations whose democratic legitimacy was dubious. Rather than regulating how those loosely bounded organizations chose their candidates, states gave the choice to party voters. Doing so was an effort to reform or purify parties, not to destroy them or to remove them from the election process as the nonpartisan ballot sought to do in municipal politics. For elections to national and state offices, with some exceptions, party labels remained even though bestowed by party voters instead of by party organizations. Indeed, the new party primary institutionalized the established parties, Republican and Democrat, by providing a state process for choosing their candidates. Institutionalization even included official governmental enrollment or registration of voters by party, in order to administer closed primaries. In that respect as in others, the new laws often reflected the continuing power of the parties whose organizations were being limited but not abolished. The Republican and Democratic legislators enacting the primary laws must, at least where party organizations were strong, have responded to their influence as well as to pressure for reform. The result, as I have suggested elsewhere, is that parties have been treated much like the privately owned companies that we regard as public utilities—heavily regulated but protected by state authority.[5] Much as an electrical company had monopoly status, our two major parties became a kind of legally recognized duopoly. Like the regulation of public utilities, the regulation of parties belongs to the era of progressive reform.

The analogy to public utility regulation was even closer in places where there was an historically established one-party dominance and where, therefore, the primary institutionalized an electoral monopoly rather than a duopoly. The most notable examples are southern states, in which Democrats won almost all elections after the Reconstruction period. Here, the primary was less a product of antimachine reform than it was of the desire to provide a convenient means for white citizens to participate meaningfully in the choice of public officeholders. Plainly, they did not do

---

[5]*Ibid.*

so in general elections that Democratic nominees always won. Nor, through caucuses and conventions, did any large number of such citizens play a part in selecting the candidates who would bear the Democratic label in the general election. Democratic party primaries provided the only way for many white citizens to cast effective ballots during the many decades of the twentieth century that one-partyism prevailed. The primaries also served to keep black citizens from casting similarly meaningful votes; southern states, when authorizing primaries, allowed Democratic parties to limit participants to whites. Only in the middle of the century were these notorious "white primaries" declared unconstitutional on the ground that they were, in effect, state elections even though southern states sought to treat them as private affairs in certain respects.

Without the racial exclusionary purpose, several northern states, particularly in the upper Midwest, may also have been influenced to adopt party primaries by one-party dominance. For at the turn of the century, Republicans tended to prevail so frequently that their statewide nominations, while not "tantamount to election" as were Democratic nominations in the South, seemed nevertheless to be almost as highly valued. So it was in Wisconsin when the state became the first to adopt a mandatory statewide party primary law. Here, as elsewhere in the north, direct voter participation was perceived principally as a democratic cure for organizational manipulation and possible corruption, and the primary was instituted for both major parties. Its appeal was enhanced by the special significance of the dominant Republican party's nominations.

The party primaries established early in this century in most states were used to select candidates for Congress, major statewide offices, state legislatures, and many local offices. In a few states, major-party conventions continued to nominate candidates, at least for certain offices, sometimes on an optional basis (as in Virginia today), but these practices became more exceptional in the last several decades as primaries, in one form or another, were adopted in hold-out states. At the same time, primaries became increasingly individual contests as party organizations lost much of their earlier capacity to turn out enough votes to nominate their slates of candidates. Occasionally they still display that capacity, but since the 1960s less frequently in what have become candidate-centered campaigns where party organizational endorsements may or may not constitute advantages. Of course, the more striking recent change is the use of the party primary in selecting presidential nominees. Until the 1970s, presidential nominations were the great exception to prevailing twentieth-century American candidate-selection practice; the minority of states conducting meaningful presidential primaries could influence but not regularly determine nominations at national party conventions. Now, with most convention delegates committed to candidates as a result of primaries, the nomination is effectively made by party voters even though the formal choice is at a national convention. Given the serial nature of presidential primaries as well as the role of the convention, which includes some delegates not chosen in primaries, the process does not have the simplicity of the *direct* primary that progressive reformers substituted for the state nominating convention. Rather, it is a hybrid in which the primary strain is dominant. Operating under rules established, confusingly, by state laws, state parties, and national parties—but not national laws except with respect to campaign finance—the presidential nominating system remains a procedural anomaly even as primaries have for a quarter century produced party nominees.

HOW IMPORTANT HAS IT BEEN?

Determining the impact of the party primary in shaping American politics in the twentieth century is more complicated than describing and explaining its peculiarity. Consider, first, the broad matter of the primary's contribution to candidate-centered campaigns and so to candidate-centered politics. Plausible as it is that the primary encourages candidate-centered campaigns to a greater degree than does organizational control of nominations, it is hardly the sole cause of such campaigns and perhaps not even the principal cause. Other well-known modern developments contribute to the same results. The United States has a long-standing individualistic tradition associated with the popular election of executives as well as legislators, and that practice leant itself to personalized candidate campaigns even during the nineteenth century. In that light, the primary itself is a consequence of an American predilection for candidate-centered politics. Once established, the primary itself probably became a causal force in promoting such politics since it often requires candidates to build their own campaign organizations in order to win nominations.

Similar complications arise when contemplating more specific effects of the party primary. Even the impact on extragovernmental party organizations is not entirely straight-forward. Generally regarded as weaker in our time than a century ago, despite recent signs of revival, they have suffered other blows besides the loss of their power to bestow the party label. State regulations impinge on various of their structures and activities, not just on their nominating procedures. Developments in mass communications reduce the dependence of candidates on party organizations; it is now often easier and more fruitful for candidates to reach voters directly, especially on television. Nevertheless, a plain and separable disadvantage does follow from an organization's loss of power to select candidates. There is less incentive to be a member of such an organization, in the usual dues-paying, meeting-attending sense, if one can become a candidate selector merely by voting in a party primary. Perhaps that has made it harder for American than for European parties to build mass-membership organizations during the twentieth century. As our nineteenth-century patronage organizations waned, they were seldom replaced by regularized dues-paying members. Of course, as I noted earlier, such memberships were not characteristic of American parties in 1900, when they might well have legitimized organizational candidate selection as the old machines ceased to do. But it is not inconsistent to believe that they would have been more likely to develop in the twentieth century without the primary, or that the looser party organizations that we do have would be more substantial if they could actually bestow their labels rather than merely endorse candidates seeking those labels.

A more often argued matter is whether primaries produce a different kind of candidate than do organizational selectors. The issue became prominent during the last few decades of controversy over the post-1968 change in presidential selection practice. Reacting to the Democratic presidential nominees who lost most elections in the 1970s and 1980s, many critics of the new system blamed the primaries. They preferred less widely participatory means (usually caucuses and state conventions) to select delegates and a brokered national convention that such means would tend to produce.[6] The results, it was thought, would be consensual nominees likelier to be elected and to become effective presidents. To a considerable extent, any such outcome assumed a greater success for moderate or centrist candidates in caucuses than in primaries. But while that assumption was

---

[6]Nelson W. Polsby, *Consequences of Party Reform* (New York: Oxford University Press, 1983).

probably valid in earlier years when party leaders controlled or decisively influenced many caucuses, it was hardly applicable to the open caucuses that prevailed after 1968 and that were often dominated by ideological and other interest groups. Indeed, just the opposite is suggested by the somewhat greater success of both Pat Robertson and Jesse Jackson in caucuses than in primaries during the 1980s. In modern circumstances, primaries (particularly open primaries) appear to offer more favorable opportunities for moderate and centrist candidates than do the smaller self-selected electorates in caucuses and conventions. This holds for other offices besides the presidency. It is not hard to find instances of moderates winning primaries for gubernatorial and senatorial nominations against candidates endorsed by ideologically zealous state party conventions.

Critics of nominees produced by primaries seem to have a better case when they stress nonideological characteristics. The need to wage a broad public campaign in order to win nomination favors candidates who are media celebrities, wealthy, telegenic, or able to raise large amounts of money and willing to devote many months to soliciting votes. Less consequential is the kind of peer review of a candidate's governmental experience that was supposed to have been a major factor in an organizational selection process. That much can be granted without denying that the characteristics useful in winning primaries—celebrity, money, energy, and telegenic attraction—are also so useful in winning competitive general elections that the same kind of candidates would tend to be chosen even by many organizational leaders.

An entirely different role of the party primary is at issue when trying to evaluate its relationship to interparty competition. Here, it is reasonable to start with the hypothesis that the primary, when established, was meant to maintain a state's existing system—either two-party competition, Republican against Democrat, or Republican or Democratic one-partyism. By the first decade of the twentieth century, one or another of these systems prevailed in every state as it had more or less for the preceding half century. Other parties certainly appeared, significantly in the late decades of the nineteenth century and occasionally later, but they were not the principal subjects of the new primary laws. The purpose of the laws was to allow voters to choose candidates for parties whose nominees were either regularly elected or at least had a serious chance of being elected. That usually meant primaries for both Republicans and Democrats, except in some southern states, and only for those minor parties that also qualified for ballot placement by virtue of a specified share of the total vote obtained by their candidates in a previous election. Having no primary would not itself seem to disadvantage a minor party. It is the difficulty of qualifying for ballot placement that has been a burden. Without a previously strong electoral performance, a party has had to gather signatures, often in very large numbers, on petitions seeking to put its label on general election ballots. But without any primary laws, that burden could have been (and was) imposed once the Australian ballot made it possible. The same can be said for the legislation that banned fusion, or cross-listed, candidacies; it was plainly intended to disadvantage third parties when enacted before as well as after the establishment of primaries.[7] Thus, having primaries provided at most a convenient means to enforce the ban.

Indirectly, however, primaries may have discouraged the development of third parties simply by providing electoral competition within the existing major parties. Protest movements can mount campaigns to win Republican or Democratic primary nominations for their candidates at least as readily as they can launch a new party or use an existing minor party. In many places, it has probably been easier to obtain the number of signatures required for primary nominating petitions than to obtain the often large number of signatures required for a new party's ballot placement. Moreover, it is my firm impression that protest candidates of one kind or another have won major-party nominations and subsequent general elections more often than third-party candidates have won elections. Often, to be sure, neither avenue is likely to produce electoral success, but even then entering a major-party primary may be an appealing alternative especially if a primary campaign can attract more media attention than a third-party candidacy in a general election.

Supporting the speculation that primaries have discouraged third-party development is the absence in twentieth-century America of a persistently successful rival to the Republican and Democratic parties. Although such a rival was also absent in the half-century before primaries, it can be argued that it would have emerged, much as third parties did in Canada and elsewhere, if the United States had not opened its party candidate-selection procedure to protest movements. In that perspective, major-party primaries

---

[7]Peter H. Argersinger, "A Place on the Ballot: Fusion Politics and Antifusion Laws," *American Historical Review* 85 (April 1980): 287-306.

appear to have channeled the kind of protest that the Populist party had begun to mobilize late in the nineteenth century and the Socialist party early in the twentieth century. But with or without primaries, Populists and Socialists might well have failed in the United States. There are many possible explanations for their failure, as there are for the failure of other third parties, national and state. For example, primaries do not seem to explain the history of the Farmer-Labor party in Minnesota and the Progressive party in Wisconsin. Each third party won control of its state government in the 1930s, when primaries were already well-fixed, and then, after losing power on its own, ended its separate existence in different ways.

Similarly uncertain is whether the primary serves to perpetuate one-partyism. For many decades, it seemed to do so in the South where its adoption was most evidently a means to provide electoral competition when Republican voters were too few to matter. But when finally, about a century after the Civil War, southern voters responded in new ways to national political issues, Republicans became effective competitors. Having primaries was not sufficient to preclude change from one-partyism to two-party competition. Still, primaries might have been necessary, or at least useful, in helping to maintain one-party Democratic politics for so long.

Generally, insofar as primaries tended to preserve prevailing party systems, be they one-party or two-party systems, their impact was almost certainly intended. When enacting primary laws, Republican and Democratic legislators, however much they yielded to anti-organizational purposes of reformers, were hardly motivated to reduce the electoral value of their party labels. They may, in fact, have enhanced the value of those labels by allowing voters to bestow them, thus helping to perpetuate existing party dominance in winning elections. What we now call the party-in-the-electorate was thus strengthened as the party organization's power diminished. Significantly, party-in-the-electorate came often to be legally defined by Republican or Democratic enrollment prior to a primary, or by public declaration of party preference at the polls.

PARTY CHALLENGES

My concern here is with challenges by political parties to the constitutional power of states to run primaries according to legislated rules that contravene party organizational rules. Implicitly, such challenges cast doubt on the general legitimacy of state-run primaries even though only particular rules have so far been at issue. Relevant cases arose in the last few decades under broadened interpretations of the First Amendment to the U.S. Constitution. Until then, for many years the authority of states to establish and regulate party primaries had almost always been taken for granted even while opposition to the exercise of that legislative authority continued in several states whose party organizations were able to resist legislative efforts to enact or extend primary laws.

To be sure, primaries were the subject of litigation in the U.S. Supreme Court before the 1970s and 1980s. Most important during the middle years of the century were the cases in which the Court ruled that southern white primaries were unconstitutional. In doing so, however, the Court was not responding to a party's challenge to state authority. Instead, individual black citizens were challenging a party as well as a state by seeking to vote in a Democratic primary; their judicial victory limited rather than expanded the power of a party to make its own rules for the conduct of primary elections. In order finally to invalidate white primaries, the Supreme Court, in *Smith v. Allwright,*[8] treated them as state elections even when a southern state allowed parties to establish voter-eligibility rules and otherwise manage the process. A party acting under state law could not, any more than the state itself, preclude blacks from voting in a primary election. The Court went even farther when it dealt with the all-white Jaybird Democratic Association whose straw-ballot (a "preprimary primary") regularly produced eventual Democratic nominees and general-election winners in a Texas county. Because the Jaybird primary effectively determined the results, the Court regarded it as an integral part of the elective process

---

[8]321 U.S. 649 (1944). At issue in this definitive case was an arrangement in which the Texas Democratic party convention restricted its membership to whites and thus barred blacks from voting in a primary paid for and largely run by the party. Holding that the party was conducting its primary election under state statutes authorizing that election and was in this respect a state agent, the Court ruled the arrangement unconstitutional—thus reversing its decision in *Grovey v. Townsend,* 295 U.S. 45 (1935). Still earlier, the Court had invalidated a Texas statute barring blacks from voting in the state's Democratic primary, *Nixon v. Herndon*, 273 U.S. 536 (1927), and then a ban on such voting imposed by the Texas Democratic party's executive committee acting under a statute authorizing such a committee to prescribe its own qualifications for membership and voting, *Nixon v. Condon*, 286 U.S. 73 (1932).

despite the absence of legal recognition of the Jaybird Association on a state ballot or elsewhere.[9]

With or without the extremity of the Jaybird case, the judicial doctrine emerging from the white primary cases treats parties as state agencies rather than as private political associations. In other contexts, the Court has treated parties as political associations entitled to First Amendment rights. So it has, as will be shown, in dealing with some of the challenges to state laws regulating primaries.

1. Limiting State Authority

In the late 1950s, the U.S. Supreme Court, in important cases unrelated to primaries, treated freedom of political association as a right, under the First and Fourteenth Amendments, to be asserted against state regulation. Not until the 1970s and 1980s, however, did the major political parties successfully invoke this right in challenging state primary laws as well as other state laws limiting parties—notably California's regulation of internal party organization and its prohibition of party endorsements of candidates. The significance of the latter case is discussed elsewhere in this volume by Jack Peltason,[10] and I put it aside in order to concentrate on challenges only to state-run primaries though they are part of a broader attack on the power of states to impinge on the asserted associational rights of political parties.

Parties successfully asserted associational rights at odds with state primaries in three important Supreme Court cases. The first two, *Cousins v. Wigoda*[11] and *Democratic Party of the U.S. v. La Follette*,[12] are also treated in Peltason's chapter, but I must say enough about them to set the stage for discussing the third case. In both *Cousins* and *La Follette*, the issue concerned state-run presidential primaries that were, in different ways, in conflict with national party rules. The cases did not pit state parties against state authority; the state parties accepted the state authority at issue.

---

[9]Terry v. Adams, 345 U.S. 461 (1953).

[10]See his chapter for a summary of *Eu v. San Francisco County Democratic Central Committee* 489 U.S. 214 (1989) and of other cases related to state regulation of parties.

[11]419 U.S. 477 (1975).

[12]450 U.S. 107 (1981).

It was a national party that claimed an associational right to impose its rules against the results of party primaries conducted by the states as part of a delegate-selection process in which state parties participated. Or, put the other way around, states and state parties sought to impose their primary results on a national party whose rules they were violating. Thus, the national party could be perceived as opposing an extraterritorial reach when it resisted state intrusion into associational affairs generally. "Resisted" is an appropriate term since in each case it was the state, first Illinois and then Wisconsin, that initially sought through the courts to enforce its rules. Nonetheless, in responding to legal suits by the states, the national party was, in effect, challenging state primary results. And because the opinions of the U.S. Supreme Court upheld broad associational rights, not merely rights against extraterritorial regulation, they set important precedents. In *Cousins*, the Supreme Court effectively overrode the primary results even though the nature of the primary was not at issue. More significantly, it did so by proclaiming: "The National Democratic Party and its adherents enjoy a constitutionally protected right of political association,"[13] and by elevating that right over the state's asserted interest in protecting the integrity of its electoral processes.

In *La Follette,* the issue was clearly the primary itself, for, in advance of its 1980 convention, the Democratic National Committee announced that it would enforce a national party rule by refusing to seat delegates selected as a result of an open primary like Wisconsin's. What made the Wisconsin primary offensively open, by DNC criteria, was that the state did not even require voters to declare their party before receiving a primary ballot. This is the only kind of party primary that Wisconsin has ever used for state-office nominations as well as for presidential preferences. Adopted in the early years of the century, when the first Robert M. La Follette, as governor, was its principal advocate, the open primary was so firmly fixed an institution that the state legislature, even with Democratic majorities, had refused to modify the presidential primary to suit DNC rules. Instead, the state through Attorney General Bronson La Follette, a Democratic grandson

---

[13]419 U.S. 477 (1975), at 487. The broad language was Justice Brennan's for the Court majority of five justices. Three other justices concurred, thinking only that the language was unnecessarily broad (at 491-96), and the remaining justice concurred in part (at 496-97).

of the law's chief promoter, sought a judicial decision to prevent the exclusion of delegates selected according to Wisconsin rules allotting delegates to presidential candidates in proportion to votes cast for those candidates in the primary. After an initial victory in the Wisconsin Supreme Court in early 1980,[14] and an acceptance of its delegates at the 1980 convention during the appeal process, Wisconsin lost in the U.S. Supreme Court in 1981.[15] In reaffirming the *Cousins* doctrine that a national convention could exclude delegates selected in accord with state law but in violation of national party rules, the Court now declared that a party had a constitutional right to reject the results of a particular kind of primary. To be sure, the U.S. Supreme Court did not declare the open primary unconstitutional. It even suggested that the Wisconsin Supreme Court might well have been correct when it upheld the constitutionality of the state's primary law. Wisconsin could keep its open presidential preference primary, but it could not enforce its results on an unwilling national party convention.[16] Significantly, however, the Court's opinion did not read as though the party's constitutional right could be exercised only because the state was trying to impose its power extraterritorially. The language was broad enough to encourage a state party to challenge a state primary law.

Ideally, from the standpoint of party organizational critics of primaries, a state party challenge should, like the DNC's case, be against a law that permitted voters to cast primary ballots without identifying themselves as party adherents. In nonpresidential elections, several states use the Wisconsin-style open primary, or a variant of it; others merely require party declarations that are so readily changed from one election to the next that their primaries are often called open or crossover primaries; and still others, though having party enrollments, allow independents to cast ballots in a

---

[14]La Follette v. Democratic Party of the United States, 93 Wis. 2d 473 (1980); 287 N. W. 2d 519 (1980).

[15]Only for the 1984 convention did Wisconsin Democrats have to comply with the national party rule by using caucuses to record presidential preferences as well as to select delegates representing those preferences. By 1988, the DNC relented and allowed Wisconsin, along with Montana, to use its open primary. The DNC rule remains applicable, unless subsequently waived, to states that have not, like Wisconsin and Montana, traditionally used open presidential primaries.

[16]450 U.S. 107 (1981), at 121. Justice Stewart spoke for the Court.

party primary. Nevertheless, no arrangement like any of those was the subject of the state party's challenge that reached the U.S. Supreme Court after *La Follette*. Instead, in *Tashjian v. Republican Party of Connecticut*,[17] it was a state's closed primary, requiring party registration as a condition for voting, against which a state party asserted the right to open its primary to unaffiliated (independent) registrants. Much as most proparty political scientists prefer closed to open primaries, more of them appeared to support than to oppose the state party's case if only to establish party rights generally.[18]

The political context of *Tashjian* is relevant. In Connecticut during the mid-1980s, Democratic registrants outnumbered Republicans, but about a third of the registered voters listed themselves as unaffiliated. They were particularly important to the state's independent-minded Republican U.S. Senator, Lowell Weicker, who sponsored the party rule, adopted in 1984 by the state Republican convention, that would permit unaffiliated voters as well as Republican registrants to vote in Republican primaries for U.S. Senators, U.S. Representatives, and six statewide offices. Only after failing to secure enabling legislation from the state—specifically, from the Democratic majorities in both houses of the Connecticut legislature—did the Republicans take their case to the federal courts. They won first in a federal district court,[19] then in the ruling of three circuit judges hearing an appeal,[20] and finally in the opinion of a five-to-four majority of the U.S. Supreme Court. Each decision viewed the state's interest in the conduct of elections as not so compelling as to justify its intrusion on the Republican party's freedom of association.

In the decisive Supreme Court opinion, the party's prevailing right was closely related to the particular facts of the case. Speaking for the Court majority, Justice Thurgood Marshall rejected the state's claim that its ban on independents' voting in a party primary actually served an interest in preventing raiding or avoiding voter confusion, and he also denied that the

---

[17]479 U.S. 208 (1986).

[18]Briefs submitted by political scientists, on each side, are discussed in my "Will American Political Parties Be Privatized," *The Journal of Law & Politics* 5 (Winter 1989): 239-74, at 254-59. Most of the article is about *Tashjian*.

[19]Republican Party of Conn. v. Tashjian, 599 F. Supp. 1228 (D. Conn. 1984).

[20]Republican Party of Conn. v. Tashjian, 770 F. 2d 265 (2d Cir. 1985).

state could here substitute its judgment for the party's in protecting party integrity. Raiding by independents, presumably to help nominate a weak candidate, seemed improbable, as did any confusion of voters because independents voted in a party primary. Significantly, Justice Marshall did not exclude the possibility that a state could in some circumstances constitutionally substitute its judgment for that of party. And, in a footnote, he described the different problem that would be posed by a party that sought, in a closed-primary state, to open its primary not merely to independents but to voters from another party.[21] Accordingly, in *Tashjian,* the Court seemed to assume the state's authority to require a primary rather than a nominating convention. Making that assumption explicit, Justice Scalia, in his strong dissent, argued that the validity of a state-imposed primary presupposes that the state should be able to enforce its rules.[22] Two of the other three dissenters, Chief Justice Rehnquist and Justice O'Connor, joined in the Scalia opinion, while Justice Stevens dissented only on the ground that the Connecticut Republican rule violated the U.S. Constitution by making the qualifications to vote for Congress different from the qualifications to vote for state legislators.[23]

It may be relevant to note that as of this writing (late 1997) Justices Scalia, Rehnquist, and O'Connor (as well as Justice Stevens) remain on the Court, whereas the five members of the *Tashjian* majority (Justices Marshall, Brennan, White, Blackmun, and Powell) do not. Predicting future outcomes of major party challenges to state primaries, difficult anyway given the reliance in *Tashjian* on the particular circumstances, is made even more uncertain because of the changed composition of the Court.

Nevertheless, *Tashjian* is a party success worth a little more elaboration. It confirmed the Court's regard, in *Cousins* and *La Follette,* for the rights of an extragovernmental party organization, and in a context involving a state party's objection, rather than a national party's. In upholding against state authority a rule of the Connecticut Republican party convention, as it did rules of the national Democratic party convention, the Court again treated the loosely defined American party "organization" as

---

[21]79 U.S. 208 (1986), at 224-25, n. 13.

[22]*Ibid.*, 236-37.

[23]*Ibid.*, 230-34. Justice Stevens did not indicate here his views with respect to party rights that he had upheld in other cases.

the holder of associational rights. For this purpose, at least, it seems more tangible than the party-in-the-electorate (all party voters or registered party voters). But it cannot be assumed to represent that broader party. A state party convention, like a national party convention, consists of activists of one kind or another. The Court has referred to them as associational "adherents," but they might be regarded as "members," even without dues-paying, because they participate in party affairs. At any rate, it is their rights, not those of ordinary party voters, that the Court was effectively upholding.[24]

To my knowledge, the impact of *Tashjian* has been modest. At least in the first legislative year (1987) following the decision, I learned of only seven states, including Connecticut, that changed their closed primary laws to enable a party to allow unaffiliated voters to cast ballots in its primary. Two other states made equivalent administrative rulings. In only some of these states did a party immediately make use of the option. The rest of the 21 closed primary states made no changes in 1987.[25] Although some may have acted subsequently to allow independent voters in a party primary, there is no indication that *Tashjian* led to any broader change in primary rules. Nor has there been a Supreme Court case in which a party challenged a state's closed primary because it excluded another party's registered voters from participating in its primary. That issue remains unresolved. So does the question, more important for proparty advocates, whether *Tashjian* can be successfully used by a state party seeking, in an open-primary state, to limit its primary electorate to declared party members.[26] *La Follette* and *Tashjian*, together, seem to provide precedents for that challenge. Although state parties have usually had good political reasons to refrain from raising the issue—no matter how much proparty political scientists want them to do so—a few have challenged the blanket primary version of the open

---

[24]For a full appraisal of Court opinions in *Tashjian* and other cases, see Daniel Hays Lowenstein, "Associational Rights of Major Political Parties: A Skeptical Inquiry," *Texas Law Review* 71 (June 1993): 174-92.

[25]In "Will American Political Parties Be Privatized," *op. cit.,* 260-70, I discuss at greater length the early responses to *Tashjian*.

[26]*Tashjian* itself is criticized by a strongly proparty political scientist because it facilitated open primaries. David K. Ryden, *Representation in Crisis* (Albany: State University of New York Press, 1996), 154-66.

primary. I discuss the three relevant cases below even while the third and most consequential may remain unsettled.

2. Questioning the Blanket Primary

Established for several decades in Washington and Alaska, the blanket primary has become more salient since California voters, by initiative, adopted it in 1996 and since California parties challenged it in federal court. A blanket primary resembles other fully open primaries in that a voter need not register in advance by party nor declare a party preference at the polls. But unlike the others, which require a voter to select candidates from only one party at a given primary election, a blanket primary allows a voter to select from among different party candidates for each office. Instead of a ballot on which each party's candidates are listed in party columns, the ballot in a blanket primary lists under each office the candidates and their different party labels. Yet candidates contest party nominations only against other candidates bearing the same label. For example, with two Democrats and two Republicans seeking gubernatorial nominations, one Democrat and one Republican will be nominated even though conceivably the two top vote getters are of the same party. Accordingly, the blanket primary is a *party* primary despite the fact that voters do not, even in the secrecy of the voting booth, have to choose a party ballot.

Before the current California suit, both Washington's and Alaska's primary laws were the subjects of unsuccessful challenges that were not resolved by the U.S. Supreme Court. The Washington Supreme Court upheld the blanket primary in 1980, as it had in the 1930s when the law was new, but in the later case, *Heavey v. Chapman*,[27] it did so after two decades of federal constitutional developments with respect to rights of political association. State Democratic party leaders argued that the law, by allowing any voter to participate in the nomination of Democratic candidates, deprived their party members of the right, under party charter, to choose their own nominees. The claim, it should be noted, could be made against any open primary. In denying it, the court found no substantial burden on associational activity, and it viewed the law as justified by a sufficiently compelling state interest in open electoral participation. The decision,

---

[27]611 P. 2d. 1256 (Wash. 1980).

which the U.S. Supreme Court did not review, came after *Cousins* but before *La Follette* and *Tashjian*.

The challenge to Alaska's blanket primary did occur after *La Follette* and *Tashjian*, but it too was unheard by the U.S. Supreme Court. In 1990, opposing the state law, the Republican Party of Alaska (RPA) adopted a rule that only registered Republicans, registered Independents, and registered voters who state no party affiliation may vote in the Republican primary election—in other words, a partially open or partially closed primary from which only registered Democrats were excluded.[28] Initially, under a tentative decision of a federal district judge who cited *Tashjian,* RPA succeeded in getting the state to provide a separate party-rule ballot for the 1992 and 1994 primary elections. But a voter, arguing against the legality of such elections, in *O'Callaghan v. State,*[29] eventually obtained in 1996 a state Supreme Court ruling that the blanket primary was constitutional and that subsequent primary elections, to be legal, would have to be conducted in accord with the law. In an opinion similar to *Heavey*, three of the four state Supreme Court justices ruled against the RPA challenge, distinguishing it from the successful post-*Heavey* challenges in *La Follette* and *Tashjian*. The former, the Alaska court noted, did not invalidate Wisconsin's open primary when it held that a state may not control how a national party selects its national convention delegates. And *Tashjian*, the state court observed, did not assert that all state party rules could override state primary laws. For a party to keep voters out of its primary, when a state law let them in, was evidently different from allowing voters in when a state law excluded them (as Connecticut's had done). So it is, but whether the difference should be crucial constitutionally is less obvious. The majority in *O'Callaghan* thought it was because of the state's interest in broadening electoral participation through its blanket primary, but the dissenting justice regarded *Tashjian* as controlling.[30] How the U.S. Supreme Court would hold we do not know, for it denied *certiorari* for *O'Callaghan* in May 1997.[31]

---

[28]Gerald A. McBeath, "Transformation of the Alaska Blanket Primary System," *Comparative State Politics* 15 (August 1994): 25-42.

[29]14 P. 2d. 1250 (Alaska 1996).

[30]*Ibid.*, 164-68.

[31]5 U.S. Law Week 3749.

Still uncertain is whether the California suit will reach the U.S. Supreme Court. Adopted by nearly 60 percent of state voters in March 1996,[32] the California blanket primary took effect in 1998 despite continuing legal challenges from the California parties. The new law drastically changed California's traditionally closed primary in which registration by party has been a requirement for voter participation. A principal motivation for the change was the belief of its sponsors that an open primary would facilitate the nomination of more moderate and centrist candidates than a closed primary, on the plausible assumption that crossover voters as well as independents would tend, more than regular partisans, to choose such candidates. The presence of increasing numbers of independents, now about 1.5 million Californians registered without party affiliation, was itself an argument for a change if only to enhance participation for those disenfranchised by closed primary rules. To be sure, similar purposes would tend to be served by an ordinary open primary. But the blanket version probably induces more partisans (and perhaps independents also) to cross over because voters can choose to support one or more candidates of a party other than their own while choosing candidates bearing their preferred party label for other offices.

In seeking to enjoin California's new primary law (Proposition 198), the state's Democratic party, Republican party, and two minor parties directly challenged only the blanket primary though they appeared to raise implicit questions about ordinary open primaries that permit the partisan crossovers that the parties find objectionable. The parties lost their case, *California Democratic Party v. Jones,*[33] at the federal district level in late 1997, but have appealed the decision. In the district court, both the submitted testimony and the judge's opinion were substantial. Expert evidence and analyses, mostly by political scientists, came from each side. Defenders of the new law claimed that open primaries elsewhere lead to greater as well as freer voter participation, and to more fairly representative results. On the side of the parties, it was argued that the choices not merely of party organizations but also of party voters can be thwarted especially by crossover voting. That such voting occurs is taken for granted by propo-

---

[32]*Congressional Quarterly Weekly Report* 54 (March 30, 1996): 926.

[33]No. CIV-S-96-2038 DFL, decided November 17, 1997, by Judge David F. Levi in the U.S. District Court for the Eastern District of California.

nents of open primaries; indeed, they support open primaries partly because of it. What they do contest, however, is that any significant amount of the crossover voting is to sabotage the opposing party by helping to nominate weak candidates. Evidence of such sabotage is much harder to find than evidence of ideologically motivated crossovers. Against any crossover, the party organizations assert their constitutional right and that of "their members" to select candidates who "best represent each PARTY's ideologies and preferences."[34] Just who these "members" are is not clear. If defined as all registered party voters, a majority probably cast ballots for Proposition 198. Their views might well differ from those of the active party adherents whose rights as "members" had previously been upheld by the U.S. Supreme Court. Members in that sense are directly represented by party conventions and party committees. And it is such members, more clearly than party voters, whose constitutional rights against state authority are asserted by the party organizations challenging the blanket primary.[35]

Judge David Levi's district court opinion carefully weighed party organizational claims against the state's interests in the conduct of elections. Before doing so, he distinguished, as the parties probably would not do, the California case from *Tashjian* where the state was defending a closed primary against a party that wanted to open it to independent voters.[36] And he emphasized that recent higher court rulings provided a flexible balancing test for deciding between the sufficiency of state interests and the degree of burden placed on associational rights.[37] Paying close attention to expert

---

[34]*Ibid.*, First Amended Complaint for Declaratory and Injunctive Relief, p. 6.

[35]In expert testimony, submitted in support of the California parties, Bruce E. Cain analyzes the definitions of party membership proposed by political scientists, "Report on Blanket and Open Primaries," 15-16. Also in his submission, at 1-2, Cain suggests that a state could achieve greater voter participation in primaries by less drastic means than the blanket primary—specifically by an ordinary open primary as well as by merely allowing independents to vote in a party primary. This suggestion assumes that the constitutional challenge to the blanket primary would not implicitly apply to any primary that allowed partisan crossovers. Not everyone would make this assumption. Judge Levi did not think that the parties showed that the blanket primary is significantly different theoretically or practically from the open primary. California Democratic Party v. Jones, *op. cit.*, 31.

[36]California Democratic Party v. Jones, *op. cit.*, 12-13.

[37]*Ibid.*, 13-14.

testimony, especially that which described Washington state's half-century experience with the blanket primary, Judge Levi found that the new law's burden on parties was "significant but not severe," and that the state's interests, notably in greater electoral participation, were substantial enough to justify the burden. He even thought those interests compelling though he did not require that they be so.[38] At any rate, Judge Levi concluded, "a blanket primary serves sufficiently weighty interests that the State of California should not be precluded from ever trying such a procedure."[39]

If the California case should reach the Supreme Court, after an appeal at the Ninth Circuit, the outcome may be influenced by another case that the Court decided in 1997. It did not concern the constitutionality of the blanket primary, or of any open primary, but it did involve questions about the validity of a particular provision of state election law that had been thought vulnerable to party challenge after *Tashjian* and other rulings upholding associational rights. I take note of it under the next heading.

3. The Failed Attack on Antifusion Legislation

On its own, the third-party effort to obtain judicial invalidation of antifusion laws posed a significant issue, and I shall say a little about it before taking up its indirect relevance to the challenge to state primary laws. Laws banning candidates from nomination by more than one party prevail in 40 states, and in states without such laws fusion candidacies are uncommon except importantly in New York. As I observed earlier, these laws, adopted both before and after the introduction of direct primaries, were evidently meant to disadvantage third parties seeking political leverage (in the manner of New York's third parties)[40] by nominating selected major-party candidates. Banning multiple-party nominations in general elections, as antifusion laws do, is often accomplished by prohibit-

---

[38]*Ibid.*, 30, 32, 38.

[39]*Ibid.*, 40.

[40]A full and clear explanation of New York's "cross-endorsement" procedure is to be found in Howard A. Scarrow, *Parties, Elections, and Representation in the State of New York* (New York: New York University Press, 1983), 55-79. Crucial in its use is the power of a party organization to permit or deny its nomination to a candidate of another party.

ing candidates from filing in more than one party primary, but, in the absence of a primary (not always required for a small party), states also prohibit a party from nominating by nonprimary means a candidate nominated by another party. Thus, antifusion laws do more than ban cross-filing. And it is not cross-filing in the style that California allowed in much of the first half of the century that third parties have lately sought. The old California practice simply allowed candidates to file without regard to their own party affiliation or the wishes of the party organizations in whose primaries they filed. Frequently, as a result, candidates won both major-party nominations. Reflecting no desire to produce that result, recent third-party challenges to antifusion laws would seem to tolerate bans on major-party nominations of the same candidate or to make it possible (as it is in New York) for any party organization, major or minor, to reject a candidate who was not an adherent.[41] The latter is consistent with the claim of a third-party organization, as it challenges an antifusion law, to have the right to nominate a candidate who is the candidate of another party.

Closely related to the antifusion case that the Supreme Court decided in 1997 is another, *Swamp v. Kennedy*,[42] decided earlier in the decade by the U.S. Court of Appeals for the Seventh Circuit. The issue was the same though it involved cross-filing in a primary as the second case did not. *Swamp* is a Wisconsin case that arose in 1990 when the Labor-Farm party wanted to nominate a well-known Democratic Secretary of State willing to have his name entered in the Labor-Farm primary as well as in the Democratic primary. After his second filing was rejected by the State Elections Board because of Wisconsin's legal ban on cross-filing, Labor-Farm went to the federal district court, where it lost, and then to the Seventh Circuit, where it again lost over a year later. Further appeals, to the full Court for the Seventh Circuit and to the Supreme Court, did not lead to any decisions on the merits of the challenge.

The case that did produce a Supreme Court decision, *Timmons v. Twin Cities Area New Party*,[43] came from Minnesota. The New party, represent-

---

[41]See a model statute suggested by William R. Kushner, "Fusion and the Associational Rights of Minor Political Parties," *Columbia Law Review* 95 (April 1995): 683-723, at 721-23.

[42]950 F. 2d 383 (7th Cir. 1991).

[43]117 S. Ct. 1364 (1997).

ing left-of-center views similar to those of the 1990 Labor-Farm party in Wisconsin, sought to nominate for the November 1994 general election an incumbent state legislator, Andy Dawkins, who was also the unopposed candidate in the primary of the Democratic Farmer Labor party (DFL). Unlike the DFL or any other major party in Minnesota, the New party was legally a "minor party" that did not hold a primary but filed a nominating petition to gain a place on the general-election ballot for a candidate selected by its organized membership. When the New party chose Dawkins, with his consent and without DFL objection, the nominating petition was rejected by local election officials because Dawkins had already filed for the DFL nomination. Minnesota law, like Wisconsin's, banned such a fusion candidacy. The New party failed to persuade a federal district court that its associational rights were thus violated, but it did win the next round when the Court of Appeals for the Eighth Circuit ruled in its favor in early 1996.[44] Now, with a different result in the Eighth Circuit from that in the Seventh, Minnesota election officials appealed to the U.S. Supreme Court. Just before and while the Supreme Court heard arguments in the case, the New party's cause attracted editorial support from those who hoped that invalidation of antifusion laws would help revitalize third parties generally.[45]

The Court disappointed third-party proponents in April 1997 by its six-to-three decision upholding the Minnesota law. In an opinion delivered by Chief Justice Rehnquist, the Court found the state's regulatory interests sufficiently weighty to justify a ban whose burden on a party's associational rights did not seem severe.[46] To support this opinion, the Chief Justice cited other fairly recent decisions upholding state authority to conduct elections in ways that limited associational rights, and he distinguished those, like *Tashjian*, that had invalidated the exercise of state authority in particular circumstances. Of the several party rights cases decided by the Court in the two decades before 1997, not all pointed in the same direction. Accordingly, Justice Stevens, dissenting in *Timmons,* was able to cite and interpret

---

[44]Twin Cities Area New Party v. McKenna, 73 F. 3d 196 (8th Cir. 1996).

[45]Jason Gray Zengerle, "Hot Fusion," *The New Republic* 215 (October 28, 1996): 10-12; Theodore Lowi, "A Ticket to Democracy," *New York Times*, Op-Ed, December 28, 1996, 21.

[46]Timmons, *op. cit.*, 1367-75.

precedents, including *Tashjian,* in an opinion that looks to be about as persuasive as the chief justice's.[47] In balancing party rights and state authority, not all justices vote consistently on one side or the other. Still, there is some continuity. Like Chief Justice Rehnquist, both Justices O'Connor and Scalia had been dissenters (that is prostate) in *Tashjian* and now they were in the majority in *Timmons* along with Justices Kennedy, Thomas, and Breyer, who joined the Court after *Tashjian.* No justice really switched positions from *Tashjian* to *Timmons* although Justice Stevens, the only other member who heard both cases and the champion of party rights in his *Timmons* dissent, had not been a member of the majority upholding those rights in *Tashjian* because he had dissented then on a different issue. In *Timmons,* his dissent was joined by Justice Ginsburg while Justice Souter dissented separately and on narrower grounds.[48]

One cannot confidently predict that the justices who upheld state authority in banning fusion candidacies would, if still on the Court, also uphold state authority to conduct a blanket primary opposed by political party organizations as a violation of their associational rights. The issues are distinguishable. Nevertheless, Timmons cannot encourage advocates of party organizational challenges. Nor can they be encouraged by Judge Levi's quotation from *Timmons* on the standard and manner of review that should be applied when a state election law is challenged by a political party on the basis of the First Amendment.[49]

THE BROADER CHALLENGE

Whatever the outcome of the California blanket primary case, it will hardly be the end of litigation and other conflict between party rights and state conduct of party primaries. No one expects the Supreme Court to abandon party rights altogether if it should decide that a state can hold a blanket primary for parties that do not want it. The Court seems likely to retain the *Tashjian* rule that a party has a right to open its primary to independents when state law specifies a closed primary even though it might not accord what party advocates really want: the right of a party to

---

[47]*Ibid.,* 1375-81.
[48]*Ibid.,* 1381-82.
[49]California Democratic Party v. Jones, *op. cit.,* 13-14.

close a state's open primary. Thus, the Court would not be following the logic, implied by Justice Scalia's dissent in *Tashjian*, that leads either to accepting state rules simply because of the state's authority to conduct party primaries, or to rejecting that authority altogether. More probably, the Court will continue the observably difficult judicial choice between party rights and state authority as long as we have state-run party primaries.

Will we always have such primaries? Peculiar though they are as a mixture of state and party that occurs in no other country, they have now prevailed for about a third of our national history. A widespread return to convention nominations seems unrealistic, despite the preferences of some proparty political scientists. A little more feasible politically, because it extends the evidently popular principle of a blanket primary, is the alternative that Louisiana has used for the last two decades. Called an "open-elections system," it provides for a first election in which candidates, with party labels of their choice, appear on a ballot grouped by office rather than by party, as in a blanket primary.[50] But, unlike a blanket primary, candidates do not compete for party nomination. They seek actual election, obtainable by winning over half the votes at the first election, or, without such an initial outcome, enough votes to win one of two run-off positions in a subsequent second election. Both candidates in a second election may be from the same party, as they are not after a blanket primary in which candidates compete only against others from the same party. There is no *party* primary. Nor is there an entirely nonpartisan primary. Rather, the system, because of the inclusion of party labels on the ballot next to candidate names, resembles the French presidential arrangement in which candidates with party labels compete in a first election and in a second run-off between the top two candidates if no one wins over half the votes in the first election. And, in large part, the system also resembles elections for the French National Assembly. Moreover, in allowing candidates to list their party labels, it is similar to the familiar procedure in Britain for its single-member, simple-plurality parliamentary elections.

---

[50]Open elections came to Louisiana not from a progressive good-government movement but because of the political concerns of Governor Edwin W. Edwards. See Charles D. Hadley, "The Impact of the Louisiana Open Elections System Reform," *State Government* 58, no. 4 (1986): 152-57. John C. Kuzenski provides a recent description of the system, *PS* 30 (June 1997): 207-08.

Like most of us, I am more inclined to favorable views of Louisiana's cuisine than of its politics, but I became interested in the open-elections system when, after *Tashjian*, it seemed likelier than now that the courts would make it difficult for states to conduct party primaries by rules of their own. Louisiana avoided that difficulty since, without a *party* primary, its system seemed immune to successful challenge by an assertion of associational rights. It was, however, constitutionally vulnerable on another issue, and in late 1997 the U.S. Supreme Court invalidated the Louisiana law with respect to its inclusion of elections to the U.S. House and Senate. The Court found that the first election in October could and usually did produce majority winners and thus at an earlier date than the Tuesday in November that Congress fixed for those elections.[51] How the Louisiana legislature will respond is uncertain as I write. Trying to adjust the dates so as to keep the system for congressional as well as state elections is one possibility. Another is to limit the system to state offices. Still another is to return to party primaries as some Louisiana politicians prefer.

For the state and congressional contests in which the open-election system has been used in Louisiana,[52] party organizations have often endorsed candidates. At any rate, with party labels on the ballot, the system is not as obviously hostile to parties as is the usual nonpartisan election. Yet party organizations probably perceive disadvantages relative to party primaries. And political scientists may find that the system contributes to local one-partyism and to the re-election of incumbents. I know of no other states considering the Louisiana example, and they now seem unlikely to be led to such consideration by judicial rulings against the conduct of party primaries. On the other hand, conventional party primaries, particularly but

---

[51]*Foster v. Love*, 96-670, decided unanimously December 2, 1997. The Court thus upheld a Court of Appeals decision, *Love v. Foster*, 90 F. 3d 1026 (5th Cir. 1996). In the absence of state legislative response to this decision in 1998, a federal district court ordered the "first election" for national offices (Congress) to be held in November with any run-offs at a later date.

[52]Louisiana has not used the open-elections system in the process of selecting delegates to presidential nominating conventions, where a national party, given the *La Follette* precedent, could refuse to seat delegates chosen by so open a method. A similar barrier could be raised if the new California blanket primary were to be used, as was the state's traditionally closed primary, to determine the commitment of delegates to presidential candidates.

not only in their closed form, may no longer suit a voting public less strongly attached to party labels than it was when primaries were adopted. The most striking evidence is the large majority of California voters who preferred to substitute a blanket primary for the state's traditionally closed primary. Would they also vote for a Louisiana-type system if the blanket primary were invalidated? Or would they, or voters in other states, prefer it in any case? Because such possibilities now seem almost as remote as any other alternative to the state-run party primary, that peculiar institution will certainly survive into the next century.

CHAPTER 3

Political Parties and the Courts in a New Era

Lawrence Baum

Ohio State University

Austin Ranney's contributions to the understanding of politics are impressive in many respects, but one of their most striking qualities is their breadth. Ranney has carried out influential research on subjects that range from popular referenda to public policymaking to the political impact of television. If a single interest does stand out, it is the one with which his scholarship began: the role and functioning of political parties in the political system.

The significance of Ranney's research on parties reflects both the originality of his insights and his concern with the relationship between parties and democratic government. Because of these qualities, to take one example, his work has changed scholars' thinking about both the prospects for achieving party reforms and the impact of such reforms if they are adopted.[1]

I had the good fortune to study with Ranney at the University of Wisconsin. His generosity of spirit and his commitment to open inquiry made him an extraordinary model for young scholars. Among the many things I learned from his teaching and writing was the significance and complexity of the roles that political parties play in the governing process.

---

[1] See, for instance, Austin Ranney, "Toward a More Responsible Two-Party System: A Commentary," *American Political Science Review* 45 (June 1951): 488-99; and Austin Ranney, *Curing the Mischiefs of Faction: Party Reform in America* (Berkeley: University of California Press, 1975).

In this essay I will explore the role of parties in the judicial branch, a role that has been changing in interesting and important ways.

Students of American political parties give considerable attention to court decisions about parties. That attention is appropriate, because these decisions have had considerable impact on parties.[2] In contrast, party scholars traditionally said relatively little about the activities and roles of parties *in* the courts. The debate over responsible party government, for example, focused on the executive and legislature. Indeed, the famous 1950 report of an American Political Science Association committee, one that advocated "a more responsible two-party system," never mentioned judges or courts.[3]

This limited attention to parties in the courts stemmed in part from the perception that courts stand outside the mainstream of both politics and policymaking. But it has become increasingly clear that the judiciary plays an integral part in public policymaking. Like other participants in politics, political parties are attracted to power, so we would expect them to take an interest in the courts—as, indeed, they always have. The question is what kind of role they actually play.

Based in part on the tenets of the responsible party model, we might set up the following criteria for a strong relationship between parties and courts in the making of public policy:

1. The Republican and Democratic parties would take clear and differing positions on the major issues that come before the courts. Those positions would be reflected in the stances of candidates for elective judgeships and for other offices whose incumbents participate in the selection of judges.

2. Once in office, officials with the power to select judges would choose people who shared their party's positions on judicial issues.

3. Democratic and Republican judges would decide cases and adopt legal doctrines consistent with their parties' positions.

4. In making their choices for judgeships and for offices involved in the selection of judges, voters would give significant weight to the parties' positions on judicial issues.

---

[2] See the essays by Leon Epstein and Jack Peltason in this volume.

[3] Austin Ranney, "Toward a More Responsible Two-Party System," *American Political Science Review* 44 (September 1950), Supplement.

A role for the parties that meets these four criteria is not necessarily desirable; even those who favor a central role for the parties in the other branches of government might disapprove of such a role in the courts. In any case, the relationship between political parties and courts in the United States has never come close to meeting those criteria fully. The primary reasons for the absence of a strong party-court linkage are the forces that limit the role of parties in government generally. In the judiciary, these forces are reinforced by institutional characteristics of courts such as the life terms of federal judges and the widespread view that direct party influence on the courts is illegitimate.

Even so, political parties have always had a significant impact on the courts. In a noteworthy development, their involvement in the third branch has grown substantially in recent years. In this essay I will consider that development.

PARTIES AND COURTS IN A QUIET PERIOD

There is no "normal" relationship between parties and courts in the United States. At any given time that relationship varies among court settings, and its overall strength has waxed and waned over the course of American history. In the early 1950s, the relationship between parties and courts as policymakers could be characterized as meaningful but fairly weak.

Partisan considerations were most evident in the selection of judges. Federal judgeships went overwhelmingly to lawyers from the president's party. In appointments and party nominations to state judgeships, potential judges benefited from links to party organizations and their leaders. But the views that candidates for judgeships held about the policy issues that they would address in the courts typically were of limited interest to those who chose among them.

Of course, the Supreme Court was something of an exception. Historically, the views of potential justices about major issues of judicial policy often were of great concern to presidents and others who participated in the appointment process. Yet this concern, critical to Franklin Roosevelt's early appointments to the Court, had declined considerably by the early 1950s. Truman's appointments to the Court were used primarily to reward political friends. And Eisenhower's most important judicial appointment, to the position of chief justice, was first of all a reward for

Governor Earl Warren's critical support of Eisenhower at the 1952 Republican convention.

Once on the bench, Republican and Democratic judges behaved differently in some respects. Judges' loyalty to the party that had put them on the bench meant that in many courts, they could be expected to support the electoral interests of their party in cases that implicated those interests. As a reflection of ideological differences between the parties, Democratic judges as a group had more liberal records across the array of legal issues than did their Republican colleagues. But this partisan difference was not overwhelming.[4]

Nor was judicial policy an important partisan issue in the other branches of government or in the electorate. Once the Supreme Court abandoned its opposition to government regulation of the economy in 1937, there were no issues of constitutional law to which the parties gave priority and on which they took differing positions. Nor did partisan disputes over judicial policy typically play much of a role in elections, even elections of judges.

The particular weakness of the links between parties and courts as policymakers during that period reflected two conditions. Courts were not widely viewed as having a major influence on the resolution of the key issues in government and society. Further, the absence of sharp ideological differences between the parties made partisanship less relevant to the issues that judges addressed.

SOURCES OF CHANGE IN THE RELATIONSHIP

To a considerable degree, the relationship between courts and political parties today resembles that relationship in the early 1950s. But the links between the parties and courts as policymakers have strengthened. That strengthening has occurred because the courts increasingly are perceived as important policymakers with a distinct role and because the parties have developed clearer ideological identities.

As many people see it, the courts' role today is primarily one of liberal activism. The courts are viewed as holding substantial power to shape

---

[4]Robert A. Carp and C. K. Rowland, *Policymaking and Politics in the Federal District Courts* (Knoxville: University of Tennessee Press, 1983), 35.

policy on important issues, especially issues that fall under the broad rubric of civil liberties.   Courts are viewed as taking chiefly liberal policy positions, those that favor individual rights over competing interests. On the whole, people who participate in politics probably exaggerate both the extent of judicial power to shape national policy and the extent of judicial liberalism. But both aspects of the courts' image are rooted in real changes that began in the mid-1950s.

The degree of judicial activism is difficult to measure, because activism has been given so many meanings and because the term is applied so loosely; as Joel Grossman has noted, "basically, judicial activism is what the other guy does that you don't like."[5]   Yet courts in the current era certainly intervene in the policy process more than they typically did in the past, perhaps more than in any prior era.

Brown v. Board of Education (1954) was the first in a series of major interventions by the Supreme Court, one that was followed by other decisions on an array of civil liberties issues. Since 1960, the Court has declared unconstitutional nearly as many federal statutes as it had through-out its entire prior history; the same is true of state statutes. Equally striking is the number of major national issues on which the Court's decisions limit the options available to the other branches, such as abortion and campaign finance.

The Supreme Court's own activism has brought greater activism to the lower federal courts, in part by example and in part by giving greater responsibility to those courts. The enhanced role of the lower courts is reflected most dramatically in their direct supervision of government institutions such as school districts and state prison systems.

The growth of activism in the state courts has been less dramatic, and it does not extend to every state. On the whole, however, state supreme courts are more willing to intervene on major public issues. Many courts have given new life to state constitutions as mechanisms to test and sometimes to strike down legislative policy. Since the 1970s, for instance, most state supreme courts have decided cases in which property tax-based school funding systems were challenged under state constitutions, and

---

[5]Richard Willing, "'Activist' Label Actively Applied," *USA Today*, March 10, 1997, 3A.

supreme courts have required major funding changes in about one-third of the states.[6]

While the growth in the courts' activism has been striking, even more striking is the content of the policies they support. Historically, judicial activism served primarily conservative interests and values. In 1941, U.S. Attorney General and future Supreme Court Justice Robert Jackson concluded that "never in its entire history can the Supreme Court be said to have for a single hour been representative of anything except the relatively conservative forces of its day."[7] If Jackson exaggerated, certainly he was accurate in describing the Court's general tendency. On the whole, the same tendency existed in other levels of the federal and state court systems.

In contrast, judicial activism in the last four decades has served primarily liberal interests and values. When the Supreme Court strikes down laws, most often it is expanding legal protections for civil liberties. State courts have supported economic "underdogs" through means such as enhancing the legal rights of people who suffer personal injuries. This does not mean that, overall, judicial policy is more liberal than conservative. And both federal and state courts have become more conservative over the past two decades. Still, just as the level of sustained judicial activism over the past four decades may have no parallel, a case can be made that American courts during this period have been more liberal than they were during any other lengthy period.

In any event, it is the perception that counts more than the reality. And the most common perception among people who follow the courts is one of liberal activism. In turn, that perception has changed the ways that people in government respond to the courts.

Most directly, the perception of activist courts has greatly increased the interest of other political actors in judicial policies. Court decisions are the object of much greater attention and discussion. And since the stakes of various political groups in judicial policies have increased, so have efforts to influence those policies. For example, interest groups participate in

---

[6]See Bill Swinford, "Shedding the Doctrinal Security Blanket: How State Supreme Courts Interpret Their State Constitutions in the Shadow of *Rodriguez*," *Temple Law Review* 67 (1994): 981-1001.

[7]Robert H. Jackson, *The Struggle for Judicial Supremacy* (New York: Alfred A. Knopf, 1941), 187.

Supreme Court cases through *amicus curiae* briefs and seek legislative redress from unfavorable Court decisions far more often than they did 40 years ago.[8]

Attention to the policy preferences of candidates for judgeships has also increased greatly. In the nomination of federal judges, presidents and their advisers give heavy weight to the preferences of possible Supreme Court nominees more regularly than they did in some past eras, and interest in the preferences of potential lower-court nominees has achieved a high level that may be unprecedented.[9] For its part, the Senate makes much greater use of its confirmation power to scrutinize the policy views of nominees for federal judgeships than it did in the 1950s. In the states, the growing importance of policy issues in judicial elections is illustrated by the efforts of interest groups on both the plaintiffs' and defendants' sides in personal injury law to secure the election of sympathetic judges.

The perception of judicial liberalism has brought about a degree of polarization in attitudes toward courts and their work. In particular, political leaders and activists with conservative views tend to view the courts negatively. For the federal courts, that view has survived the increasingly conservative stance of the Burger and Rehnquist Courts and the large number of lower-court appointments by Presidents Reagan and Bush.

Both activism and liberalism make it attractive to attack the courts and their policies for electoral advantage. Courts have made a number of decisions that significant segments of the electorate view quite negatively, on issues ranging from abortion to flag burning. Candidates for judgeships and other offices, as well as interest groups, may benefit by identifying their opponents with unpopular judicial policies.

This is especially true of criminal procedure. Rightly or wrongly, courts have developed an image of undue leniency toward criminal defendants. In a 1994 national survey, three percent of the respondents

---

[8]Lee Epstein, "Interest Group Litigation During the Rehnquist Court Era," *Journal of Law & Politics* 9 (Summer 1993): 639-717; William N. Eskridge, Jr., "Overriding Supreme Court Statutory Interpretation Decisions," *Yale Law Journal* 101 (November 1991): 331-455.

[9]See Sheldon Goldman, *Picking Federal Judges: Lower Court Selection From Roosevelt Through Reagan* (New Haven: Yale University Press, 1997).

thought that "the courts in this area deal too harshly" with criminals, while 85 percent thought "not harshly enough."[10] Given the depth of concern about crime, an issue on which opinion is so heavily weighted on one side is quite attractive to candidates and interest groups.

Disagreement with court policies and perceptions of electoral advantage have spurred strong attacks on particular judges and courts. Since the late 1950s the Supreme Court has been the target of heavy criticism from conservatives in Congress, criticism that flares up with each controversial decision broadening legal protections for civil liberties. In the 1980s and 1990s, state judges increasingly have been challenged by electoral opponents for alleged softness on crime—particularly on use of the death penalty. Some of those challenges have led to defeats of incumbent judges, who ordinarily enjoy a great deal of electoral safety.

Controversy over the courts need not divide the parties sharply. Indeed, for many years it did not. Congressional battles over Supreme Court decisions in the late 1950s and 1960s typically cut across party lines. In the Senate defeats of President Nixon's Court nominees Clement Haynsworth and G. Harrold Carswell, substantial minorities of Democrats voted for the nominees and substantial minorities of Republicans opposed them.

Thus something more than change in the courts was needed to strengthen the linkage between parties and judicial policy: the parties themselves had to change. Of course, change *has* come, in that the ideological character of the parties has evolved. With fewer liberal Republicans and conservative Democrats, the two parties are further apart in their collective views about public policy. As a result, the parties are more divergent in what they want from the courts and in how they react to court policies. Moreover, party leaders, party activists, and the interest groups associated with each party typically give greater weight to ideological concerns—especially on "social issues" that are related to judicial policy on civil liberties—than they did a few decades ago. In this way the conditions developed for courts and their policies to become not only major political issues but important partisan issues as well.

---

[10]Kathleen Maguire and Ann L. Pastore, eds., *Sourcebook of Criminal Justice Statistics 1995* (Washington, D.C.: U.S. Government Printing Office, 1996), 172-73.

Lawrence Baum

PARTIES AND THE COURTS IN THE NEW ERA

The linkage between political parties and the judicial branch is stronger today than it was in the 1950s or even in the 1970s. That stronger linkage appears both in the selection of judges and in reactions to court decisions.

Selection of Judges

The selection of federal judges has become more partisan. To begin with, the parties' increasing homogeneity and heightened concern with judicial policies have led to greater emphasis—for the lower courts, far greater emphasis—on ideological considerations in making nominations. As a result, the policy preferences of Democratic and Republican nominees to federal judgeships differ from each other more consistently than they did a few decades ago. In the district courts, for instance, what had been only marginal ideological differences in the decisional tendencies of Republican and Democratic judges before 1969 have become more substantial differences.[11]

Senate reaction to judicial nominees also is more partisan. In contrast with Haynsworth and Carswell, the battles over confirmation of Supreme Court nominees Robert Bork in 1987 and Clarence Thomas in 1991 essentially pitted the two parties against each other. Only two Democrats voted for Bork, only six Republicans against him. And since the 1970s, senators have been increasingly willing to challenge lower-court nominations by presidents of the other party even when home-state senators approved of the nominees.

Interest groups have been important to this development, encouraging partisan differences and partisanship in the selection process. Liberal groups for which judicial policy is a high priority lobby Democratic administrations for nominees who share the groups' positions, as conservative groups do in Republican administrations. In the Senate, groups help to mobilize opposition to nominees from senators who share the groups' partisan sympathies.

---

[11]C. K. Rowland and Robert A. Carp, *Politics and Judgment in Federal District Courts* (Lawrence: University of Kansas Press, 1996), 31-38.

Partisanship in the selection of federal judges has reached a high point since 1995, with a Republican Senate majority pitted against President Clinton. A Senate controlled by the opposition party always shows some reluctance to confirm nominees during a presidential election year, but the Senate's resistance in 1996 was unusually strong. The Senate continued to confirm nominees at a slow pace in 1997 and 1998, indicating that at least some Republican senators simply want to limit the number of Clinton appointees on the federal courts.

There are signs of growing partisanship in the selection of state judges as well. In some states, governors have given greater weight to ideology in their judicial appointments and thereby increased the overall differences in policy positions between Republican and Democratic judges. In some states, party organizations participate in judicial elections more extensively than in the past, through campaign contributions and direct support for candidates. Battles over seats on state supreme courts between the two sides in the personal injury debate sometimes involve the state parties as well.

The liberal image that makes some incumbent judges vulnerable to defeat has spurred party involvement in judicial elections. When judicial incumbents are attacked for alleged softness on crime or for other pro-civil liberties positions, Republican leaders and interest groups linked with the Republican party often help to lead the attacks. In 1996, for instance, conservative groups and the Tennessee Republican party combined to defeat a Democratic state supreme court justice in a retention election by creating a perception that she had been unduly favorable to criminal defendants.[12]

Because of such successes, similar efforts are likely to become more common in the future. This is particularly true in the South, where growing Republican strength and voter conservatism make Democratic judges increasingly vulnerable to defeat. Perceptions of vulnerability help to

---

[12]Tom Humphrey, "White Ouster Signals New Political Era," *Knoxville News-Sentinel*, August 4, 1996, A1. In retention elections, voters cast "yes" or "no" votes on incumbent judges; typically, judges retain their offices if they win a majority of votes.

account for the defections of some Democratic judges to the Republican party in Texas and Alabama.[13]

Reactions to Courts and Court Decisions

Related to partisanship in the selection of judges is the use of courts and their decisions as a partisan issue. To a growing degree, the parties—primarily the Republican party—have criticized court policies with which they disagree and that they perceive as unpopular.

Richard Nixon's presidential campaign in 1968 was something of a landmark in this respect. One theme of the campaign was an attack on the courts for what he depicted as undue sympathy for criminal defendants: "our judges have gone too far in weakening the peace forces as against the criminal forces."[14] Republican candidates for president and Congress used the same theme in later campaigns.

Other judicial policies on civil liberties have been used as partisan issues. The parties became increasingly polarized in their positions on *Roe v. Wade*, and to a degree each party has sought to use the abortion issue to build electoral support. In contrast with abortion, on which opinion is heavily divided, public support for flag burning is somewhat limited. When the Supreme Court struck down the Texas law that criminalized flag burning in 1989, President Bush and Republicans in Congress recognized the electoral value of this issue: if congressional Democrats with civil libertarian sympathies voted against a constitutional amendment to prohibit flag burning, Republican challengers might have a potent issue to use against them. The Democrats largely defused this issue by supporting a federal flag-burning statute; by the time that the Supreme Court struck down the statute, passions over the issue had declined.[15] But the effort to adopt a flag-burning amendment has been revived and has developed

---

[13]Kevin Sack, "10 Alabama Judges Stage a Mass Defection to the G.O.P.," *New York Times*, January 4, 1996, A8.

[14]Richard M. Nixon, "What Has Happened to America?" *Reader's Digest*, October 1967, 50-51.

[15]See Robert Justin Goldstein, *Burning the Flag: The Great 1989-1990 American Flag Desecration Controversy* (Kent, Ohio: Kent State University Press, 1996).

considerable strength since the Republicans gained control of Congress in 1995.

Bob Dole's 1996 presidential campaign attacked liberal activism in the courts, with emphasis on criminal procedure. The Republican platform denounced federal judges and their decisions on several issues; among other things, it said that "the American people have lost faith in their courts, and for good reason."[16] In an April 1996 speech, Dole criticized positions taken by four Clinton appointees to the lower federal courts.[17] One of those judges was Harold Baer, a New York district judge. Baer already had been strongly criticized by Republicans for a January 1996 ruling that drugs seized from a suspect were inadmissible as evidence. President Clinton joined the attack on Baer's decision, and Clinton argued that he was actually tougher on crime than the congressional Republican party. Partly as a result, crime proved not to be a powerful issue for Dole.

But attacks on the courts survived the 1996 elections. The continued slow pace of confirmations for Clinton judicial nominees in the Senate in 1997 was accompanied by continued Republican attacks on sitting federal judges. House Majority Whip Tom DeLay and other congressional Republicans proposed that the House consider impeachment of several Democratic appointees whom they accused of judicial activism.[18] Senator John Ashcroft of Missouri held hearings on judicial activism in which liberal judges and their rulings were the primary target.[19]

Just as in the battles over selection of judges, interest groups allied with the parties play a significant part in attacks on sitting judges. Conservative groups have expressed considerable unhappiness about what they view as the apostasy of some Republican Supreme Court justices, especially Reagan appointee Anthony Kennedy. They have also charged Democratic judges with excessive liberalism.

---

[16]"Prosperity, Self-Government and 'Moral Clarity,'" *CQ Weekly Report* 54 (August 17, 1996): 2322.

[17]Dan Balz, "Dole Warns of Liberal Judiciary; Clinton Appointees Soft on Criminals, Majority Leader Says," *Washington Post*, April 20, 1996, A1.

[18]Harvey Berkman, "Spiking Judges for Rulings," *National Law Journal* (June 10, 1997): A1, A11.

[19]Tim Poor, "Ashcroft Hearings Targeting Judicial Activism," *St. Louis Post-Dispatch*, June 13, 1997, 2F.

Republican governors and other state political leaders increasingly criticize judicial liberalism. Such criticism seems to reflect both disagreement with court policies on the merits and a perception of political advantage from attacks on unpopular decisions. Where criticism of courts is part of an effort to defeat judges at the polls, governors who participate in successful campaigns against incumbent judges can put ideological allies on the courts and, in states that use retention elections, can appoint new judges themselves. In this way, to take one example, Governor George Deukmejian was able to reshape the California Supreme Court in the late 1980s.

Parties and the Courts Today

All these developments have not produced a situation that even vaguely resembles a responsible party system for the courts. What they *have* done is to create more meaningful links between political parties and the courts as policymakers. The essence of the change is twofold. The parties assign a higher priority to issues of judicial policy than they did in the 1950s, and they take more distinct positions on judicial policy.

In combination, these changes cause the parties' electoral fortunes to have greater impact on judicial policy than they did in the past. A voter who chooses a Republican candidate for president can have considerable confidence that a victory for that candidate will lead to the appointment of more conservative federal judges. To the extent that the party balance in the Senate affects the appointment of judges—as it increasingly does—a voter could expect that the larger the number of Republican senators, the more the Senate will move appointments in a conservative direction.

On the whole, it appears, the impact of parties on the state courts has not grown to the extent that it has in the federal courts. Still, significant changes have occurred in some states. As a result, a voter in Texas today knows that in most instances, choosing a Democrat for the state supreme court will make state legal doctrines on personal injury law more favorable to plaintiffs. A California voter knows that a Republican governor is likely to choose appellate judges with conservative positions on a wide array of judicial issues.

That voters have clearer choices concerning the courts does not mean that they cast their votes for public officials with judicial issues in mind. Policy issues of any kind are only part of any voter's calculus, and the issues that come before the courts typically are not the most salient for voters. Where voters choose judges directly, the limited availability of information on candidates for judgeships reduces their ability to engage in issue voting. At the least, however, the higher priority of judicial issues for the parties and the increasingly distinctive positions of the two parties give voters a better chance to take judicial policy into account when they choose between Republicans and Democrats.

This is an important change in itself. After the Supreme Court handed down *Brown v. Board of Education*, a voter who favored or opposed that decision would have had a difficult time determining whether its implementation would be hastened by the election of Democrats or of Republicans to national office. In contrast, a voter today who cares a great deal about abortion or school prayer or interpretation of the civil rights laws finds it much easier to cast a vote with that issue in mind.

CONCLUSION

The relationship between political parties and courts as policymakers has become stronger in the past few decades, and that trend is likely to continue in the near future. This is a significant development for the parties and for the courts. For the parties, it represents an extension of influence and, to a degree, of responsibility as well. For the courts, it represents a reduction in independence, both in the general sense that political trends have greater impact on court policies and in the more specific sense that judges have become more accountable.

The extent of this change should not be exaggerated. All in all, the linkage between parties and courts is still a loose one. As Austin Ranney has shown, characteristics of the American political system serve to limit the extent of party government in any arena. One of those characteristics, an unwillingness to accept full-fledged majority rule, is especially relevant to the courts; ultimately, it may serve as a brake on the trend toward heightened party influence over the courts.

Through his work, Ranney has demonstrated the value of studying the parties for our understanding of the political system as a whole and of its various components. This is true even of the courts, distant though they may seem from the mainstream of political action. In this way, as in so many others, Ranney has enriched our comprehension of politics.

II. Recruiting, Deliberating, Governing

CHAPTER 4

Parties and Candidate Recruitment in American Politics

Malcolm E. Jewell
University of Kentucky

One of Austin Ranney's most valuable contributions to our understanding of representative government was *Pathways to Parliament* (Ranney 1965). In this study, Ranney challenged the conventional wisdom that the cohesion of British parliamentary parties resulted largely from the ability of the national party organizations to control the selection of candidates for the House of Commons. He explored in detail the process by which candidates were actually selected by party constituency organizations and the influence of national parties on that selection, a subject that had been almost entirely ignored by scholars.

He found that the selection was largely determined by small groups of activists on the screening committees of constituency parties. "One of this book's principal findings is that the national organizations' actual influence over candidate selection is substantially weaker than their formal supervisory powers allow" (Ranney 1965, 272). But he also found that the leaders of local parties usually are loyal to the national party leadership and therefore select candidates for M.P. who will usually support their parliamentary party.

More research has been done on American political parties and the recruitment of congressional and state legislative candidates than had been done in England before Ranney's work. But the role of national and state parties has been changing, and the research on recruitment has left many questions unanswered. The purpose of this chapter is to summarize what has been learned about parties and recruiting and to examine some of the theoretical and methodological issues that need to be resolved if we are to gain a fuller understanding of the recruitment process.

RECRUITMENT IN THEORY

The recruitment of candidates is one of the most important functions of political parties—at least in theory. The political party obviously wants to run a slate of candidates who have the best possible chance of being elected. It may also prefer candidates who share its values and viewpoints and who will be attractive to the groups and interests that are predisposed to vote for that party. But in practice the performance of national, state, and local parties in recruiting candidates for legislative bodies appears to be uneven.

Maisel and his colleagues (1994, 147) list several reasons "for so much diversity in the capacity of parties to recruit competitive candidates." American parties are so decentralized that national and state organizations can provide relatively little tangible help to the local parties that are chronically weak and unable to recruit effectively. Many parties "have limited incentives to encourage prospective candidates to run" and "even fewer sanctions to protect their preferred nominee from a primary challenge." "Given the prevalence of candidate-centered elections, parties may find themselves with either an embarrassment of ambitious candidates or a dearth of willing contenders."

These limitations on effective recruiting by political parties are well understood. There is an obvious linkage between the recruitment and nomination of candidates. If party leaders recruit the best candidate they can find, they want that candidate to get nominated. In fact, it may be difficult to persuade someone to run for office if the party cannot help that person to get nominated. But the party's ability to influence the selection of nominees is limited by the primary elections used almost exclusively for nomination in this country. Recruitment used to be the job of state and local party organizations, some of which were powerful enough to pick the candidate they wanted and make sure that person was nominated. Today very few state and local party organizations have the political power or resources to control nominations.

But there is scattered evidence that some party leaders and organizations are becoming more active in legislative recruiting. The president or a state governor may actively encourage specific candidates to run for Congress or the state legislature, particularly in an effort to get or keep a legislative majority. As the party leader he or she may be able to appeal to the party loyalty of potential recruits, or to offer them various kinds of assistance, such as campaigning for them.

The leaders of congressional campaign committees have considerable resources available that may be used to support potential candidates whom they are encouraging to run. In many of the states, the leaders of the state party organizations, the leaders of legislative parties, or both, raise substantial funds and distribute some of these resources to nonincumbents whom they have encouraged to run for legislative seats.

Where local party organizations are strong and active, they may search for candidates to run for the legislative districts in their city or county, though there are probably fewer such active organizations than was the case 30 or 40 years ago.

What we lack is detailed, specific, up-to-date information on the role that national, state, and local parties are playing in recruiting candidates. How extensive are these recruitment efforts, and what difference do they make? At a time when most candidates at both the congressional and state legislative level appear to be self-selected, little is known about how they actually emerge and how they interact with recruiters from the political parties.

Recruiting is not a very precise term, and it may be difficult to define which candidates have been recruited and which are self-starters. It seems likely that recruiters in a district often turn to persons who hold some public office and/or are active in politics or community affairs. It is probably unusual for persons who have never given any thought to running for legislative office to be approached by party leaders. In other words, the job of the recruiter is often one of encouraging and promising support to someone who has some interest in entering the race.

It is particularly important for the political party to recruit candidates when it is more difficult to find them—in districts where the party has relatively few loyal voters and often very little organizational strength. Unless the party becomes involved in recruitment, it may have no candidate running, or at least not a viable one. It is likely to be difficult to find anyone who has any interest in running or any obvious qualifications as a candidate. Anyone with enough ambition to run for legislative office may be registered with the majority party. In some of these districts, where the prospects look hopeless, the party may make little or no effort to recruit, choosing to target more promising districts.

Recruitment may also be important in districts where the two parties are almost evenly balanced and the race is likely to be close. Although there may be several candidates available to challenge the incumbent or to run for an open seat in such a swing district, the party needs to find and encourage the strongest candidate available.

Recruitment is least important when a party has a comfortable margin in a district. But, if the party's incumbent is not running, it may need to recruit the strongest possible candidate in order to block potential candidates who are outside the mainstream, who might embarrass the party, or who might precipitate a divisive and expensive primary battle.

Some state party leaders in recent years have developed relatively sophisticated systems of targeting districts where a good candidate may stand a chance of running at least a competitive race. Their aim is not to find a warm body to run for every seat, but to recruit a viable candidate for every district where such a person might be competitive and to provide some help to such a candidate.

If a party is serious about recruiting candidates for legislative office, it must be prepared to offer them some kind of tangible assistance. This might be, for example, financial aid or assistance in raising money, advice on running a campaign, or access to polls, precinct voting lists, and information about the voting record of the incumbent. A well-known party leader, such as the governor or house speaker, might be available to speak or attend a fundraiser in the candidate's district.

UNANSWERED QUESTIONS

Two types of questions need to be answered about why candidates run for legislative office at the national or state level. The first concerns the reasons why candidates emerge; the second concerns the role that political parties play in the recruitment of legislative candidates.

We should recognize that there may not always be a hard and fast distinction between self-starters and recruited candidates, and the distinction may sometimes be an artificial one. Sorauf (1963, 103), in a study of state legislative candidacies in Pennsylvania, concluded: "Under the flattering stimulus of party hints and overtures, the candidate-to-be may develop ambitions or at least make the party's will his own. By the same token, he may become the object of party encouragement only after he has carefully hinted his availability or his contemplation of a candidacy."

Political scientists are interested in the characteristics of persons who are likely to run for political office: their family and educational background, occupation, and early interest in politics. Have they run for, or held, any office before running for the legislature? We are also interested in the circumstances that lead potential candidates to actually run for legislative office—what is often referred to as their emergence as candidates.

We are also interested in how candidates are recruited for legislative office, particularly recruited by political parties. This leads to a number of specific questions. How extensively do political parties engage in recruiting candidates for Congress or state legislatures? Is this responsibility handled primarily by national, state, or local party organizations, or by congressional or state legislative campaign committees?

What strategies do the parties follow in recruiting candidates? How do they choose how many, and which, districts to concentrate on? What kinds of qualifications do party leaders look for in a potential candidate? What kinds of assistance are parties most likely to offer to candidates they are trying to recruit?

Ultimately, we are interested in evaluating the effectiveness of party recruitment. If a national or state party is actively involved in recruiting congressional or legislative candidates, what difference does it make? Does the party run more candidates or better candidates, and does it focus its efforts on close districts? Does the party's recruiting effort result in winning seats that would otherwise be lost?

These are difficult questions to answer. One reason is that party leaders and legislative candidates may have different perceptions of the recruitment process. Leaders may exaggerate the effectiveness of their recruiting efforts, while candidates may be reluctant to admit that they were not entirely self-starters. Most efforts by political scientists to study recruitment of legislative candidates are based on questionnaires from, or interviews with, party leaders.

Studies by Frendreis and Gitelson (1995) illustrate this problem. They have found that state legislative candidates in a number of states rate various state and local party organizations and legislative campaign committees as having a relatively modest influence on their decision to run for office even though various studies (Frendreis et al. 1996) have shown that such party groups frequently list recruiting as a high-priority activity.

It is difficult to get detailed answers about party recruiting of legislative candidates, partly because party leaders who are quite willing to tell us that they recruit are sometimes reluctant to be much more specific, perhaps fearing that they will give away trade secrets to leaders of the other party.

Most information on candidate emergence comes from candidates, usually the successful ones. Information on recruitment may come from either candidates or party leaders, but more often the latter.

The next few pages summarize what has been learned about congressional emergence and recruitment. Then we will turn to the state legislative level, summarizing previous research and discussing more fully recent findings on political party recruitment of legislative candidates.

THE EMERGENCE AND RECRUITMENT
OF CONGRESSIONAL CANDIDATES

Research on the Emergence of Candidates

In an effort to understand the entire recruitment process, and not just the role of parties, political scientists have tried to learn more about what motivates individuals to consider becoming candidates and what factors determine whether they will actually run. Because of the complexity of this process, the case study of one or a few congressional races has often been used. Fowler and McClure (1989), for example, studied one district in New York in the 1984 and 1986 elections. They found that personal motivations of potential candidates were intertwined with a number of district circumstances, such as the variety of opportunities for individuals to run for other offices. They found that in this particular district local leaders of both parties were able to influence the process of selecting candidates.

Maisel (1982) found a way to combine a case study of candidate emergence with a larger study. In his book, aptly titled *From Obscurity to Oblivion,* he describes his unsuccessful 1978 campaign for a congressional district in Maine and summarizes information collected from other candidates running in primaries that year, using both questionnaires and interviews. Maisel is particularly interested in what motivates candidates to run and how much information new candidates have about what they will face. He found that many candidates were unrealistic about their chances of winning, but many others recognized from the start that their chances were poor. Some of this latter group ran to present an alternative or to air their views or because they thought that particular race presented them with a better chance of winning than usual.

Kazee (1980), interviewing a group of candidates who ran for Congress more than once unsuccessfully in the mid 1970s, found some common motivations. Some candidates had unrealistic expectations about their chances of winning. Some thought that campaigning was a rewarding experience, whatever the outcome. Negative comments frequently expressed by the losers included the high cost of campaigning and the lack of assistance received from party organizations, particularly those in the minority in the district.

Jacobson and Kernell (1983) have emphasized that nonincumbents who are potentially the strongest candidates, including those holding other elective offices, are likely to make careful strategic decisions about the best time to run for Congress. They recognize that their prospects are brighter when their national party's chances are greater. By contrast, Kazee (1980) found that weaker candidates, who lost several times, often seemed oblivious to unfavorable national trends.

Political scientists studying the emergence of congressional candidates have long been frustrated by the difficulty of identifying, in a large number of congressional districts, potential candidates, including those who ultimately decide not to run and not merely those who choose to run in any given election. As far back as 1986, the National Science Foundation sponsored a conference of congressional scholars who wrestled with this problem. Within a large sample of congressional districts, a survey of all state legislators might be a good starting point but would miss many potential candidates; only about half of the current members of Congress have served in state legislatures. Another source of information might be political activists, journalists, or other "experts" in each congressional district.

In 1992 Maisel and Stone (1997) led a team of researchers who persuaded delegates to the two national conventions from 75 districts in nine states to fill out questionnaires identifying up to five "good candidates" for Congress in their district. These informants identified a total of 890 potential candidates, including every candidate in these districts who won more than 90 percent of the vote in a primary and 90 percent of all candidates who ran in 1994. Obviously they identified many others who chose not to run, as they were expected to.

About 29 percent of those identified as potential candidates responded to a questionnaire, two-thirds of whom said there was no chance that they would run in 1994, while only 12 percent said there was a chance. Respondents said that the better their perceived chances of winning the primary and the general election, the more likely they were to run; this perception was related to the presence or absence of an incumbent in the race and the party balance in the district.

Having completed this pilot project, Maisel, Stone, and Maestas (1997) undertook a more comprehensive search for potential candidates. They drew a sample of informants in a national sample of 200 House districts. They sought, as informants, 10 Democratic and 10 Republican activists in each district, to provide detailed information about the district, the incumbent, and potential candidates for the 1998 election. They drew largely on lists of delegates to the 1996 national conventions and county chairs. The questionnaire sent to these informants asked them to identify potentially strong candidates for the congressional seat in 1988; in addition, they were asked to judge the likelihood that these persons would actually run, their chances of winning nomination and election, and their chances of running over the next decade. The next step was to send a questionnaire to the potential candidates who had been identified as well as to all state legislators residing in the 200 congressional districts.

This ongoing, comprehensive study of the emergence of congressional candidates is important for several reasons. On the methodological level, it should prove whether local party activists can adequately identify a substantial number of the most likely candidates and how well incumbent state legislators serve as another source of congressional candidates. On the substantive level, much can be learned about this pool of potential candidates: what are their characteristics, what factors affect their decision to run or not run, how realistically do they assess their chances of winning, to what extent do they act "strategically" (in Jacobson's terms)? Perhaps the most intriguing finding would be what separates those who decide to run from those who give it serious consideration but reach a negative conclusion.

A strong case can be made for a longitudinal study, extending beyond the 1994 and 1998 elections. The perceived chances of defeating the incumbent (or the chances that he or she will not run again) change over time. How much does the pool of potential candidates change over several elections? How has the process of candidate emergence been affected by the change in partisan control of the House? In those states where term limits on state legislators are taking effect, will the pool of potential congressional candidates increase and will those forced out of the legislature be more willing to accept the costs of running for Congress? The fact that potential congressional candidates are asked if they have some long-term interest in running makes longitudinal research on candidate emergence more feasible.

Research on Party Recruitment of Candidates

In the last two decades the Republican and Democratic House and Senate campaign committees have become increasingly important players in congressional elections. They have raised increasing large sums of money and contributed funds and services to incumbent and nonincumbent candidates. These committees must decide how to target their resources, particularly among challengers and open-seat candidates, and their major criterion is usually the candidate's chances of winning the seat.

As part of this process, the congressional campaign committees have become active in recruiting candidates. They are particularly concerned with locating the strongest possible candidates in competitive districts and persuading them to run; in less competitive districts they try to find candidates who seem capable of running a respectable campaign. The committees must work closely with state and local parties and members of Congress from each state, both to avoid conflicts and to get the best possible information about possible candidates and district politics (Herrnson 1988, 48-56).

Herrnson (1988, 49) quotes an official at the National Republican Senate Committee as saying: "Candidate recruitment is the biggest thing we do. We start early, looking for candidates through the maze of state and local party organizations and at elected officeholders and other prominent civic leaders. We consult with these people and take surveys to try to find out who the best potential candidates are."

Because these campaign committees have substantial resources, they are in a position to make assurances about funding to those they recruit. Similarly, on occasions when a committee is trying to discourage a weaker candidate from entering the race against its preferred candidate, the withholding of campaign resources can be a persuasive argument. If the preferred candidate is challenged by someone else in a primary, however, the national campaign committees usually avoid becoming openly involved in the primary election, with either endorsements or funds.

Herrnson (1988, 85-87) surveyed candidates in the 1984 elections, and found that nonincumbents did not usually believe that parties played a big role in their recruitment, although Republican candidates who were challenging incumbents were more likely to perceive party recruiting activities, particularly by the national campaign committees. Herrnson notes that measuring party recruitment efforts through candidate perceptions is difficult because candidates may not always be fully aware of those recruitment activities that only indirectly affect them, such as efforts to discourage other candidates from running.

Congressional Competition and the Effectiveness of Recruitment

A starting point for judging the success or failure of recruitment efforts is to look at the proportion of congressional seats that a party fails to contest. Some of the uncontested seats might be in districts where the party has no realistic chance of winning. A more accurate way of evaluating recruiting might be to determine in how many of the districts where the party had substantial voting strength did it run a candidate and how many of these were viable candidates.

Jacobson (1990) concluded from a study of competition for U.S. House districts that during the 1980s, when Republicans controlled the presidency, they failed to win control of the House "because they did not field enough challengers capable of exploiting favorable partisan trends" (45). Republicans in the 1980s left more northern Democratic incumbents unchallenged than in the past and failed to take advantage of the southern electoral strength of Reagan and Bush to challenge significantly more Democratic incumbents in the South than they had done in the 1970s. Moreover, the Republicans in the 1980s failed to recruit strong enough challengers in those districts where they did run candidates.

During the 1990s, however, the Republican party began to run candidates against almost all Democratic candidates, in both northern and southern states. The number of Democratic House incumbents in northern states unchallenged by Republicans was consistently less than 15 (often much less) from 1958 through 1972, rose to an average of 23 from 1982 through 1990, and dropped to an average of less than 10 from 1992 through 1996. The number of unchallenged Democratic incumbents in southern states averaged 66 in the 1958-62 elections, began dropping sharply when Goldwater ran in 1964, and ranged from the mid 20s to the high 30s in most elections from 1964 through 1990. The number of unchallenged southern Democrats averaged only three from 1992 through 1996. To put it more dramatically, in the South Republicans left 81 Democratic incumbents unchallenged in 1958 and only one in 1996. In the 1992-96 elections there were more uncontested Republican than uncontested Democratic incumbents in the South.

The Republican proportion of southern House seats increased from close to a third in the 1980s to 51 percent in the 1994 election and 57 percent in the 1996 election. This suggests that the Republican party organizations at the national level and in many southern states were not only recruiting challengers, but were recruiting credible candidates and supporting them with adequate resources. The Republican parties were also targeting southern districts that had enough Republican voters so that they could be competitive if there was a strong enough Republican candidate.

THE EMERGENCE AND PARTY RECRUITMENT OF STATE LEGISLATIVE CANDIDATES

Previous Research on Emergence and Recruitment

Most of what we have learned about the emergence and recruitment of state legislative candidates comes from in-depth, and often book-length, studies of a single state, and several of the best ones date back 30 years or more. These studies have often included both analyses of how potential candidates become seriously interested in running and descriptions of the role that political parties play in recruiting them. One common thread running through most of these studies is that the emergence and recruitment process differs along an urban-rural continuum and from competitive to noncompetitive districts.

Frank Sorauf's (1963) study of the 1958 election in Pennsylvania demonstrated how important a role a strong party organization can play in recruitment, particularly in competitive districts and those in urban areas. "In Pennsylvania, the political party dominates the candidate and legislator selection system. . . . [I]t intervenes freely in the primary elections and supervises the preprimary recruiting activities" (118). Sorauf found that the parties were more likely to play a role in encouraging losers to run (two-thirds) than winners (one-third), presumably because there was greater need for the party to recruit in districts where the party was not dominant. However, he also found, "In the hard-core minority parties, recruitment often involves little more than harried efforts by the chairman and a few henchmen to fill the party ticket" (57).

In Pennsylvania the party organizations very often helped candidates they recruited to gain the nomination, either by discouraging other candidates from entering the primary or endorsing the preferred candidate in a contested primary. Sorauf noted that the party organization must try to recruit candidates who will be acceptable to the district.

Barber (1965), in his detailed analysis of the members of the 1959-60 Connecticut House, devoted considerable attention to the recruitment of candidates. The Connecticut parties, like those in Pennsylvania, at that time were very actively involved in recruitment, and the support of party leaders was very often essential for a candidate's nomination. Rural districts were often dominated by one party. A leader of the local majority party might have to choose among several aspiring candidates, but in other cases the task might be to find someone who was actually willing to serve in the legislature and had the potential to be a good legislator. A leader of the minority party in such a district might be simply looking for someone who was willing to be listed on the ballot. Because the Democratic party made major gains in the 1958 election, many candidates were surprised to find that they had become legislators. It was in more competitive districts, often in urban areas, that the party recruiters were more concerned about a potential candidate's chances of winning.

One of the most comprehensive studies of the recruitment of state legislative candidates was carried out in Oregon by Seligman (1974) and his colleagues. They found that the social and economic diversity of districts significantly affected how candidates developed and what was the level of competition within or between parties. In urban two-party districts, with greater diversity, there was heavy competition in both the primary and general election; in most other districts, neither primary nor general elections were competitive (171-74).

Because the local political parties in Oregon were generally neither well organized nor powerful and were often fragmented, they were not very influential in instigating candidacies; "political parties are neither the most important, nor are they even first among equals" in sponsoring legislative candidates (375). "Seldom were the parties solely responsible for initiating a candidate" (74). Consequently, "recruitment sponsorship in Oregon is a network of primary groups, interest groups and party factions." The "loose, freewheeling character of political life" forces most legislative candidates to rely on their own resources (376).

A variety of groups, including parties, were more likely to be active in recruitment in rural than in urban districts in Oregon. Party leaders provided some support for candidates during both primary and general election campaigns, but it was often perfunctory, and the candidates seldom considered it very important (95-107).

The four-state study, *The Legislative System* (Wahlke, Eulau, et al. 1962) examined the political socialization and experience of legislators in California, New Jersey, Ohio, and Tennessee. They found that from one-half to two-thirds of the members had some governmental experience before being elected to the legislature, and from one-third to almost two-thirds had been active in their party. When asked how they became legislators, over two-thirds in New Jersey said they were sponsored (presumably recruited) by their party; the comparable figures are about one-third in California, about one-fifth in Ohio, and less than one-fifth in Tennessee. It is surprising that the proportion sponsored by the party was not higher in Ohio, which has long had a strong party organization.

Tobin and Keynes (1975) found that political parties were much more likely to be active in recruiting state legislative candidates in Pennsylvania and Connecticut, states with strong parties and closed primaries, than in Minnesota and Washington, states with less strong parties and open primaries. The proportion of legislative candidates (responding to a survey) who reported early contact by parties was over one-third in the strong-party states, and only one-fourth in the others. The proportion who received a preprimary endorsement from the party was from one-third to three-quarters in the strong primary states, less than half in Minnesota, and only one-fourth in Washington. (The Minnesota parties are more active in preprimary endorsements now than 25 years ago.)

One of the major advantages of single-state case studies such as those conducted by Sorauf, Barber, and Seligman is that they demonstrate how complex and varied the process of candidate emergence and recruitment can be in the real world. One obvious disadvantage is that we are unable to make comparisons among a large number of states with different political cultures and party systems. Another major problem is the acute shortage of such studies over the last 20 years.

Recent Research on Party Recruitment of State Legislators

In the past some state party organizations and many local parties were active in recruiting state legislative candidates. Some of the well-organized local parties virtually dictated the selection of legislative nominees. In recent years there appears to have been some decline in proportion of local parties that give high priority to recruiting legislative candidates, and some state parties appear to concentrate on statewide and congressional races. But there has clearly been an increase in the number of state legislative parties and individual legislative leaders that raise funds and provide support for legislative candidates. The recruiting of candidates is an important component of that activity.

There is evidence from a number of sources that legislative leaders and party caucuses have been active in recent years in recruiting and providing tangible support to legislative candidates in at least three-quarters of the Democratic and the Republican parties in both the state senate and house. Such activity is least likely to be found in states where one party has safe control over the legislature, such as a few states in the Deep South. There is evidence that state party organizations play some role in recruiting and supporting legislative candidates in at least one-third of the Democratic parties and one-half of the Republican ones. In southern states where the Republican legislative party is less well organized, the state Republican party is more likely to be active in recruiting and supporting legislative candidates.

To learn more about how legislative candidates are recruited, in 1997 I sent questionnaires to legislative leaders in both parties in both chambers of most legislatures and to those state party organizations that seemed most likely to be involved in recruiting legislative candidates. The response rate was low, but about 50 legislative leaders and 17 state party organizations reported that they were involved in recruiting and answered questions about the process. The state party organizations usually reported that they shared the recruiting responsibilities with leaders of the legislative party; some reported close coordination between the two groups, while others reported that they worked independently.

About two-thirds of the legislative leaders believe that recruiting legislative candidates is an important part of their job, in some cases a very important part.

State legislative leaders usually rely on local sources to help identify potential legislative candidates: leaders and activists in the party organization, local officeholders, and legislators from nearby districts (such as districts in the same city or county). Many of them also seek advice from leaders of various organizations, such as labor unions or businesses. State party leaders rely on similar local sources.

An overwhelming proportion of legislative leaders said that, among the districts controlled by the other party, they would focus on trying to recruit, and provide support for, candidates in those districts where the party has a realistic chance of winning or running a close race, rather than focusing on as many districts as possible. Most agreed that they would give the highest priority to close races. Because leaders usually try to provide campaign funds and services to those they recruit, they often stressed that the limits on available resources forced them to carefully target the districts where they made serious efforts to recruit candidates. Most respondents from state party organizations reported that they had the same priorities, though some indicated that they try to find candidates for as many districts as possible to put pressure on the other party.

There is considerable agreement among legislative leaders about the qualities they look for in candidates. They want persons who have a strong commitment to run and are willing to campaign hard. It is important that they be able to raise money. Another important factor is their standing in the community. They should be well known, with a good reputation, and a record of service in community activities. A candidate should also know the district well and share its views and values, but not very many leaders are concerned about stands on specific issues. Some mention experience in elective office or the ability to get party organizational support. Leaders often stress the personal qualities of prospective candidates: judgment, intelligence, and integrity.

The Effectiveness of Recruitment and State Legislative Competition

The proportion of seats that are contested at the state legislative level should be a rough measure of the success of Democratic and Republican party recruiting, as it is at the congressional level. An even better measure of success would be the proportion of seats a party contests in those districts where it has a realistic chance of running a competitive race. Unfortunately it is much more difficult to compile and analyze such data comprehensively for state legislatures than for Congress. The proportion of contested races in any recent time period varies considerably among the states, and therefore it is risky to draw conclusions about contests based on data from a few states. Jewell and Breaux (1988), in a study of both legislative chambers in 13 states with single-member districts, found that between the early 1970s and the mid 1980s in almost every chamber there was a decline in the proportion of contested races with incumbents running. The decline in the proportion of contested house races for open seats was much smaller and less consistent; there were too few open seat races in state senates to make a valid comparison. Weber, Tucker, and Brace (1991), studying the lower house in 20 states from 1950 through 1986, found that the proportion of contested races was declining in 14 states, nearly steady in four, and increasing in California (because cross-filing ended) and in Tennessee (the only southern state studied).

The decline in the proportion of contested seats appears to be linked to the growing electoral strength of incumbents. Jewell and Breaux found that the decline was much greater in races with incumbents running. Weber, Tucker, and Brace found that the proportion of contested races declined more in states where there were greater increases in collective and individual legislative expenses, resources that could aid incumbent legislators.

Another explanation for the decline in contested races might be that party organizations are becoming less effective in recruiting legislative candidates. Several of the states that still have relatively strong party organizations that are likely to be active in recruiting, such as Connecticut, New York, New Jersey, Pennsylvania, and Michigan, have had higher proportions of contested races than most—though some of them have had significant declines in recent years. In many states legislative leaders and campaign committees did not begin to become active in fundraising and recruiting candidates until the early or mid 1980s. The impact of this development will not become evident until more comprehensive data on contested races are available for elections in the 1990s. We should remember that, if parties target their recruiting efforts on districts that are potentially winnable, their efforts will not necessarily reduce the proportion of uncontested races.

If we are searching for evidence about the success of a party in recruiting legislative candidates, the obvious place to look is at the Republican party in southern states. Because the Democratic party had held large and often overwhelming majorities in most southern legislatures for decades, the Republican party needed a major recruiting effort to become competitive. Because in recent years the Republicans have made major gains in legislative seats in most states, there is reason to believe that such recruiting efforts have been underway.

This analysis of Republican competition for southern legislative seats is based on 10 states: the traditional 11, plus Kentucky, and minus Arkansas and Louisiana, where Republican gains have come more slowly than in other southern states. Table 1 shows that, in these states as a whole, the Republican party rather consistently contested a little less than half of the seats from 1968-71 through 1984-87. In the 1980s the Republicans began to win an increasing share of the contested races, which suggests that they were targeting districts more skillfully and recruiting stronger candidates to take advantage of Republican gains in national and statewide races in the South. By the 1992-94 period, the Republicans were contesting over 60 percent of the seats, and by 1994 they were winning two-thirds of those contested. (In the 1996 elections the Republicans generally held the gains made in 1994.)

Between the 1980-83 period and the 1994 elections (1992 in Mississippi and 1993 in Virginia) in the lower houses, there was a 29 percent increase in the proportion of seats the Republicans contested, a 94 percent increase in the proportion of all seats won, and a 50 percent increase in the proportion of Republican candidates who won. These data provide an even stronger indication that the Republicans were not only recruiting more southern legislative candidates, but recruiting better candidates and focusing on districts where they had the potential for winning.

There are some differences among the states in the pattern of Republican gains between 1980-83 and 1994. (Only Tennessee had little increase in contests or victories.) Kentucky, Texas, and North Carolina started with over half the seats contested, had modest increases in the number of candidates and large increases in seats won (very large in North Carolina). Florida and Virginia, which also began with over half the seats contested, had modest increases the number contested, and somewhat larger increases in victories. In these states, where the Republican party had some need to run more candidates, it had a greater need to target districts better and run stronger candidates; it succeeded, particularly in North Carolina, Texas, and Florida.

Table 1. *Proportion of Legislative Seats Contested and Won by Republican Candidates, over Time, in Ten Southern States*

Election Years	Percentage of Seats Contested	Won	Percentage of Candidates Who Won
STATE SENATES			
1968-71	44.3	16.7	37.8
1972-75	44.3	15.1	34.8
1976-79	43.0	12.8	29.6
1980-83	47.3	17.0	36.0
1984-87	47.7	21.4	44.8
1988-91	60.6	28.0	46.2
1992-93	68.1	32.2	47.4
1994	64.8	44.3	68.5
STATE HOUSES			
1968-71	45.4	18.1	39.7
1972-75	50.0	18.5	36.9
1976-79	43.0	16.5	38.4
1980-83	47.8	21.6	45.1
1984-87	47.0	26.8	57.1
1988-91	55.4	32.4	58.6
1992-93	60.2	35.0	58.1
1994	61.8	42.0	67.7

Georgia, South Carolina, Alabama, and Mississippi started with one-third or fewer of the seats contested, approximately doubled the number of candidates running (though increasing only 69 percent in Alabama), and at least tripled the number of seats won. Here the need was to recruit much larger numbers of candidates, and stronger ones, as well as to target skillfully. In each of these states, the Republican party was very successful.

In eight of these nine states (except Mississippi) where there were significant Republican legislative gains, we have evidence that Republican state political parties or legislative leaders, or often both, in recent years have been actively involved in targeting districts and recruiting candidates for the legislature. Most of this evidence is based on the questionnaires I received from state parties and legislative leaders and some comes from previously published sources (Cassie 1994; State Legislative Leaders Foundation 1997).

It is impossible to estimate from such sources how much of the Republican gains in southern legislatures comes from increased efforts and more skillful techniques in recruiting candidates. But, if the small size of Republican legislative gains in the 1980s can be plausibly attributed to the weakness of recruiting efforts, it seems plausible to conclude that the gains made in the 1990s have been caused to a considerable degree by a more aggressive and sophisticated Republican effort to target winnable districts, recruit viable candidates, and provide them with adequate support.

As we undertake more studies of state legislative recruiting, we need to better understand the consequences of recruiting efforts. This requires more hard evidence about recruiting strategies and outcomes, and closer study of the linkages between recruiting and election results. We need more district-level longitudinal studies showing how candidates emerge and how recruitment actually occurs. We need to recognize that recruiting is affected by trends in the role of parties, campaign techniques, and the costs of campaigning; all these trends, and particularly changes in levels of two-party competition and the impact of term limits, have different impacts in the various states.

REFERENCES

Barber, James David. 1965. *The Lawmakers: Recruitment and Adaptation to Legislative Life.* New Haven, Conn.: Yale University Press.

Cassie, William E. 1994. "More May Not Always Be Better: Republican Recruiting Strategies in Southern Legislative Elections." *American Review of Politics* 15: 141-55.

Fowler, Linda L., and Robert D. McClure. 1989. *Political Ambition: Who Decides to Run for Congress.* New Haven, Conn.: Yale University Press.

Frendreis, John, and Alan R. Gitelson. 1995. "Parties, Candidates, and State Electoral Politics." Paper prepared for presentation at the annual meeting of the American Political Science Association.

Frendreis, John, Alan R. Gitelson, Gregory Fleming, and Anne Layzell. 1996. "Local Political Parties and Legislative Races in 1992 and 1994." In *The State of the Parties*, 2d ed., ed. John C. Green and Daniel M. Shea. Lanham, Md.: Rowman and Littlefield.

Herrnson, Paul S. 1988. *Party Campaigning in the 1980s.* Cambridge, Mass.: Harvard University Press.

Jacobson, Gary C. 1990. *The Electoral Origins of Divided Government: Competition in U.S. House Elections, 1946-1988.* Boulder, Colo.: Westview Press.

Jacobson, Gary C., and Samuel Kernell. 1983. *Strategy and Choice in Congressional Elections*, 2d ed. New Haven, Conn.: Yale University Press.

Jewell, Malcolm E., and David Breaux. 1988. "The Effect of Incumbency on State Legislative Elections." *Legislative Studies Quarterly* 13: 495-514.

Kazee, Thomas A. 1980. "The Decision to Run for the U.S. Congress." *Legislative Studies Quarterly* 5: 79-100.

Maisel, L. Sandy. 1982. *From Obscurity to Oblivion: Running in the Congressional Primary.* Knoxville: University of Tennessee Press.

Maisel, L. Sandy, Linda S. Fowler, Ruth S. Jones, and Walter J. Stone. 1994. "Nomination Politics: The Roles of Institutional, Contextual, and Personal Variables." In *The Parties Respond*, 2d ed., ed. L. Sandy Maisel. Boulder, Colo.: Westview Press.

Maisel, L. Sandy, and Walter J. Stone. 1997. "Determinants of Candidate Emergence in U.S. House Elections: An Exploratory Study." *Legislative Studies Quarterly* 22: 79-96.

Maisel, L. Sandy, Walter J. Stone, and Cherie Maestas. 1997. "Candidate Quality in Congressional Elections: A Preliminary View from the Candidate Emergence Study." Paper prepared for presentation at the annual meeting of the American Political Science Association.

Ranney, Austin. 1965. *Pathways to Parliament.* Madison: University of Wisconsin Press.

Seligman, Lester G., Michael R. King, Chong Lim Kim, and Roland E. Smith. 1974. *Patterns of Recruitment: A State Chooses Its Lawmakers.* Chicago: Rand McNally.

Sorauf, Frank J. 1963. *Party and Representation.* New York: Atherton Press.

State Legislative Leaders Foundation. 1997. *The Handbook of State Legislative Leaders, 1997-98.*

Tobin, Richard J., and Edward Keynes. 1975. "Institutional Differences in the Recruitment Process: A Four-State Study." *American Journal of Political Science* 19: 671-76.

Wahlke, John C., Heinz Eulau, William Buchanan, and LeRoy C. Ferguson. 1962. *The Legislative System.* New York: John Wiley.

Weber, Ronald E., Harvey J. Tucker, and Paul Brace. 1991. "Vanishing Marginals in State Legislative Races." *Legislative Studies Quarterly* 16: 29-48.

CHAPTER 5

Parties, Interests, and Narratives: The Decline of Deliberation

Burdett Loomis
University of Kansas

Throughout his career, Austin Ranney has consistently explored the central element of democratic government: how the governed are linked to those who govern them. Even as his research and writing have mapped out the uneven terrain of American democracy, Ranney has communicated an optimism of spirit, in his scholarship, his activism, and his devotion to both politics and political science. Political institutions do matter, as they arc between citizen and congressman, voter and presidential candidate, even—arguably—viewer and pundit. It is no accident that Ranney, the long-time student of parties and elections, turned his attention to television in the 1980s; in an age of actor-president Ronald Reagan and weakened political parties, this rapidly maturing mass medium constituted a powerful form of linkage between political elites and the people.

In 1983, when Ranney's *Channels of Power* was published, television derived its power from its capacity to allow a huge audience to experience, simultaneously, the same event or appeal. Most of the traffic over these channels traveled from the elites—political and media—to a mass audience. Sometimes, of course, the audience would respond—with "rally round the flag" effects to national crises[1] or with judgments about the legitimacy of presidential candidates from Kennedy to Goldwater to Muskie to Carter. Likewise, the compelling drama of Watergate transfixed an entire nation, as we learned, day by day, of presidential misdeeds.

---

[1] John Mueller, *War, Presidents and Public Opinion* (New York: John Wiley and Sons, 1973), Chs. 9, 10.

Although Ranney generally concluded that the three major networks would remain dominant and that the most important media effects would remain mass-oriented, he could see the growing possibilities for more selective mobilization of particular interest-group constituencies. He observed that

> cable and closed-circuit television formats, with their abilities to target specific audiences, are likely to enable . . . groups to mobilize their members more rapidly and effectively than ever. . . . Hence, the main political impact of television's new devices may be, not to make ordinary citizens better informed, but to fragment the policy-making processes of government even further.[2]

Even in the 1980s, applications such as satellite uplinks (for groups like the Chamber of Commerce) and the establishment of Pat Robertson's cable-based Christian Broadcast Network allowed interests to communicate to group members (the Chamber) or to the faithful (CBN) with their own extensive versions of events and related calls to action.[3] Indeed, many interests invest heavily in framing issues and setting the policy agenda by articulating their own versions of policy problems and solutions (e.g., global warming, electricity deregulation). Even though the daunting promise of 500 channels of cable television has not yet materialized, fragmentation within the policymaking process has increased, as our checks-and-balances constitutional framework has encouraged the "demosclerosis" of hyperpluralism.[4]

Moreover, as myriad interests defend their respective turfs, our institutional capacity for civil discourse has declined,[5] replaced by rigid

[2]Austin Ranney, *Channels of Power* (New York: Basic Books, 1983), 164.

[3]See Burdett Loomis, "Groups and the Grassroots," in *Interest Group Politics,* ed. Allan J. Cigler and Burdett A. Loomis (Washington, D.C.: CQ Press, 1983), 169-90.

[4]See, for instance, Jonathan Rauch, *Demosclerosis* (New York: Times Books, 1994); Theodore Lowi, *The End of Liberalism* (New York: Norton, 1979); and Mancur Olson, *The Logic of Collective Action* (Cambridge: Harvard University Press, 1965).

[5]Eric Uslaner, *The Decline of Comity in Congress* (Ann Arbor: University of Michigan Press, 1993).

partisan rhetoric and interest-group pleadings in the form of stories, such as the health insurance industry's "Harry and Louise" advertisements, that leave little room for discussion. Still, parties must seek to aggregate varying points of view and at least attempt to govern; even in the Republican congressional era, this means that face-to-face deliberation remains a frequent fact of life for members of the party in government. For organized interests, however, there is no clear need to deliberate, even in the face of a clear public policy problem, such as the lack of health care insurance for 40 million Americans. Indeed, to defeat a proposed piece of legislation, an interest group is well advised *not* to deliberate, in that the outcomes of the deliberative process are not predictable and may well alter the status quo. With no need to aggregate and little incentive to deliberate, organized interests are left free to advocate on behalf of their own carefully constructed positions through lobbying, access-building campaign contributions, advertising, and public relations.

In *Golden Rule*, Thomas Ferguson expounds an "investment theory" of political parties in which "a tiny minority of the population—major investors—[dominate] the political system."[6] He points out that large investors hold natural advantages in both acquiring and analyzing information of importance to them. He posits the control of political parties (and the party system in general) as a goal of these investors, who seek a hefty return on their capital. To the extent that parties link institutions, they tie wealthy elites to their political servants. Though overstated, such an interpretation offers real insights, especially given the coordinated contributions and corporate soft money that has flowed to both Republicans and Democrats.[7] And even weak parties are worth capturing. Still, major economic interests rarely place all their bets on a single set of institutions, and political parties represent only one option among many. For example, interests will invest directly in individual politicians, through campaign contributions, and in various lobbying initiatives. This is especially true for corporations in large, concentrated industries, where investment—by either one firm or a tightly-knit trade association—will likely provide tangible

---

[6]Thomas Ferguson, *Golden Rule* (Chicago: University of Chicago Press, 1995), 29.

[7]See, for example, Elizabeth Drew, *Whatever It Takes* (New York: Viking, 1997), 252-53.

dividends. Many industries, such as weapons/aerospace, blend the marketing of their products to the government with efforts to influence policy decisions.[8]

It may be a mistake to make too much of a distinction between an organized interest spending money by investing in candidates through contributions and providing information to elected officials through a lobbying, advertising, or public relations campaign. As Schlozman and Tierney documented in the 1980s, interests employ a wide array of tools in pressing for advantage.[9] Nevertheless, information exchanges between interest groups and legislators can be posited as distinct from the seeking of influence through contributions or favors. Jack Wright notes that interests

> achieve influence in the legislative process not by applying electoral or financial pressure, but by developing expertise about politics and policy and by strategically sharing this expertise with legislators through normal lobbying activities. . . . [Organized interests] can and do exercise substantial influence even without making campaign contributions and . . . contributions and other material gifts or favors are not the primary sources of interest group influence in the legislative process.[10]

Even if information, and not favors or contributions, reflects the basis for interest group influence, does that mean that money is unimportant? Or that all information is equal? Hardly. Beyond advertising and public relations campaigns that seek to hammer home a group's perspective, a lot of policy and political information represents the views of well-heeled interests that fund think tanks, pay for surveys, and subsidize grassroots voices.[11]

---

[8]Ferguson, *Golden Rule*, 30; Burdett Loomis and Eric Sexton, "Choosing to Advertise: How Groups Decide," in *Interest Group Politics*, 4th ed., ed. Allan J. Cigler and Burdett Loomis (Washington, D.C.: CQ Press, 1995), 193-214.

[9]Kay Lehman Schlozman and John T. Tierney, *Organized Interests and American Democracy* (New York: Harper and Row, 1986).

[10]John R. Wright, *Interest Groups and Congress* (Boston: Allyn and Bacon, 1996), 8.

[11]Among others, see Oscar H. Gandy, *Beyond Agenda Setting: Information Studies and Public Policy* (Norwood, N.J.: Ablex Publishing, 1982).

INTERESTS AND INFORMATION

Organized interests and legislators engage in a continuing set of exchanges—or what look like exchanges. Much attention has been placed on the alleged exchange of material benefits: interests provide campaign contributions, trips to Palm Springs and other plush resorts, and (formerly) honoraria to legislators in exchange for favorable treatment in the legislative process. Although this linkage has proved difficult to pin down in extensive studies of congressional voting, we occasionally get glimpses of these exchanges in the journal entries of former Sen. Bob Packwood (R-Ore.) or the openly political operations of the agricultural giant, Archer-Daniels-Midland, whose jets were routinely used to ferry former Senate Majority Leader Bob Dole (R-Kans.) around the country. In addition, much influence may well exist below the surface of congressional operations, within the confines of informal deliberations in committees, subcommittees, and informal conversations.[12]

Without dismissing the importance of corporate investments in politicians' careers and political parties, the emphasis here turns to another set of exchanges—the information that passes, almost continually, between legislators (and their staffs) and organized interests. The world of legislative politics is an uncertain one, and reliable information, especially on complex, politically thorny issues, is always at a premium, for both interests and lawmakers. Lobbyists need information that they can glean only from careful monitoring of the legislative process. "Lobbyists," writes Jeffery Berry, "are the nerve endings of an interest group, [as they] spend most of each day carrying messages back and forth between their environment and their organization."[13]

Information that can be easily obtained is of little worth; scarce and reliable information in uncertain situations is highly valued. Indeed, uncertainty is the governing condition of much legislative activity, in that agendas, bill content, legislative strategies, constituent responses, and interests' reactions are often unpredictable on a single complex bill, to say

---

[12]Richard L. Hall and Frank W. Wayman, "Buying Time: Moneyed Interests and the Mobilization of Bias in Congressional Committees," *American Political Science Review* 84 (September 1990): 797-820.

[13]Jeffery Berry, *The Interest Group Society* (Boston: Little Brown, 1984), 118.

nothing of the uncertainties generated by a host of difficult issues, considered simultaneously.

Although policy expertise is important, other intelligence can be equally useful. In recent studies, Wright and David Whiteman distinguish among three types of valuable information: policy, political (re-election), and procedural (internal to the legislative process).[14] Legislators and lobbyists continually attempt to reduce uncertainties by seeking out all of these kinds of information and engaging in long-term relationships to remain well-informed. Lobbyists frequently convey policy and political information to congressional enterprises (made up of members and their respective staffs), and lobbyists will often provide regular communication linkages among a number of members' enterprises.[15] At the same time, lobbyists garner policy and procedural information from legislators and staff. In particular, knowledge of key procedural moves can only be obtained from congressional sources near the heart of the legislative process. The mutual, long-term needs of groups and lawmakers to reduce uncertainties often forge strong bonds between them, bonds that would be cut if either partner seriously misinformed the other. Nevertheless, interests do advocate; that's what they do. In that advocacy is rarely neutral, it must be packaged in useful and palatable ways. So lobbyists wrap their information in stories.

NARRATIVES: CLARITY IN A CONFUSING WORLD

But stories also protect us from chaos, and maybe that's what we, unblinkered at the end of the twentieth century, find ourselves craving. Implicit in the extraordinary revival of storytelling is the possibility that we need stories—that they are a fundamental unit of knowledge, the foundation of memory, essential to the way we make sense of our lives: the beginning, middle, and end of our personal and collective trajectories. It is possible that narrative is as important to writing as the human body is to representational painting. We have returned to narratives—in many fields of knowledge—because it is impossible to live without them.

Bill Buford, *The New Yorker*, June 24/July 1, 1996

---

[14]Wright, *Interest Groups and Congress*, 88; David Whiteman, *Communication in Congress* (Lawrence, Kans.: University Press of Kansas, 1996), 40.

[15]Whiteman, *Communication in Congress*, 47.

More than three decades ago, E. E. Schattschneider pointed out the importance of the audience in establishing the outcome of conflicts between competing interests. He proposed that "the outcome of *every* conflict is determined by the extent to which the audience becomes involved in it" and that "*the most important strategy of politics* is concerned with the scope of the conflict"—that is, the extent to which the conflict is socialized or privatized.[16] If Schattschneider was even close to being correct, then the relationships between political actors and various audiences lie at the core of understanding who wins and loses in American politics. As issues develop, problems emerge, agendas become established, and alternatives take shape, the linkages between audience and actors are forged through narratives—stories about what is a problem, what the problems look like, what solutions might exist.[17]

On occasion, party leaders can construct overarching, integrative narratives of "evil empires" or "great societies," but day to day, no political figures have more at stake than lobbyists in polishing policy narratives that will work to their advantage. Although distinctions have long been made between inside and outside lobbying, the lines have become blurred in an age of instant communication.[18] The best recent take on this development comes from Jeffrey Birnbaum's close-up account of contemporary lobbying, as a host of separate professionals combine to convey messages that will resonate beyond the Beltway and echo back to Capitol Hill.

> There are still plenty of gladhanders and fundraisers. But right behind those classic types of lobbyists are people with more targeted and potentially more potent skills: economists, lawyers, direct-mail and telephone salespeople, public relations experts, pollsters, and even accountants. All these skills play a role in information gathering. . . [and] lobbyists see it as their job to persuade lawmakers that voters are on the

---

[16]E. E. Schattschneider, *The Semi-Sovereign People* (New York: Holt, Rinehart and Winston, 1960), 2-3, emphases added.

[17]Gary McKissick, "Issues, Interests, and Emphases: Lobbying Congress and the Strategic Manipulation of Issue Dimensions," paper presented at the 1995 Midwest Political Science meetings, Chicago, Illinois.

[18]Kenneth Kollman, *Outside Lobbying* (Ann Arbor: University of Michigan Press, forthcoming); Hedrick Smith, *The Power Game* (New York: Random House, 1988).

lobbyists' side. To that end, *Washington has become a major marketing center.*[19]

More generally, Birnbaum argues that, due to their pervasiveness, "Lobbyists provide the prism through which government officials often make their decisions."[20] This is not because these officials have too little information to sort out, but because they often must confront far too much.

For elected officials, audiences come in all shapes and sizes; a legislator may pay attention to a few local notables, the district's constituents, a single important organized interest, or a set of political action committee managers. In virtually every instance, the linkage is cemented through a common understanding, based on a narrative that ties the actor to the audience. Rarely is there a single dominant narrative or one given story that dictates a legislator's position. Rather, a good tale will include the fodder for a set of acceptable explanations, constructed to fit various groups of voters and interests. As Richard Fenno points out, a legislator must stockpile many explanations for a whole range of actions, especially votes. "There isn't one voter in 20,000 who knows my voting record," he quotes one House member, "except on the one thing that affects him."[21]

In a related vein, Grant Reeher finds that legislators use stories as ways to think through issues of justice—issues that they often do approach head on. Even sophisticated policymakers, such as lawmakers, use stories to process information. Cognitive psychologists would predict as much in their characterization of individuals as "cognitive misers."[22] Narrative, Reeher notes,

> supplies cognitive shortcuts, provides an organization for the other, more specific organizations of attitudes, and places them in a familiar context. It tells us what items of information are to be treated as evidence and what

---

[19]Jeffrey Birnbaum, *The Lobbyists* (New York: Times Books, 1993), 5-6 (emphasis added).

[20]*Ibid.*, 4.

[21]Richard Fenno, Jr., *Home Style* (Boston: Little, Brown, 1978), 144.

[22]Grant Reeher, *Narratives of Justice* (Ann Arbor: University of Michigan Press, 1996), 31.

items are irrelevant. It also invests the information with both meaning and purpose.[23]

Organized interests of all stripes take seriously the task of providing material for congressional explanations. Lobbyists and grassroots advocates offer up stories that members can incorporate in their communications with constituents. Or legislators and their staffers may draw upon public themes articulated by interests through advertisements and public relations campaigns To the extent that their stories are adopted, interests tend to claim credit—both internally and externally—for influencing the policy discourse.

NARRATIVES: STRUCTURING THE PAST AND THE FUTURE

Lawmakers and lobbyists share the desire to reduce uncertainty as they make policy. In an era when most "iron triangles" (linking Congress, the bureaucracy, and organized interests) have disintegrated, to be replaced by much looser, more inclusive issue networks, alternative means of organizing the policymaking process have grown in importance. Drawing on the work of Robert Cover, literary scholar Jay Clayton focuses on the capacity of narrative to organize policy formulation. Moving beyond Richard Neustadt's conclusions about the importance of persuasion for presidents, Clayton states, "[Narrative] is an important source of power in society but the state has no monopoly on that power." Indeed, the availability of a "multiplicity of stories . . . allows narrative to work *against* an agreed upon social order."[24] Such a perspective fits with Schattschneider's notion of drawing the audience into a conflict, with the possibility that the less-powerful can use numbers to counteract position and wealth. Still, narratives are spun out by myriad interests in a crowded and competitive political world, and many of them—even when conflicts are social-ized—defend the status quo, as with 1997 ads on global warming.

As Deborah Stone observes, in order to cut through the multitude of voices and rhetoric, "causal stories" play increasingly important roles in

---

[23]*Ibid.*, 31.

[24]Robert Cover, "Forward: *Nomos* and Narrative," *Harvard Law Review* 97 (1983): 16.

shaping agendas and particular decisions;[25] such stories are usually more specific than the narratives that are put forward to organize the discourse (and structure the conflict) within broad policy communities. Indeed, many causal stories are spun out in relatively private settings of congressional subcommittees or executive agencies, where sophisticated, complicated arguments can be made and understood.

If narratives are powerful, what is the nature of that power? Clayton sees their strength as "not individual but neither . . . precisely collective; it arises from one's participation in established networks of expertise. . . ."[26] But many actors and interests participate within dozens, even hundreds, of distinct networks. Participation merely allows an individual or interest the chance to employ narrative powerfully. All messages are not created—or delivered—equally. Resources are crucial in developing and conveying meaningful communication. Survey research and focus groups help determine what message is most palatable or most powerful; political consultants, public relations firms, and advertising professionals craft themes that appeal to policymakers, partisans, and the public audiences, though rarely to all simultaneously.

COMPETING NARRATIVES AND THE POLICY PROCESS

> Many public policy issues have become so uncertain, complex, and polarized—their empirical, political, legal, and bureaucratic merits unknown, not agreed upon, or both—that *the only things left to examine are the different stories* that policymakers . . . use to articulate and make sense of that uncertainty, complexity and polarization. (emphasis added)
> Emery Roe, *Narrative Policy Analysis*

In the end, there is more to examine than "the different stories." Different policies have objective dimensions, and other potential elements of influence, such as campaign contributions, congressional structure, and presidential involvement, can and do make a difference. Still, the framing

---

[25]Deborah Stone, "Causal Stories and the Formation of Political Agendas," *Political Science Quarterly* 104 (1989): 281-301.

[26]Jay Clayton, *The Pleasures of Babel* (New York: Oxford University Press, 1993), 27.

of past and future policies remains central to most struggles over important decisions.

In terms of shaping the policymaking process, two types of competition among narratives come into play. First, there are competing "causal stories" that imply very different policy choices on such issues as welfare, violence, and trade. Second, and equally important, are those narratives that socialize (expand) or privatize (limit) the scope of conflict.

Narratives are important on both of these dimensions (causality; socialization of conflict) because they ordinarily mix together empirical and normative elements. Thus, causal stories both "purport to demonstrate the mechanism by which one set of people brings about harms to another set" and "blame one set of people for causing the suffering of others."[27] It is no wonder that so many narratives flow from Washington think tanks with distinct ideological leanings (e.g., the conservative Heritage Foundation, the libertarian CATO Institute, or the "New Democrat" Progressive Policy Institute). Almost invariably, we get either social science with a point of view (e.g., Brookings) or a point of view with some social science trappings (e.g., Heritage Foundation). Stripped bare, however, the analyses are both stories in themselves and the grist for many other stories—as with Charles Murray's welfare studies presented in *Losing Ground* and *The Bell Curve* and the many responses inspired by these works.

Lobbyists appeal to legislators and other policymakers through their preferences for communicating through stories much of the time. Although data and related analyses are plentiful and important, anecdotes often provide both lobbyists and legislators with a way to blend both policy and political information as well as combining empirical and normative approaches to a problem.[28] Even when addressing elites, interests often condense their stories and present them publicly through advertisements or public relations campaigns.

For example, the Business Roundtable's advertisement (in the Capitol Hill newspaper *Roll Call*) opposed the expansion of health care benefits to

---

[27]Stone, "Causal Stories and the Formation of Political Agendas," 283.

[28]Legislators and other policymakers should not be considered easy targets for even the most attractive narratives. They spend their days reacting to individualized stories generally resist the temptation to "govern by anecdote," as one Republican lawmaker put it.

include mental illness. Although this ad was directed at the congressional community, rather than toward a mass audience, its story line was simple; the text employed medical terminology, including the Hippocratic Oath, to caution the Congress against doing harm. The Roundtable, identified only at the bottom of the ad as the sponsor, borrowed the normative authority of the medical profession, while simultaneously noting the empirical accounting ("Price Waterhouse") conclusion that 1.7 million people would lose their health care benefits under a federal mental health mandate. The same study also predicts a steep rise (8.7 percent) in health insurance premiums, and the political information warns that most voters would be adversely affected by such a mandate. Finally, the message argued for reforming health care "one step at a time," a policy reference to traditional incrementalism, rather than the more comprehensive approach embodied in the Clinton plan. In this single advertisement, the Roundtable conveyed policy and political information, with an empirical base and a normative overlay, all in the context of a traditional style of federal policymaking.

Especially beneficial for the Business Roundtable in this advertisement is the group's ability to maintain complete control over its message. The price of such control is two-fold—the literal expense (about $6-7,000) and the unknown (but real) costs of presenting the information in a paid format, which dilutes the power of the communication. Overall, however, with its clean presentation and clear message, the ad does not set off alarm bells of warning among readers, who may well retain the information without recalling its source. In addition, the Business Roundtable presented its mental health coverage message in various other contexts—including distributing copies of the study, having CEO's call their friends on the Hill, and obtaining publicity in free media stories.

At the same time, the Business Roundtable did have to contend with alternative narratives. Among the most powerful were the highly personal pleas of fiscally conservative senators such as Pete Domenici (R-N.M.) and Alan Simpson (R-Wyo.), whose family experiences with mental illness became dramatic stories in support of federal mandates.

Still, there are narratives and there are narratives. An extended, complex story spun out at length and in private for a congressional staffer would not work when presented to most average citizens. In these instances, narratives are ordinarily truncated, leaving little more than metaphors or symbolic appeals.[29] As Murray Edelman observes, "Unless their audience is receptive to the depiction of a condition as a problem, leaders and interest groups cannot use it to their advantage."[30] A complex, detailed narrative may, by definition, restrict the receptivity of a mass audience. What remains to be seen, then, is how various audiences are addressed in constructing problems and posing solutions. As Ross Perot and political scientist John Kingdon have pointed out, many proposed solutions have often existed long before the problems of the moment have been defined.[31] Thus, interested narratives can be spun around either problems (global warming), solutions (tax credits for emissions), or both, depending on the audience.

NARRATIVES AND AUDIENCES

In hopes of shaping the policy thoughts and political considerations of political elites, organized interests fashion their narratives to suit particular audiences. As the scope of the conflict broadens, narratives become less complex and meaning is more frequently conveyed by metaphor and symbol. What this means is that different policy arenas, as framed by the scope of the conflict and the number of individuals ultimately affected by policy decisions (see Table 1), will encourage distinctive communication patterns. The policy and political information conveyed by interests (among other actors) to the multiple audiences varies greatly from quadrant to quadrant; at the same time, the overall themes of the messages remain at least roughly consistent.

In the symbolic and public confrontation arenas, the audiences are extensive, although only occasionally would the great majority of all citizens be included within the audience (e.g., during the Great Depression or the Second World War). Still, for interests (and leaders) to influence

---

[29]George Lakoff, "The Contemporary Theory of Metaphor" in *Metaphor and Thought*, ed. Andrew Ortony (New York: Cambridge University Press, 1993), 202-51; Murray Edelman, *The Symbolic Uses of Politics* (Urbana: University of Illinois Press, 1964), and *Constructing the Political Spectacle* (Chicago: University of Chicago Press), 1988.

[30]Edelman, *Constructing the Political Spectacle*, 33.

[31]John Kingdon, *Agendas, Alternatives, and Public Policies* (Boston: Little Brown, 1984), Ch. 6.

Table 1. *Narratives, Interests, and the Scope of Conflict*

Number of individuals and interests affected	Scope of Conflict	
	Narrow	**Broad**
	Niche Politics	**Symbolic Politics**
Few	—detailed private narratives —sketchy public narratives —pure political "muscle"	—truncated narratives —highly public reliance on symbol and myth
Many Politics	**Policy Community Politics** —detailed narratives, available to public, but not widely disseminated —coalitions unified around agreed-upon narratives	**Public Confrontation** —combination of detailed narratives (personal lobbying, including local elites) and truncated narratives (public relations, ads, astroturf) —highly visible coalitions

these audiences, they must tap into well-developed societal myths. As John Nelson observes, "political myth-making provides crucial requirements for the virtuous practice of mass persuasion."[32] But tapping into myths does not mean that they cannot be changed. In fact, constructing arguments around myths and metaphors may well encourage changes in meaning.

In the end, however, politicians usually employ metaphors that reinforce societal stereotypes, or those of dominant interests within a policy community.[33] Audiences responded to Ronald Reagan's description of the Soviet Union as an "evil empire" and his desire to protect us with "Star Wars" technologies. Presidents possess great advantages in employing such

---

[32]John S. Nelson, no date, typescript, "What If the Government Was Never a Machine or a Man? Myth as Cognition and Communication in Politics," University of Iowa.

[33]Murray Edelman, *Political Language* (New York: Academic Press), 1977.

symbols and metaphors, when compared to legislators or lobbyists. On occasion, however, an individual legislator (e.g., Newt Gingrich on various issues, Bill Bradley on tax reform) can succeed in shaping the nature of a policy debate, as can an interest group, such as the Health Insurance Association of American (HIAA) on health care reform or the AFL-CIO on NAFTA (and later "fast track" procedures for trade bills), especially when the news media elevate alternate narratives to positions of prominence.

INTERESTS AND NARRATIVES

Although public lobbying campaigns are important, they do not determine policy results, at least on their own. Still, these efforts can affect outcomes, both by conveying certain kinds of information to various audiences and by having the potential to change the scope of the conflict. The narratives articulated by organized interests, ordinarily directed at external audiences, can be of great significance inside the interest as well. For a large corporation or institution (e.g., a university) or a mass membership organization, narratives offer the possibility of promoting a shared mission at a relatively low cost.[34] Either by design or by default, all interests develop core narratives that help hold the organization together. Such narratives are especially important for large, highly complex institutions (e.g., General Motors or the University of Michigan), in that disparate parts of the organization can refer to, either consciously or not, the basic set of stories that define it.

What, then, is the relevance of such narratives to policymaking processes and decisions? Interested narratives can tell us a good deal about the nature of communication in different contexts and the ways in which information is employed at different stages of policy formulation. Narratives have internal as well as external audiences, and this affects the ultimate possibility of deliberation within the policymaking process.

---

[34]Conversely, counter narratives within an interest may prove costly, as with many rank-and-file union members who supported Reaganesque views of many policy issues.

NARRATIVES AND THE SCOPE OF CONFLICT

Building on the four-celled combination of scope of conflict and extent of impact (Table 1), we see an interest drawing on its core narratives in distinct ways, both in terms of affecting the debate in a given context and seeking to redefine the nature of an issue to a different, more favorable, context. To the extent that an organized interest has a core narrative or a set of such narratives, they will be modified to fit into a particular context.

Archer-Daniels-Midland, for example, has proven itself an aggressive player in niche agricultural policymaking and hotly contested policy community politics (e.g., ethanol subsidies), while articulating highly public narratives and symbols (based on its "supermarket to the world" theme) when conflict has become highly socialized. ADM found a new way to break down barriers between paid advocacy and news by hiring David Brinkley as its corporate spokesperson on the ABC interview show that he formerly hosted.[35] ADM's approach stands in contrast to the major privately held grain companies, which assiduously avoid public presentations.[36]

Some anti-abortion groups and environmental organizations incorporate few private narratives into their lobbying; their narratives remain public, in part because they may be distrusted by their own members if they are seen as offering private stories in a context of negotiation. In 1997, for example, the leader of the antitobacco group came under sharp criticism for his willingness to engage in settlement negotiations with state attorneys general and the tobacco industry.[37]

Organized interests—especially those with substantial resources—will shape their messages and their delivery to the nature of conflict. More and more, this means that they opt for expensive outside lobbying campaigns that put forth public narratives that shape the nature of policy decision making, to say nothing of their extensive (and expensive) forays into

---

[35]Maureen Dowd, "Good Night, David," *The New York Times*, January 7, 1998, A21.

[36]See Dan Morgan, *Merchants of Grain* (New York: Viking Press, 1979).

[37]See reactions to prosettlement positions advanced by Campaign for Tobacco-Free Kids at www.tobaccofreekids.org.

electoral politics, through so-called independent expenditure advertising campaigns.[38]

INTERESTS, NARRATIVES, AND THE POLICYMAKING PROCESS

Although policymaking is a messy process, there are some regularities.[39] Roughly speaking, societal conditions come to be defined as problems, which are coupled with potential "solutions" to the problems, many of which have been kicking around for years, if not decades. Policy alternatives are floated, and in the end, a host of forces affect the decision that is ultimately made by the Congress. In most analyses, the defining of issues and the shaping of agendas offer the greatest opportunities for interested narratives (and public narratives, in particular) to affect policymaking.[40] In the era of congressional committee government and closed policy subsystems, which ran from the late 1930s into the 1960s, crucial decisions on specific alternatives and final passage were often made far from the light of day.[41] Schattschneider could thus assume that expanding the scope of the conflict, to bring the audience into the policymaking process, would ordinarily benefit the mass of citizens at the expense of organized interests who labored with quiet success in the corridors of power.

Given the policymaking process in and around the postreform Congress of the 1980s and 1990s, Schattschneider's emphasis on expanding the scope of conflict, while still relevant, plays out in very different ways. Although policy narratives continue to affect the nature of problems and agendas,

---

[38]The 1996 experience—both expensive and successful for some groups—has spawned an aggressive approach to 1998 campaigning. See, for example, Richard L. Berke, "Interest Groups Prepare to Spend on Campaign Spin," *The New York Times*, January 11, 1998, A1.

[39]Among others, see Kingdon, *Agendas, Alternatives, and Public Policy.*

[40]See, for example David Rochefort and Roger Cobb, eds., *The Politics of Problem Definition* (Lawrence, Kans.: University Press of Kansas), 1994.

[41]Kenneth Shepsle, "The Changing Textbook Congress" in *Can the Government Govern?*, ed. John E. Chubb and Paul E. Peterson (Washington, D.C.: Brookings Institution, 1989), 238-66; and Richard F. Fenno, Jr., *The Power of the Purse* (Boston: Little Brown, 1973), among others.

they have become increasingly important in shaping well-articulated policy alternatives and even the final, specific, versions of legislation.

As budgetary concerns grow in significance, interests put forth highly public narratives that compete with each other to fashion future visions that can only be regarded as speculative. What will happen if NAFTA is adopted? What will be the upshot of a balanced budget? How can welfare reform usefully proceed? What will happen in the wake of telecommunications or electric utility deregulation? Even the best policy analysis can take us only a few steps down the road to answering these questions, yet all participants—legislators, executives, lobbyists, and journalists—want more fully blown explanations. In various forms, narratives can satisfy the yearnings for certainty, even when it cannot be guaranteed.

Thus, when the scope of the conflict is expanded, especially on high stakes issues, the best-financed interests tell their stories, over and over again, to a series of overlapping audiences. The old trusting relationships between lobbyist and legislator remain important, but so is the overlay of public narrative—on medical savings accounts, the virtues of deregulation, the importance (or danger) of free trade—in which the moneyed interests can tell their tales, through anecdotes, scientific studies, or symbolic appeals, again and again. Schattschneider's heavenly chorus of moneyed interests has become more vocal, in more venues, with more sophisticated harmony. Much of its influence rests upon the power of narrative to organize information in ways that ultimately serve some interests at the expense of others, to say nothing of the community at large, even as the stories tell a tale of public benefit and a better future for all.

INTERESTS, AUDIENCE, AND THE
POSSIBILITY OF PUBLIC DELIBERATION

Calvin: Doesn't it seem like everybody just shouts at each other these days?

Hobbes: I think it's because conflict is drama, drama is entertaining, and entertainment is marketable.

Calvin: Finding consensus and common ground is dull! Nobody wants to watch a civilized discussion that acknowledges ambiguity and complexity. We want to see fireworks. We want the sense of solidarity and identity that comes from having our interests narrowed and exploited by little-minded zealots. The talk show hosts, political candidates, news programs, special interest groups . . . become successful by reducing debates to the level of shouted rage. Nothing gets solved, but we're all entertained.

Hobbes: Hmm, you may be right.

[silence]

Calvin: What a boring day this turned out to be!

As usual, Calvin and Hobbes (before their untimely demise) have gotten it right. Debates over issues often end up being shouting matches, with little value save entertainment. Even when voices are muted, there is often no significant deliberation, no substantive exchange of view. Still, hope springs eternal. Benjamin Page argues that professional communicators, such as reporters, writers, commentators, pundits, and experts from academia and think tanks, can facilitate *public* deliberation, both by assisting policy experts to communicate with each other, but also to "assemble, explain, debate, and disseminate the best available information and ideas about public policy, in ways that are accessible to large audiences of ordinary citizens."[42] Relying on several case studies, Page finds that public deliberation is highly mediated by visible communicators; despite some biases and an occasional tendency to be out of touch, he concludes that "the marketplace of ideas actually works reasonably well, most of the time, so long as there is sufficient competition and diversity in the information system."[43]

Examining recent public discussion on major issues scarcely makes one sanguine over the possibility that public communicators can effectively deliberate through press releases, talk shows, op-ed pieces, and the like. For example, if the stakes of a decision are high and the level of understanding of the policy choices, even among elites, is relatively low, can we hope that public deliberation can be of any assistance? Thus, in the 1992-1996 fight over telecommunications reform, the only time the public weighed in at all was in 1992 when the debate focused narrowly on the price of cable service. Subsequently, after the passage of the 1992 bill reregulating cable rates, the policy debate shifted to either a highly symbolic plane—more choice for consumers—or to arcane, often incomprehensible, topics of market penetration, accessibility to spectrum, and the particulars of

---

[42]Benjamin I. Page, *Who Deliberates?* (Chicago: University of Chicago Press, 1996), 5.

[43]*Ibid.*, 124.

competition. All of the major players did, however, hold a clear vision of what short-term gains they wanted to obtain from the complex legislative package. For example, the regional Bell companies desired rapid approval of their bids to provide long-distance service. Their contribution to the public discourse was to bombard elites with highly simplified narratives about offering increased choices to consumers; the long distance coalition (ATT, MCI, Sprint) produced a seemingly similar public message, but its short-term goal was to keep the regional Bells at bay as along as possible. Other elites contributed only marginally to the public discourse, and the important (if highly complex) set of decisions that made up the Telecommunications Act of 1996 was finally passed with many deals, numerous compromises, but little serious public deliberation.

Conversely, the Clinton health reform package seemingly enjoyed a great deal of public deliberation. A host of journalists and scholars have weighed in with their interpretations of the demise of the Clinton plan; despite various differences in their emphases and conclusions, their conclusions scarcely offer much hope for public deliberation contributing to a reasoned policy decision. In particular, the evidence is strong that the so-called professional communicators—and not the public at large—were unduly affected by the HIAA's "Harry and Louise" advertising campaign. With a limited budget ($20 million overall; $14 million for advertising), HIAA successfully "misinformed" policy elites about both the political implications and the policy content of the Clinton proposals.[44] To make matters worse, as one study concludes, "Media coverage reinforced the messages of interest group advertising, and thus an electorate poorly informed about a complex policy area found it difficult to disentangle truth from falsehood."[45]

In the end, the simplifying narratives of "Harry and Louise" or the apparent simplicity of the Canadian-style system (along with dozens of other specific stories, put forth by dozens of interests) did little to move

---

[44]This sum is clearly "generous" among those seeking to influence policy outcomes, but in terms of marketing an idea or product to the public at large, it is very small; see, for example, Darrell West, Diane Heith, and Chris Goodman, "Harry and Louise Go to Washington: Political Advertising and Health Care Reform," *Journal of Health Politics, Policy and Law* 21 (Spring 1996).

[45]West, Heith, and Goodman, "Harry and Louise Go to Washington."

elites or the public toward some set of reasoned health care decisions. The very scale of the decisions surely worked against the possibility of adopting an integrated package of reforms, as many groups could support a story that called for health care reform, but not *this* one. What happens, then, when only one component (or a few parts) of the health care system is targeted for change?

The very uncertainty of many high stakes outcomes (and how to influence them) may well lead to an increasing reliance on narratives among the interested parties. Narratives provide some comforting coherence in highly uncertain situations, when large numbers of interests and complex issues combine to render incomplete any firm understanding of either policy substance or political linkages. As cozy triangles have given way to loose, ill-defined policy communities, all kinds of relevant information (policy, political, and process) have grown in importance, both to members of Congress and to those who would influence these legislators.[46] This lack of structure opens up the possibility for narratives to provide coherence to a messy and uncertain policymaking process, in that a narrative requires both a speaker (writer) and an audience. In the end, stories may seem concrete, but their very construction and interpretation derive from the intangible relationship between narratives and audiences. Stories remain open to change and reinterpretation.

Anyone who has spent much time with legislators or lobbyists will appreciate that they communicate through stories much of the time. Although data and related analyses are plentiful and important, anecdotes often provide both lobbyists and legislators with a way to blend both policy and political information as well as combining empirical and normative approaches to a problem. In private settings among political veterans, narratives can surely convey clear, agreed-upon meanings that can serve as the basis for meaningful deliberation. But when interests "go public" with their stories, nuance is often lost, as with the Harry and Louise's interpretation of the Clinton health care plan. Likewise, interests enjoy less policy and political flexibility when their positions are well-publicized. The

---

[46]See William Browne, *Cultivating Congress* (Lawrence, Kans.: University Press of Kansas, 1995); Whiteman, *Communication in Congress*; and Wright, *Interest Groups and Congress*.

opportunities for deliberation and compromise decline, and confrontation becomes more likely.

INTERESTS, AUDIENCES, AND DELIBERATION

> The role of the press, as Lippmann saw it, was to circulate information, not to encourage argument. . . . His point was that information precluded argument, made argument unnecessary. Arguments were what took place in the absence of reliable information.
>
> Christopher Lasch, *Revolt of the Elites*

As interests craft their messages for given audiences—congressional staffers, op-ed readers, constituents of a committee chairman—they are much more likely to convey information than engage in an argument. Even when there seems to be a real debate, messages ordinarily do not address the meat of opponents' positions. After all, as Lasch notes, "Argument is risky and unpredictable, therefore educational." Indeed, he points out that argument "carries the risk . . . that we may adopt [our opponents'] point of view."[47]

When interests convey information, they ordinarily do not engage in deliberation or argument; rather, they work to marshal their own evidence. Compromise may occur, as with the 1996 telecommunications bill, but that does not imply any deliberation took place. Legislative results are often purely opportunistic—political deals, virtually unrelated to any consideration of the merits of the policy at hand.

In conveying information, the group universe scarcely offers equal representation to all interests. Schattschneider noted this most forcefully, of course, but even Page observes the inequalities and biases in the mediated marketplace of ideas. In particular, "large, dispersed groups of citizens" are disadvantaged in the information they convey relative to the "political knowledge and/or propaganda bought by businesses and other concentrated interests."[48] Page does not even argue that deliberation occurs. In addition, despite conceding the information produced by private sources "may be quite important," he observes that direct information about

---

[47]Christopher Lasch, *The Revolt of the Elites* (New York: Norton, 1996), 170.
[48]Page, *Who Deliberates*, 9.

possible "antidemocratic biases" in interest group communication is difficult to come by.[49] So he essentially dismisses this element of communication, even as he proceeds to detail optimistically the possibility for mediated deliberation.

More productively, Jane Mansbridge incorporates interested narratives into her notion of deliberation. Although not endorsing a corporatist model, she argues that "Empirical research on the deliberative aspects of interest representation should begin to describe and model existing mechanisms both for deliberation among rank-and-file members and for interchange between members and their formal and informal representatives."[50] Mansbridge wants to transcend competitive frameworks for communication among interests, but she does not give much of a hint how interests may move from conveying information to engaging in argument.

In the end, narratives—especially expensive ones—seek to convey a version of information to a given audience. And the more public the performance, the less likely will there be any meaningful deliberation. As more and more interests incorporate public presentations—on television, in newspapers, and in magazines, even when the audience is dominated by policy elites, these interests may well discover that they cannot easily deliberate, given the stories that they have spun. To be sure, the media allow for the construction of narratives and the framing of issues, but they also encourage a stasis, once a story has been established. Where politicians desire flexibility, interests want certainty. Skillfully designed narratives, publicly repeated over and over, may well serve the particularistic goals of interests, but the give-and-take of politics will surely suffer.

---

[49]*Ibid.*, 9.

[50]Jane Mansbridge, "A Deliberative Theory of Interest Representation," in *The Politics of Interests*, ed. Mark Petracca (Boulder: Westview, 1992), 54.

CHAPTER 6

President Clinton, Newt Gingrich, and the 104th Congress

James P. Pfiffner
George Mason University

In January 1995 after the Republican sweep of the midterm elections Bill Clinton was in a world of hurting. The Republicans had just won a historic victory, giving them control of both houses of Congress for the first time in 40 years. Republicans gained 52 seats in the House and eight in the Senate in a clear electoral rejection of President Clinton and the Democrats. Not one Republican incumbent lost his or her seat. President Clinton's approval ratings had dropped to the low forties, and if he had been up for reelection in 1994, it is likely that he would have been defeated. Newt Gingrich, considered the architect of the House takeover, was seen as the agenda setter for the government, and he was orchestrating a 100-day drive to legislate the Contract with America. In April of 1995 President Clinton was reduced to asserting that the president was still "relevant" to the policy process.

The author would like to thank George Mason University for granting an academic study leave in the spring of 1997 and the Governmental Studies Program at the Brookings Institution for providing a congenial atmosphere, stimulating colleagues, and a home to carry out this research. Several colleagues provided helpful comments on this research whom I would like to thank: Sarah Binder, George Edwards, Chris Foreman, Jacob Hacker, Steve Hess, John Kingdon, Eric Lawrence, Tom Mann, Pietro Nivola, Bruce Oppenheimer, John Owens, Steven Shull, Barbara Sinclair, Kent Weaver, Margaret Weir, and Joe White.

Fast forward one year to January 1996 and the positions are reversed. Newt Gingrich and the Republicans had been blamed by the public for unnecessarily shutting down the government twice in the previous three months. Gingrich had the highest negative poll ratings of any major national leader. Most of the Contract had not become law. Conservative House Republicans blamed Gingrich for their failure to win broader victories and talked openly of a revolt against the Speaker. President Clinton had rebounded in the polls, with some of the highest ratings of his presidency, and he was unopposed in the Democratic primary races. He would go on to a relatively easy victory in his campaign for reelection against Robert Dole.

This turnaround is one of the most striking reversals of fortunes in recent American political history, and its explanation is intertwined with the nature of the U.S. party system. This essay will take up the question of how President Clinton went from being an extremely vulnerable incumbent whom the Republicans were certain could easily be beaten in 1996 (most Democrats agreed) to an easy victory over Robert Dole by November 1996. The parallel story is how Newt Gingrich plunged from being the hero of the 1994 elections who had master-minded the Republican takeover of Congress to one of the most unpopular politicians in the national government.

In his classic analysis of responsible party government, Austin Ranney catalogues the defects of the U.S. political party system according to its critics and advocates of responsible party government.[1] U.S. parties do not often "stand" for anything and seldom offer voters clear programmatic choices at election time. Parties seem to pursue power as an end in itself rather than for the purpose of enacting systematic programs. Members of Congress see themselves as individual delegates responsible to their own constituencies rather than members of a party with collective responsibilities. Once in office they cannot command the votes of their members and thus cannot enact a coherent policy program.[2]

---

[1]Austin Ranney, *The Doctrine of Responsible Party Government* (Urbana, Ill.: University of Illinois Press, 1962). See also Austin Ranney, *Curing the Mischiefs of Faction: Party Reform in America* (Berkeley: University of California Press, 1975).

[2]Ranney, *Responsible Party Government*, Ch. 2.

But in 1994 it seemed that the Republican party was offering the voters a clear choice in accord with some of the principles of responsible party government. In contrast to the complaint that U.S. political parties do not "stand" for anything, the Republicans had run on the Contract for America. In contrast to the complaint that U.S. parties put emphasis on individuals rather than collective responsibility in the party, the Republican leaders said explicitly that if they did not deliver on their promises that voters should vote against them in the next election. In contrast to the complaint that U.S. political parties only seek political power and are not committed to policy results, Republican candidates, especially the freshmen, often seemed to be more committed to policy outcomes than to winning reelection. Thus the Republican victory in 1994 seemed to be an exception to politics as usual.

In another perspective on American political parties, David W. Rohde has argued that the political circumstances of the 1994 elections and the 104th Congress created the conditions for "conditional party government." According to Rohde the necessary conditions include (1) a high degree of preference homogeneity within a party and (2) a high degree of preference difference between the parties. These conditions make party members willing to delegate a relatively high degree of power to their leaders because they are confident that leaders accurately reflect the will of the party.[3] The elections of 1994 resulted in greater interparty polarization and interparty cohesion than any other postwar Congress. The changes enacted by the Republicans in the House (and to a lesser extent in the Senate) resulted in greater power being delegated to congressional leaders than since the early 1900s.[4]

While Rohde's theory of conditional party government helps explain the unusual degree of delegation of power Newt Gingrich enjoyed as Speaker of the House in the first session of the 104th Congress, Ranney's insights about the party system should lead us to expect that these condi-

---

[3]David W. Rohde, *Parties and Leaders in the Postreform House* (Chicago: University of Chicago Press, 1991).

[4]John H. Aldrich and David W. Rohde, "Theories of the Party in the Legislature and the Transition to Republican Rule in the House," paper presented at the 1995 annual meeting of the APSA; David W. Rohde, "Parties, Institutional Control, and Political Incentives: A Perspective on Governing in the Clinton Presidency," revision of a paper delivered at the colloquium on "The Clinton Years in Perspective," at the Université de Montreal, October 6-8, 1996.

tions would not endure too long and that the ambitious policy aspirations of the Republicans in 1994-95 would not be entirely achieved. Ranney's trenchant critique of the responsible party government model points out that the antimajoritarian institutions created by the U.S. Constitution make virtually impossible the type of majoritarian democracy implied by the responsible party government model and by extension, the policy aspirations of the Republicans in 1995.[5]

What makes the political reversal of fortunes between the Republican Congress and President Clinton in 1995 so interesting is that the Republicans, after their impressive victories, did not seem to realize the limits inherent in the separation of powers system. In pushing their priorities further than the system would allow, they hurt themselves and handed President Clinton an advantage he might otherwise not have had.

Before examining the reasons that the Republicans acted as they did, this essay will begin with a brief analysis of the electoral underpinnings of party polarization in Congress and its institutional effects. It will then take up the Republican congressional victory in the 1994 elections and the consolidation of power in the Speaker's office in the House. The budget showdowns and government shutdowns in the fall of 1995 that positioned President Clinton for his reelection in 1996 will then be analyzed. Finally, several explanations of the Republicans' actions will be presented.[6]

POLITICAL TRENDS AND PARTISAN POLARIZATION

The building blocks of the Republican majority in the House can be traced to the partisan reversal in the South over the past three decades. This transformation led to increasing ideological cohesiveness of both parties and polarization in Congress. National policies in the 1960s led to increasing participation by African Americans in the electoral process. The

---

[5]Ranney, *Responsible Party Government*, Ch. 10. According to Ranney, the factors that undermine majority rule in the U.S. include the separation of powers, presidential veto, staggered elections, Senate filibuster, federalism, and the Supreme Court.

[6]For a more thorough analysis of these developments see James P. Pfiffner, "President Clinton and the 104th Congress: Losing Battles but Winning the War," Working Paper of The Institute of Public Policy, George Mason University (October 1997).

Voting Rights Act of 1965 and the registration of many more black voters in the South began the slow change that led to a Republican majority in Congress. Increased black voting and the creation of majority/minority districts (in which a majority of the voters were African American) led to increased numbers of African-American representatives from the South. Since black members of Congress tended to reflect the liberal orientation of their constituents, they reinforced the liberal wing of the Democratic caucus, while the new Republican representatives from the South tended to be more conservative than their Democratic predecessors.[7]

As the party identification of southern whites changed, so did the number of House seats from the South held by Republicans. In the 102nd Congress the Democrats enjoyed a margin of 85 to 44 seats representing the South in the House; in the 104th Congress the margin had reversed to a 73 to 64 Republican advantage. In the Senate southern seats were dominated by the Democrats in the 102nd Congress by a margin of 17 to 9; by the 104th Congress the Democrats were at a 16 to 10 disadvantage. Partisan representation in the other three regions of the country stayed relatively stable over the same period.[8] Thus the Republican capture of Congress in 1994, in addition to short-term factors such as Democratic vulnerability and

---

[7]For analyses of the changing electoral make-up of the South and the partisan implications, see: Earl Black and Merle Black, *The Vital South* (Cambridge, Mass.: Harvard University Press, 1992); Bruce Oppenheimer, "The Importance of Elections in a Strong Congressional Party Era," in *Do Elections Matter?*, ed. Benjamin Ginsberg and Alan Stone (Armonk, N.Y.: M. W. Sharpe, 1996); Gary Jacobson, "The 1994 House Elections in Perspective," in *Midterm: The Elections of 1994 in Perspective,* ed. Philip A. Klinker (Boulder, Colo.: Westview, 1996); Gary C. Jacobson, "Reversal of Fortune: The Transformation of U.S. House Elections in the 1990s," paper delivered at the Midwest Political Science Meeting, Chicago, April 10-12, 1997; Paul Frymer, "The 1994 Electoral Aftershock: Dealignment or Realignment in the South," in *Midterm: The Elections of 1994 in Context,* ed. Philip Klinker (Boulder, Colo.: Westview Press, 1996); Lawrence C. Dodd and Bruce I. Oppenheimer, "Revolution in the House: Testing the Limits of Party Government," in *Congress Reconsidered,* ed. Lawrence C. Dodd and Bruce I. Oppenheimer (Washington, D.C.: CQ Press, 1997), 29-60; and "Congress and the Emerging Order: Conditional Party Government or Constructive Partisanship?" 371-89.

[8]Dodd and Oppenheimer, "Congress and the Emerging Order," 396-97.

effective Republican strategies, was the result of longer-term trends in national and particular southern electoral politics.

These trends in electoral politics had an important impact on the internal dynamics of the House and Senate. As the two parties have become more ideologically homogeneous, they have become more cohesive, particularly House Republicans. Thus politics in Congress have become more polarized and partisan. There are fewer conservative Democrats (often called Boll Weevils) and fewer liberal Republicans (often called "Rockefeller Republicans"). One measure of partisan conflict in Congress is the "party vote" in which a majority of one party opposes a majority of the other party in a roll call vote. This measure of polarization has been increasing in recent years, especially in the House. From 1955 to 1965 the percentage of votes in the House that were party votes averaged 49 percent; from 1967 to 1982 the percentage was 36 percent. But after 1982 it began to climb, reaching 64 percent for the 103rd Congress.[9] Party voting reached a record 73.2 percent in 1995.[10] Party voting in the Senate roughly paralleled that of the House though at slightly lower levels, reaching a Senate record of 68.8 percent in 1995.

In the Senate the increased use of the filibuster and other dilatory tactics, such as "holds" on nominations, has developed into a "parliamentary arms race" in which each side is willing to use the extreme tactic because the other side has used it against them.[11] The recent polarization of Congress has also led to a decline of civility and comity that has led a

---

[9]See Barbara Sinclair, "Transformational Leader or Faithful Agent? Innovation and Continuity in House Majority Party Leadership: The 104th and 105th Congresses," paper presented at the 1997 annual meeting of the American Political Science Association, Washington, D.C., 5; and *CQ Weekly Reports*, (January 27, 1996), 199.

[10]It was the highest since *CQ* began keeping the data in 1954, *CQ Weekly Reports* (January 27, 1996), 199. According to John Owens' calculations party voting was the highest since 1905-06. See John Owens, "The Return of Party Government in the U.S. House of Representatives: Central Leadership —Committee relations in the 104th Congress," *British Journal of Political Science* 27 (1997): 265. Party unity scores, in which members of the two parties vote with their majorities on party line votes, also increased to unusually high levels.

[11]Sarah A. Binder and Steven S. Smith, *Politics or Principle?* (Washington, D.C.: Brookings, 1997), 10, 16.

number of thoughtful and moderate members to step down rather than to stay and fight increasingly partisan battles.[12]

Thus over the past several decades the once solid Democratic South has turned Republican, leading to the polarization of the political parties in Congress. This polarization has led to increased confrontation and the decline of comity in Congress. Although the partisan trends described above contributed to the Republican victory in the 1994 elections, the turnover of Congress to the Republicans was not foreordained by these trends. In order to understand the outcome of the 1994 elections it is necessary to review the political context of the 1994 campaigns for Congress.

The longer-term groundwork for the Republican victories in 1994 was laid by Newt Gingrich after his election to Congress in 1978. In 1983 he formed the Conservative Opportunity Society, a group of House Republicans who would fight the Democrats with harassing parliamentary tactics, such as long lists of floor amendments intended to force Democrats into making difficult votes.[13] Also in 1983 Gingrich became the chair of GOPAC, a political action committee to raise money for Republican challengers to Democratic congressional seats. GOPAC systematically set out to develop a "farm team" of congressional candidates by aiding in fund raising, and by developing ideas, issues, debating points, and campaign literature for their campaigns. By the time of the 1994 Republican election victories the newly elected freshman class felt that Newt Gingrich had played a major role in their individual elections and in the creation of a Republican majority in the House. Their gratitude would be a factor in tight House votes during the 104th Congress.

The longer-term electoral trends and the building of Republican challengers over the previous decade provided the context for the immediate issues presented by President Clinton and the 103rd Congress.[14] The

---

[12]See Eric Uslaner, *The Decline of Comity in Congress* (Ann Arbor, Mich.: University of Michigan Press, 1993).

[13]See the summary by Barbara Sinclair in "Transformational Leader or Faithful Agent?"

[14]For an analysis of the Clinton administration's legislative record, see James P. Pfiffner, "President Clinton and the 103rd Congress: Winning Battles and Losing Wars," in *Rivals for Power: Presidential-Congressional Relations*, ed. James Thurber (Washington, D.C.: CQ Press, 1996).

Clinton administration was vulnerable in 1994 because the 1992 elections had brought unified government; expectations of the electorate, encouraged by Clinton's ambitious policy agenda, were high. In his first year in office President Clinton won several significant legislative victories. But the major Clinton policy priority of the 103rd Congress, and the one that would make them most vulnerable to Republican attack, was the proposed overhaul of health care financing policy. The administration wanted to achieve universal health care insurance coverage without government financing (thus employer mandated insurance) or major tax increases.

The proposal was attacked by the Republicans as being too complex, too coercive, too costly, and too much big government. By blocking action on health care legislation in 1994 and opposing any alternative plan that might have been more acceptable, the Republicans were able to argue that the Clinton administration was in favor of big government and at the same time was not able to govern, since it could not even pass its most important legislative priority.[15]

The Republicans were able to turn the election into a referendum on the Clinton Administration and Democratic control of the government. Individual candidates ran as much against the Clinton administration as they did against their congressional opponents. Democratic candidates did not want the president to campaign for them in their districts, and Republicans ran ads that "morphed" photographs of their Democratic opponents into images of President Clinton. The Republican election themes were that President Clinton could not be trusted personally, the Democrats were not able to govern effectively, and that the government was a sinister force.

In addition to unified opposition to the Clinton administration, the Republicans sought to nationalize the 1994 elections through the Contract With America. The "Contract" was a collection of issues arranged into 10 points that had been carefully constructed under the inspiration and

---

[15]For analyses of the Clinton health care plan and the politics of Republican opposition, see: Jacob Hacker, *The Road to Nowhere* (Princeton, N.J.: Princeton University Press, 1997); Thomas Mann and Norman Ornstein, eds., *Intensive Care: How Congress Shapes Health Policy* (Washington, D.C.: Brookings, 1995); Theda Skocpol, *Boomerang: Health Care Reform and the Turn Against Government* (New York: Norton, 1996); and Haynes Johnson and David Broder, *The System* (New York: Little Brown, 1996).

direction of Newt Gingrich.[16] The Contract issues included a balanced budget, welfare reform, term limits, defense increases, tort reform, crime, congressional reform, family legislation, tax cuts, and a number of other issues; though the specific form of each of the policy proposals would depend on the legislative process. Despite the Republicans' efforts to publicize the Contract, including an ad in *TV Guide*, most voters had not heard of the Contract.[17] Nevertheless, it did have the effect of unifying the Republican candidates for Congress. They went back to their individual races and used the issues and rhetoric of the Contract to run against the Clinton administration and their Democratic opponents.

The efforts of the Republicans were successful; they won the 1994 elections in a landslide. In gaining 52 seats in the House and eight in the Senate, the Republicans took control of the Congress for the first time since 1952. Thirty-four Democrats lost their seats in the House, and no Republican incumbents lost. Perhaps more importantly, Republicans won 39 of 52 open House seats.

ORGANIZING THE 104TH CONGRESS: CONDITIONAL PARTY GOVERNMENT

Since Newt Gingrich was seen as the architect of the Republican takeover of Congress, his support was universal among House Republicans, and particularly strong among the 73 House freshmen who felt that they owed their seats to him. This strong support from the rank and file, combined with shrewd initial actions to consolidate his power in the House, gave Gingrich initial control of the agenda approaching that of a prime minister in a parliamentary system. The delegation of power to the leadership fulfilled the conditions of conditional party government, and the

---

[16]John Bader, "The Contract with America: Origins and Assessments," in Dodd and Oppenheimer, *Congress Reconsidered*.

[17]A *New York Times*—CBS poll found that 71 percent of those polled had not heard of the Contract with America, see Gary Jacobson, "The 1994 House Elections in Perspective," in *Midterm: The Elections of 1994 in Perspective,* ed. Philip A. Klinker (Boulder, Colo.: Westview, 1996), 6.

discipline of the Republican ranks resembled what might be expected under responsible party government.[18]

After the elections Gingrich lost no time in asserting his control over the House, and a number of important changes were made in House rules and structure that facilitated leadership control over the legislative process. In enhancing the Speaker's power, Gingrich built upon Democratic practice over the previous two decades, but the Republicans' changes to the House rules created the most powerful Speakership since those of "Uncle" Joe Cannon and Thomas B. Reed at the turn of the century.

The main thrust of the changes was to enhance the power of the leadership at the expense of committees. Three committees were abolished outright (Post Office and Civil Service, District of Columbia, and Merchant Marine and Fisheries), and some committee jurisdictions were changed. Twenty-five subcommittees were abolished.[19] Authority over committee assignments was changed from the committee on committees to the newly created Steering Committee that was dominated by Gingrich. In naming the chairs of committees Speaker Gingrich chose to ignore seniority in several cases. The terms of committee chairs were limited to three consecutive terms, while the speaker's would be limited to eight years, thus putting chairs on a much shorter leash than when the tenure of chairs was assumed to be indefinite and the seniority system sacrosanct. In addition, committee staffs were cut by one third, from 1,854 to 1,233 positions; committee

---

[18]For astute analyses of the leadership of Newt Gingrich in the 104th Congress, see John E. Owens, "Taking Power? Institutional Change in the House and Senate," and Barbara Sinclair, "Leading the Revolution: Innovation and Continuity in Congressional Party Leadership," both in *The Republican Takeover of Congress,* ed. by Dean McSweeney and John E. Owens (Basingstoke and New York: Macmillan, 1998).

[19]On the institutional consequences of the Republican takeover of Congress, see John E. Owens, "The Institutional Consequences of Partisan Change in Congress," in *Developments in American Politics 3,* ed. Gillian Peele, Christopher J. Bailey, Bruce Cain, and B. Guy Peters (Basingstoke and New York: Macmillan, 1998); and "Party Government and the Converging of Committee-Floor Relations in the House of Representatives: Some Preliminary Findings," paper presented at the Southern Political Science Association meeting, Norfolk, Va. (November 5-8, 1997).

budgets were also cut from \$222.3 to \$156.3 millions.[20] Notably the leadership staff was not cut (and in fact was slightly increased), and personal staff was left untouched.

With full committee chairs now more effectively controlled by the leadership, subcommittees were put under tighter control of the full committee chairs. The Republicans decided to roll back some of the reforms of the 1970s that were referred to as the "subcommittee bill of rights." In the 104th Congress full committee chairs would now be able to designate subcommittee chairs and control majority party subcommittee staffing and budgets.

Gingrich skillfully used his new leadership powers to control the legislative work of the committees. When he was not confident that he could control their behavior, he bypassed them by forming special task forces that were able to bypass regular committees in the formulation of legislation. Between 20 and 30 of these temporary task forces were created by Gingrich, and in October 1995 he went so far as to say that "eventually, it would be better if committees could be replaced by task forces."[21]

That all of these mechanisms to enhance the Speaker's power and ability to control committees were deemed necessary, demonstrates just how powerful the fragmenting tendencies are in the House and how formidable are the forces against maintaining conditional party government, let alone responsible party government. Virtually all the Republicans, and especially the 73 freshmen, gave Newt Gingrich credit for masterminding the Republican takeover of the House; they were firmly committed to the Republican policy agenda and felt grateful to Gingrich personally. Nevertheless, all of these changes were seen as necessary to ensure control of the agenda by Gingrich and his leadership team.

The opening of the 104th Congress on January 4, 1995 was accompanied by all of the spectacle and media coverage that usually accompanies a presidential inauguration. The Republicans were claiming a mandate from the 1994 elections based on the policy proposals in the Contract. The

---

[20]John E. Owens, "The Return of Party Government in the U.S. House of Representatives: Central Leadership—Committee Relations in the 104th Congress," *British Journal of Political Science* 27 (1997): 252.

[21]Quoted in Owens, "The Return of Party Government in the U.S. House," 261.

opening session lasted a record 14 and one half hours, finally adjourning at 2:25 a.m. on January 5. The enthusiasm of the House Republicans stemmed from the conviction that they were participating in an unprecedented historic event. No previous congressional class had campaigned on such an explicit policy platform, and they intended to deliver on their promises. Newt Gingrich emphasized the historical significance of the Republican agenda: "what we're doing is a cultural revolution with societal and political consequences that ultimately changes the government. That is a vastly bigger agenda than has been set by any modern political system in this country."[22]

The ambition of their policy goals was matched by the ambition of the timetable set by the Contract. It promised that the House would bring to a vote each item in the Contract within the first 100 days of the new session. Despite the large agenda, the House Republicans were successful in bringing up each of the items for a vote and passing all of them, with the exception of the term limits proposal, which entailed a constitutional amendment, requiring a two thirds majority. Of the 21 legislative actions that embodied the 10 Contract policy initiatives, the House passed 20, an impressive legislative feat, particularly within such a limited time frame.[23]

The Contract was used very skillfully to force through a lot of legislation in a short period of time. It was invoked by the leadership as a moral commitment to pressure House Republicans to move quickly, delegate power to their leaders, and vote for measures that in ordinary circumstances they might not have. The 100-days commitment added pressure to act without questioning. That the Republicans were so successful in pushing through the House so much significant legislation was due to the skillful leadership by Speaker Gingrich as well as the special circumstances that provided the opportunity for his leadership.

While the Contract sped through the House in historic fashion, the Senate was another story. Senators had not signed the Contract, and in traditional fashion, the Senate acted as the saucer that cooled the legislative

---

[22]Elizabeth Drew, *Showdown: The Struggle Between the Gingrich Congress and the Clinton White House* (New York: Simon and Schuster, 1996), 275.

[23]Bader, "The Contract with America," in Dodd and Oppenheimer.

tea (in George Washington's metaphor). Of the 21 legislative items in the Contract, only 13 passed the Senate, and eight eventually became law.[24]

THE BUDGET BATTLES OF 1995

The first several months of the 104th Congress were taken up with the push to pass the Contract items, an effort that had overwhelmed the House and pushed aside most other priorities. If the first 100 days of the session were devoted to the Contract, the second hundred days were to be devoted to bringing about the Republican "revolution" through the budgetary process. The first step was passing the budget resolution that would lay out the overall guidelines and priorities. It would set targets for expenditures (which were to be cut) and for revenues (taxes would also be cut) and for the projected deficits (which were to decline until the budget was balanced within seven years). Overlapping with the passing of the budget resolution would be the consideration of appropriations bills that would specify programs to be cut or eliminated. Finally, in the fall all of the unresolved issues would culminate in the reconciliation bills that embodied the Republican priorities and would lead to presidential vetoes and shutdowns of the government.

BUDGET RESOLUTION AND APPROPRIATIONS

The budget President Clinton sent to Congress on February 6 was pretty much a status quo document, with a modest reduction in projected deficits over five years, but also projecting $200 billion deficits over the next five years.[25] Clinton felt that he got little credit for his 1993 budget reduction efforts and saw no need to take any political risks for moving the budget

---

[24]*Ibid.*, 363.
[25]*CQ Weekly Report* (February 11, 1997), 403.

toward balance. The House and Senate resolutions each proposed the elimination of hundreds of programs and several cabinet departments.[26]

After conference committee meetings to iron out the differences between the two versions of the budget resolution, it was finally passed by both houses on June 29 on near party line votes. The resolution called for budget savings of $894 billion (over projected spending) over seven years and a tax cut of $245 billion.[27] While the budget resolution set guidelines for the serious spending cuts that would be necessary to deliver on the promise to balance the budget within seven years, the specific program-matic decisions still had to be made in committees and reported to the floors of the two houses for votes. The Republican leadership in the House decided to make many of the most far-reaching decisions through the appropriations subcommittees rather than through the standing authorizing committees that would ordinarily consider significant changes to programs.

Tight leadership control of the appropriations committee was asserted before the beginning of the 104th Congress when Newt Gingrich announced that he was going to bypass the three senior Republican members of the committee and elevate Robert Livingston (R-Louisiana) to chair the committee. In February Gingrich met with Livingston and the appropria-tions subcommittee chairs. He impressed upon them the centrality of their role to the overall Republican agenda, telling them: "You're going to be in the forefront of the revolution. . . . You have the toughest jobs in the House. If you don't want to do it, tell me."[28] He also insisted that they each write him letters to affirm that they would follow through on their mission. Majority Leader Dick Armey instructed the authorizing committee chairs that they were to work with the appropriations subcommittees in making the

---

[26]See the account by Barbara Sinclair in *Unorthodox Lawmaking: New Legislative Processes in the U.S. Congress* (Washington: CQ Books, 1997), Ch. 11. See also the account in Aaron Wildavsky and Naomi Caiden, *The New Politics of the Budgetary Process*, 3d ed. (New York: Longman, 1997), 303-08; and Drew, *Showdown*, 208-09.

[27]Sinclair, *Unorthodox Lawmaking*, 188-89.

[28]Quoted by David Maraniss and Michael Weisskopf, *"Tell Newt to Shut Up"* (New York: Touchstone, 1996), 87.

cuts. In addition, many of the substantive changes in programs sought by the Republicans would be made in the appropriations committee.[29]

THE RECONCILIATION PROCESS AND GOVERNMENT SHUTDOWNS

As the appropriations subcommittees worked on the programs under their jurisdiction, authorizing committees had to make changes in the large entitlement programs whose funding did not go through the appropriations committees. The committees had to meet to decide how to make the cuts that had been ordered by the budget resolution. All of the appropriations bills as well as the entitlement cuts were supposed to be finished by September 22 so that they could all be combined into one large reconciliation bill.[30]

The budget resolution had committed the Republicans to deep cuts in entitlement programs, and battles over the contours of the cuts were contentious among the Republicans as well as drawing the opposition of Democrats. The cuts necessary to achieve balance were particularly challenging since the Republicans had excluded a majority of federal spending for political reasons: Social Security (about 22 percent of outlays, defense—16 percent, and interest on the debt—16 percent).[31] In order to comply with the budget resolution the Republicans intended to cut $270 billion from Medicare, and $183 billion from Medicaid as well as making deep cuts in other entitlement programs.[32]

The Senate Budget Committee proposed abolishing 100 programs and eliminating the Department of Commerce. The House voted to abolish more than 280 programs and eliminate the Departments of Education and Energy as well as Commerce. Both budget committees called for severe cuts or elimination of Clinton's Goals 2000, national service program, the

---

[29]See John H. Aldrich and David W. Rohde, "The Republican Revolution and the House Appropriations Committee," Working Paper 96-08, Institute for Public Policy and Social Research, Michigan State University, presented at the Southern Political Science Association Convention, Nov. 7-8, 1996, Atlanta, Georgia, 9-21.

[30]Sinclair, *Unorthodox Lawmaking*, 190.

[31]*CQ Weekly Reports* (October 28, 1995), 3282.

[32]Sinclair, *Unorthodox Lawmaking*, 189.

National Endowments for the Arts and Humanities, and the Corporation for Public Broadcasting.[33] The reconciliation bill had to embody compromises between the two houses across many policy areas.

When the end of the fiscal year approached late in September the appropriations bills had not been completed, and as is usually done in such situations, a continuing resolution was passed in order to keep government programs funded. The CR kept the government open until November 13 while Congress deliberated about the fate and funding of the programs slated for cuts or elimination by the Republicans. During October the Republicans began to gather all of the spending cuts in appropriated programs and entitlements together in the reconciliation bill. By October 26, the compromises among the Republicans had been made, and there was tremendous pressure for them to vote for their party's budget balancing package, despite the reservations of many individual members.

Democrats, of course, were firmly opposed to the deep cuts in many programs that they had supported over the years. They argued that drastic program cutbacks had been put into the bill at the last minute without hearings and that they did not have adequate time to consider them or offer alternatives. But the House Republicans prevailed and on October 26 passed the largest reconciliation bill ever passed by 227-203.[34] According to Newt Gingrich the bill was "the most decisive vote on the direction of government since 1933."[35] The next day the Senate passed its reconciliation bill 52-47. The conference committee included 43 senators and 71 members of the House, and after weeks of negotiations covering hundreds of programs, each House had approved the final version by November 20.

The First Shutdown

But in the meantime much of the government had shut down because of a lack of appropriations. Only two appropriations bills had passed and been signed by the president by the end of the fiscal year, September 30. Of the 11 remaining bills, only three had been sent to the president. Others

---

[33]Drew, *Showdown*, 208-09.
[34]Sinclair, *Unorthodox Lawmaking*, 199.
[35]*CQ Weekly Reports* (October 28, 1995), 3282.

were still not agreed to by the House and Senate.[36] When the continuing resolution that had been in effect from October 1 to November 13 ran out, Congress passed another continuing resolution to send to President Clinton. But the bill had a number of provisions that were unacceptable to the president. While the first continuing resolution allowed for agencies to spend funds at 90 percent of their fiscal 1995 levels, the new proposal called for spending at 60 percent of that level for programs that both houses had agreed to eliminate.[37] In addition, it deeply cut funding for many programs, and it committed the president to agree to a balanced budget by 2002. The resolution also prohibited the Treasury Department from using trust funds to pay interest on the national debt. The Republicans intended to put further pressure on the president through the CR by threatening a financial crisis; the legislative ceiling for the $4.9 trillion national debt would be breached about November 15 when $25 billion in interest was due unless Congress passed a law increasing the debt limit.[38]

The strategy of the Republicans was to use the leverage of a possible government shutdown and default on the national debt to force the president to agree to their budget and policy priorities. The Constitution limits the power of Congress to make policy by providing the president with a veto that can only be overridden by two-thirds of each house. Since the Republicans did not have the votes for an override and did not want to compromise with the president, they had to find some other way to pressure the president if they were to prevail. They chose the statutory debt limit and the threat to shut down the government as their means to put pressure on the president. Their calculation was that the consequences of each of the two actions would be so serious that the president would agree to their demands. It was essentially a game of chicken in which they challenged Clinton to accede to their demands or allow unacceptable consequences to follow.

The stakes were high because the United States had never defaulted on its debts, and its failure to finance its debt (pay bondholders) could easily have led to a financial crisis that would undermine the confidence of financial markets and drastically increase the cost of future borrowing to the U.S. Treasury. That the Republicans were willing to risk the financial

---

[36]*CQ Weekly Report* (November 11, 1995), 3442.
[37]*CQ Weekly Report* (November 11, 1995), 3442.
[38]*CQ Weekly Report* (September 23, 1995), 2863.

stability of the country demonstrated their commitment to their own policy goals. The consequences of shutting down the government were not nearly as great. When appropriations had lapsed in the past (about eight times since 1980) parts of the government had been shut down, but for relatively brief periods of time. The consequences were the disruption of services, the inconvenience of citizens depending on government programs, and the administrative costs of administering a shutdown.

The political calculation of the Republicans was that if the government was shut down, that President Clinton would be blamed and that he would soon agree to their terms so as not to be blamed for resisting a balanced budget and shutting down the government. The Republican freshmen were particularly committed to having their way because they felt that they had been elected to carry out their agenda in cutting government programs and balancing the budget. In October Gingrich told a university audience that if the Democrats did not go along with Republican demands, "fine, they won't have any money to run the parts of the Government they like, and we'll see what happens."[39] He further elaborated his position, "I don't care what the price is. I don't care if we have no executive offices, no bonds for 60 days. . . . What we are saying to Clinton is: Do not assume that we will flinch, because we won't."[40]

When the continuing resolution with its unacceptable provisions reached President Clinton on November 13, he vetoed it. The political calculation of the White House was that the president would emphasize the deep cuts that the Republicans intended to make in popular programs such as Medicare, education, and environmental protection as well as programs to help the poor, such as Medicaid, food stamps, and welfare. When the government shut down on November 14, about 800,000 government workers were ordered to stay home, with only those necessary for essential services or where funds for programs had been appropriated.

Gingrich saw the Medicare cuts as crucial to the Republican agenda, and it became a key battleground between the parties. First, it was a big pot of money, and thus significant cuts were necessary since Social Security, defense, and interest on the debt were off the table. Second, the Medicare

---

[39]Jason DeParle, "Listen, Learn, Help, Lead," *New York Times Magazine* (January 28, 1996), 61.

[40]*CQ Weekly Report* (September 23, 1995), 2865.

fund was projected to go into the red within a decade, and regardless of which party did it, changes had to be made soon. Third, the Republicans wanted to shift public policy away from direct government funding of services toward private insurance. But the Republicans became politically vulnerable when President Clinton capitalized on the popularity of Medicare and accused the Republicans of slashing it.[41]

The rhetoric on both sides was misleading from a financial perspective because the estimates of future spending were not that far apart. The Republicans wanted to reduce the rate of growth of Medicare spending, which would necessarily reduce benefits as costs went up and new people qualified for benefits. And the Clinton administration knew that Medicare spending increases had to be curbed if the system was not to go broke. The Republican plan called for cutting $270 billion over seven years, which meant a reduction in the rate of spending from 9.9 percent to 7.2 percent, while Clinton had proposed in 1993 to limit the rate of increase to between six and seven percent.[42] On the other hand, the two sides did have sharply differing visions of how the U.S. should approach large public policy programs that were reflected in the dispute over Medicare. The Republicans wanted to cut governmental spending and rely on the private sector and individual savings, while the Democrats wanted to preserve governmental funding of most social programs, even if costs had to be trimmed.

The Republicans' Medicare proposals passed the House as a separate bill on October 19, and the Senate decided to include the Medicare plan in the reconciliation bill. In the battle for public opinion President Clinton had the advantage of being able to juxtapose the Republicans' target for cutting Medicare by $270 billion with their proposed tax cut of $245 billion, arguing that they wanted to cut Medicare for the elderly in order to pay for a tax cut tilted toward the wealthy. Throughout the fall of 1995 President Clinton would not let voters forget that the Democrats wanted to protect

---

[41]Some public statements by the Republican leadership exacerbated their problems. For instance, on October 25, 1995, Newt Gingrich said that the Health Care Financing Agency, which administers the Medicare Program, should "wither on the vine." Robert Dole the same day said about his opposition to the creation of Medicare in the 1960s, "I was there fighting the fight, voting against Medicare . . . because we knew it wouldn't work." (For both quotes, see Drew, *Showdown*, 318.)

[42]Drew, *Showdown*, 316.

Medicare, Medicaid, education, and the environment from the ravages of Republican cuts.

The reconciliation bill put into one piece of legislation all of the Republican priorities, including Medicare cuts, putting Medicaid into a block grant, turning welfare (AFDC) back to the states, cutting taxes by $245 billion, and the specific programs cuts and eliminations that had been included in the appropriations bills. It cut the Earned Income Tax Credit for the working poor, as well as food stamps and other welfare programs. The final bill, which proposed to cut federal spending by $894 billion over seven years, was finally approved in both Houses on November 17 and finalized on the 18th, and Gingrich proclaimed it "the largest domestic decision we've made since 1933. . . . This is a fundamental change in the direction of government."[43] When the reconciliation bill with the provisions that the president had been objecting to arrived at the White House, Clinton vetoed it on December 6. To make a symbolic statement he used the same pen to sign the veto message that President Johnson had used to sign Medicare legislation in 1965.

With much of the government shut down, pressure for both sides to negotiate began to mount, though public opinion polls indicated that the public blamed the Republicans more than the Democrats for the shutdown.[44] Finally on November 19 a deal was reached to reopen the government, and a continuing resolution was sent to the president for his signature. As the Republicans had insisted, the president agreed to a resolution that called for a balanced budget in seven years scored by CBO.[45] Each side would read

---

[43]*Ibid.*, 328. On the reconciliation bill see Sinclair, *Unorthodox Lawmaking*, 181, and Drew, *Showdown*, 326.

[44]Drew, *Showdown*, 334.

[45]According to the agreement, "The President and the Congress shall enact legislation in the first session of the 104th Congress to achieve a balanced budget not later than fiscal year 2002 as estimated by the Congressional Budget Office. . . ." But as the White House insisted, programs important to the Democrats would be protected: "the President and the Congress agree that the balanced budget must protect future generations, ensure Medicare solvency, reform welfare and provide adequate funding for Medicaid, education, agriculture, national defense, veterans and the environment." *CQ Weekly Report* (November 25, 1995), 3598.

the resolution to support its own objectives. Gingrich called the agreement, "one of the great historic achievements in modern America."[46]

So the longest government shutdown to that date ended on November 19 and the 800,000 government workers went back to work as the continuing resolution took effect; it would last until December 15. The significance of this was that President Clinton had finally agreed in outline to the major demands of the Republicans: a balanced budget in seven years scored by CBO. He was not, however, locked in to the Republican policy priorities in attempting to achieve that balance.

As negotiators for the White House and congressional leaders negotiated into December to arrive at a mutually acceptable formula for the budget, it became increasingly likely that a solution would not be found soon. The White House wanted another continuing resolution in case there was no agreement when the existing continuing resolution ran out on December 15. Robert Dole was inclined to agree to a continuing resolution, but Speaker Gingrich was under heavy pressure from Republicans in the House, especially the freshmen, not to agree to one. Dole's political instincts told him that Congress and the Republicans would again be blamed for the ensuing shutdown, but Gingrich told President Clinton in budget negotiations: "If I go back and try to get a long-term CR without a budget from you, the next time you'll be dealing with Speaker Armey."[47] The Republicans wanted to be sure that the administration would agree to a specific balanced budget containing their priorities. Representative Scott Klug (R-Wis.) said, "We felt that the only way to get the White House to be serious was by keeping the government closed."[48]

The Second Shutdown

With no new continuing resolution, the existing one ran out on December 19, and the government again shut down. But since several appropriations bills had been passed, the shutdown this time affected only 280,000 workers rather than the 800,000 of the earlier shutdown. Over the

---

[46]Drew, *Showdown*, 340.
[47]*Ibid.*, 352.
[48]*Ibid.*, 354-55.

holidays the press ran articles on the effects of the shutdown on government services and programs. Pressure continued to mount for some resolution.

On January 2 Senate Majority Leader Dole declared that "Enough is enough," and convinced the Senate to pass a continuing resolution to allow the government to reopen. While Gingrich was still under pressure from his backbenchers, he felt that negative publicity from the shutdown was hurting the Republicans and that it was time to pass a continuing resolution. On January 3 and 4 Gingrich spent 22 hours in meetings with Republican House members to hear their feelings on opening the government.

After hearing the dissatisfaction of the conservatives but realizing that some of the moderates were worried about the public reaction to the shutdown in an election year, he decided that it was time to end the shutdown.[49] He told the House Republicans, "You don't like the job I'm doing as Speaker, run against me."[50] On January 6, Congress passed a continuing resolution to open the government until January 26 and end the 21-day shutdown. On the same day Clinton delivered a proposal to balance the budget in seven years, but the Clinton proposals differed from the Republicans' and included much lower cuts in Medicare, Medicaid, and welfare. The government was open, but the issues dividing the two sides did not disappear.

A series of continuing resolutions kept the government open for the first three months of 1996 as the two sides continued to negotiate contentious issues. On April 25 an omnibus appropriation bill was passed to cover all the appropriations that had not yet been passed to keep the government open until the end of the fiscal year.

Thus at the end of 1995 Newt Gingrich and the Republicans had shifted the debate in Washington from whether to balance the budget to an agreement with President Clinton to balance the budget within seven years using CBO's numbers. Even though most of the Contract With America had not become law, the Republican Congress had made a large difference in public policy. Many domestic programs were cut, and the framework for considering public policy had clearly shifted to the right. But the Republicans were unwilling to declare victory. Through two government shut-

---

[49]David Maraniss and Michael Weisskopf, "As Time Ebbs, Futility of Talks Starts to Dawn," *Washington Post* (January 21, 1996), A16.

[50]Drew, *Showdown*, 367.

downs they insisted on winning all of their policy priorities, even (or especially) minor symbolic ones such as shutting down the National Endowments for the Arts and Humanities. Their intransigence during the fall of 1995 led to Clinton's resurrection in public opinion polls and his resuscitation as a strong contender for reelection.

WHY VICTORIOUS POLITICIANS ARE TEMPTED TO OVERREACH

President Clinton's relations with the 103rd and 104th Congresses present us with some striking ironies. In his first two years in office Clinton won many battles (laws passed and a presidential support score of 88.6 percent), but he lost the war—his health care proposals were defeated and the Republicans took over Congress in the 1994 elections.[51] In dealing with the Republican 104th Congress, Clinton lost most of the legislative battles (his legislative support score was 36.2 percent), but won the larger war by winning the public relations contest with the Republicans and by being reelected in 1996. As Richard Fenno observed, the Republicans "did something few people thought could be done when they took over the Congress—they reelected President Bill Clinton to a second term. . . . The scope of that political transformation is mind-boggling and virtually impossible to pull off. But the Republicans had done it."[52]

The big question is why things happened that way. It seems that the Republicans blew it late in the first session of the 104th Congress. In 1994 they had won a historic reversal of control of Congress, taking over for the first time in 40 years. They had come into office with an unprecedented and coherent agenda. They had pushed through the House an impressive amount of legislation and pushed much of it through the Senate. They had made significant cuts in a number of government programs. And perhaps most importantly, they had convinced Bill Clinton to agree to a balanced federal budget within seven years.

---

[51]For an elaboration of this argument see James P. Pfiffner, "President Clinton and the 103rd Congress: Winning Battles but Losing the War," in *Rivals for Power,* ed. James A. Thurber (Washington, D.C.: Brookings, 1996).

[52]Richard Fenno, Jr., *Learning to Govern: An Institutional View of the 104th Congress* (Washington, D.C.: Brookings, 1997).

They did not win all of their agenda to be sure. No departments were abolished, Medicare was not privatized, Medicaid and welfare were not turned back to the states (though welfare would be in 1996), and many of their other program cutbacks and eliminations were not achieved. Nevertheless, they might very well have seen the glass of political change as half full and declared victory in the fall of 1995. But when they realized that President Clinton would not agree to much of their ambitious agenda in the fall, they insisted on holding to their threats and refused to pass a continuing resolution that would allow the government to remain open. This allowed President Clinton to convince a majority of the public that the Republicans were being stubborn and thus responsible for the shutdown. Clinton was able to come out ahead by acting as the protector of popular government programs from "extremist" Republican plans for drastic cuts, and he was able to juxtapose their proposed cuts in Medicare funding of $270 billion with their proposed $245 billion tax cut to argue that Republicans were cutting Medicare to give tax breaks to the rich. Several explanations of the Republicans' behavior will be examined in an attempt to understand the political dynamics of 1995.

Rational Explanations

In trying to answer the question of why the Republicans would act in such a seemingly irrational manner (at least in retrospect), several avenues of explanation are possible. The Republicans' action could have been rational from several perspectives. One argument is that if you aim low, you will not accomplish as much as you might if your aim is higher than your reach. The Republicans might have realized that they would be unlikely to achieve all of their goals, but if this were the case, they did not recognize the point at which they had achieved much of what they wanted and that pressing further would hurt them.

A related rational explanation would be that the Republicans had a short time perspective because they had to demonstrate that they could govern as the majority party in Congress and that if they did not demonstrate this in two years, the voters would not return them to office. In addition, many of the freshmen believed in term limits and did not see themselves as professional politicians. Thus they wanted to win all that they could quickly, because they would not be in office for the long haul. Their time horizon was short.[53]

Another rational explanation for their behavior stems from the argument that strategic stalemate may sometimes be preferable to compromise. John Gilmour argues that at times politicians would prefer to have the issue to argue rather than to agree to a compromise and accept a partial solution.[54] This is based on the assumption that the lack of any progress and the persistence of the problem will convince the electorate to strengthen your party in the future, at which time a more complete policy victory can be achieved. This is the type of thinking that led some White House staffers to urge President Clinton in the summer of 1995 not to offer his own proposal to balance the budget, but rather continue to use the Republicans' proposed cuts to bash them and hope for future electoral advantage. The same sort of thinking led the Republicans in 1994 to work for the defeat of *any* health care reform rather than offering a plan of their own or compromising with the Democrats. They calculated that this would give them an electoral advantage in the 1994 elections. (They seem to have been right.) The problem with this approach in 1995 was that public opinion was not with the Republicans on the shutdown and many of the proposals for program cutbacks.

Hubris

It is also possible that the Republican actions did not result so much from rational calculation as from the nonrational tendency of victorious politicians to overreach. One could argue that President Clinton had overreached in 1993-94 when he pushed for a broad series of legislative programs and particularly when he proposed the sweeping health care reforms that ended up defeated. One might explain this by the Democrats

---

[53]For an argument that presidents must move quickly after inauguration if they want to be successful with their policy agendas see James P. Pfiffner, *The Strategic Presidency: Hitting the Ground Running*, 2d ed. (Lawrence, Kans.: University Press of Kansas, 1996). For an analysis of how politicians must utilize policy windows of opportunity, see John Kingdon, *Agendas, Alternatives, and Public Policies* (New York: Harper Collins, 1984).

[54]John Gilmour, *Strategic Disagreement* (Pittsburgh, Penn.: University of Pittsburgh Press, 1995).

focusing on the return of unified government after 12 years and the capture of the presidency, but ignoring the 43 percent plurality and divisions within the Democratic party. From this perspective he overreached and lost in 1994. The Republicans' behavior may have been similar in 1995.

Why do victorious politicians often tend to overinterpret their victories? Perhaps it is because the odds against winning the presidency or control of Congress for the first time in 40 years are so great that the winners see it as a miracle and a sign that they are specially favored by the voters. If the victors come out on top despite the odds against them, perhaps they become emboldened to buck the odds again and bite off more than they can chew.

It is also possible that victorious politicians tend to interpret elections as prospective mandates from the voters rather than as retrospective judgments by the voters on their opponents.[55] The Republicans could easily have seen a mandate from the voters because most House Republican candidates had run on the Contract for America. In their eyes this constituted a specific promise that they needed to keep if they were to be reelected. The problem with this, of course, was that most of what the showdown was about in the fall of 1995 was not in the Contract but went far beyond it in cutting programs and changing policy priorities.

Another problem with reading mandates into elections is that voters are often rejecting the incumbents rather than granting a broad mandate to the winners. Politicians should be sensitive to this since so much campaign strategy and media expenditures go into negative ads that portray the opposition as evil rather than touting the proposed programs of challengers. Both the 1992 and 1994 elections were waged in part on negative advertising and thus the winners should have been wary of reading too much of a mandate into either.[56] Both the 1992 and 1994 elections were also about "change," but it is relatively easy for a broad range of voters to agree that there is a problem (such as the health care system), without any consensus on what should be done to deal with the problem (which is why health care reform foundered in 1994).

———————————

[55]Morris P. Fiorina, *Retrospective Voting in American National Elections* (New Haven: Yale University Press, 1981).

[56]Robert A. Dahl, "The Myth of Presidential Mandate," *Political Science Quarterly* 105 (Fall 1990): 355-66.

It is also possible that voters listen to campaign appeals that promise all sorts of good things if certain policy changes are made, e.g., universal health care coverage. But after the election and concrete policies are proposed to deal with the problem, the costs of the changes become more apparent. Voters may then become disillusioned and turn away from their initial enthusiasm in rejecting the changes that are necessary to achieve the results they had initially favored. In 1994 voters may have favored balancing the budget but may not have agreed with the specific policy proposals that the Republicans favored in order to achieve balance.[57]

Lack of Governing Experience

Richard Fenno proposes another explanation for the overreaching of the Republicans in 1995 and their failure to realize when to stop and accept half a loaf. He argues that the root cause of the Republicans' actions was their lack of experience in governing. He points out that none of the Republicans in the House had ever served with a Republican majority and only seven of the 73 freshman had any governing experience.[58] Republican congressional veterans had spent their careers in the minority, and many had become convinced by Newt Gingrich that the best way to win majority status was a confrontational approach that included attacking the House as an institution. The tactics of the "bomb throwers" in the House were not easily transferable to building governing coalitions. Republicans in the Senate did not have the same problems, since they had been in the majority from 1981 to 1987.

The lack of governing experience was aggravated by the overbearing behavior of the Democrats over part of the 40 years they were in control. There was a tendency to deny the Republicans staffing and other resources proportional to their numbers and to use parliamentary tactics to keep the minority from achieving many of their goals, such as forcing votes on amendments they offered. As the disruptive tactics of the Gingrich-led

---

[57]For an analysis of this dynamic, see: Anthony Downs, "Up and Down with Ecology—the issue-attention cycle," *The Public Interest* 28 (Summer 1972): 38-50.

[58]Richard Fenno, Jr., *Learning to Govern: An Institutional View of the 104th Congress* (Washington, D.C.: Brookings, 1997), 25.

Republicans increased in the late 1980s, Democratic use of special rules to thwart the Republicans intensified the negative cycle.

From Fenno's perspective, the ability of the Republicans to push the Contract through the House was impressive, but short sighted. It was, "a short-run, narrowly focused, inward-looking legislative performance." In Fenno's judgment the Republicans, "had not understood the difference between passing the Contract and governing the country, but what was worse, they had mistaken one for the other."[59] The Republicans might have realized that the Constitution established a system that is not easy to change in the short run. For institutional and political reasons the Senate might have been expected to slow the Contract and modify its contents. More fundamentally, the president has the authority to veto legislation, and short of the two-thirds majority in both houses to override, must be persuaded to sign a bill before it can become a law. Fenno quotes one conservative senator as observing, "I'd feel a lot more confident about the outcome of the revolution if I were convinced all of these guys had taken high school civics."[60] In addition to misjudging President Clinton's willingness to stand firm against them through two government shutdowns, the Republicans failed to recognize the practical significance of the framers' antimajoritarian device, the president's veto power.

Newt Gingrich's Personality

Part of the problem of the Republican's miscalculations can be attributed to Newt Gingrich's personality. Just as Newt Gingrich must be given credit for leading the Republican minority in the House and orchestrating the victory of 1994, so must he be blamed for some of the negative incidents that undermined the ability of the Republicans, once in control of Congress, to accomplish all of their goals. David Maraniss and Michael Weisskopf argue that the problem stemmed from the inability of Gingrich to change his personal style once he became the Speaker of the House and leader of the majority party in Congress.[61] In the minority,

---

[59]Fenno, *Learning to Govern*, 22.

[60]*Ibid.*, 42.

[61]David Maraniss and Michael Weisskopf, *Tell Newt to Shut Up* (New York: Touchstone, 1996), Ch. 1.

Gingrich used disruptive tactics to harass and badger the majority Democrats. He used hyperbole and insult to attack the Democrats, and he made
exaggerated claims about the historical significance of his quest.

When the Republicans captured control of Congress, two things
changed: they were now in charge of attempting to govern, and Newt
Gingrich became a celebrity. While in many ways Gingrich's attitude and
personal style changed in accord with his new status, enough of his previous
"bomb-throwing" behavior from his days in the minority remained to
undercut some of the Republican progress. In seeing himself in a world-
historic role, Gingrich was tempted to hubris, and too often he let himself
become the issue.

Gingrich sometimes failed to see how he would be perceived by the
public, as when he initially accepted a $4.5 million dollar advance for a
book he was writing. Part of the problem was his inability to suppress his
voluble personality, as when he seemed to blame a murder in Chicago on
the welfare state or a mother drowning her children as a failure of liberalism
or advocating the return of orphanages as a solution to broken families. Part
of the problem was his inability to soften his stance, as when he said that
the agency that administers Medicare should "wither on the vine," or when
he complained about being snubbed by the president during the return from
Israel and said that the harshness of his stance on the CR was partly in
reaction to that.[62]

---

[62]Gingrich complained in a November 15 news conference that he had felt
snubbed by President Clinton when he and Robert Dole returned on Air Force One
from Yitzhak Rabin's funeral. He and Dole had to leave the plane through the
back door while Clinton deplaned from the front. He implied that this personal
snub was part of the reason that the continuing resolution sent to Clinton was as
harsh as it was. "This is petty. But you land at Andrews Air Force Base and
you've been on the plane for twenty-five hours and nobody has talked to you and
they ask you to get off the plane by the back ramp. . . . You just wonder: Where is
their sense of manners? Where is their sense of courtesy?" (Maraniss and
Weisskopf, *Tell Newt To Shut Up*, 152). "[P]art of why you ended up with us
sending down a tougher interim spending bill . . . " was the way he was treated on
Air Force One (Drew, *Showdown*, 331). Gingrich had a point that Clinton might
have used time on the plane to talk about the budget, and the fact that they did not
signified the administration's intention not to move toward the Republican
position. While they should have been able to leave the plane from the front door,

It is easy to see how his legitimate claim to having led the Republicans out of the wilderness and his daily press conferences during the first several months of the 104th Congress could lead him to feel that he was the center of action. But his failure to rein himself in over the next year helped to undermine the Republican cause. He let himself, rather than the Republican agenda, become the focus of attention. Thus when his public approval ratings sank well below President Clinton's, he made a tempting target for Democrats attacking the Republican agenda. With one of the lowest approval ratings of any contemporary in American politics, Gingrich was often the target of Democratic attacks. During the campaigns of 1996 Clinton and Democratic House candidates ran against Gingrich as the symbol of all they objected to in the Republican agenda. Thus while Gingrich deserved much of the credit for bringing about the Republican "revolution," he must also shoulder some of the blame for their failure to achieve all that they had hoped.

Unstable Coalitions

The above analyses assume that "the Republicans" constituted one rational actor and that Gingrich was in control of their strategy. The reality, of course, is that the Republicans were, as all political parties are, a coalition of factions. A number of issues split the Republicans, such as abortion, race, gay rights, the role of the government, prayer in public schools, etc. But the main fissure seemed to fall between southern conservative Republicans who felt strongly about social issues and were concerned with traditional social values on the one hand, and Republicans who were moderate on social issues, but economic conservatives.[63] The more extreme members of the Republican coalition wanted to undercut the capacity of the federal government by cuts in taxes, delegating major

---

the public complaining made Gingrich look like he was whining and that he was making important policy decisions out of personal pique.

[63]See the analysis by Dodd and Oppenheimer, "Congress and the Emerging Order," *Congress Reconsidered*, 403. See also William F. Connelly, Jr., and John J. Pitney, "The House GOP's Civil War: A Political Science Perspective," *PS: Political Science and Politics* (December 1997): 699.

programs to the states through block grants, and privatizing Medicare.[64] This fissure could be seen in the inordinate amount of time (from the fiscal conservatives' perspective) that was spent on trying to abolish the NEA and NEH during the budget fights. These arts and humanities programs involved relatively small amounts of money, yet were important targets of the social conservatives of the Republican party.[65]

The Republican coalition was kept together during the first several months of the 104th Congress through the skillful leadership of Newt Gingrich and the realization that, with their slim majority, they had to stick together in order to accomplish much of their agenda. But in the fall of 1995, as President Clinton attacked the Republicans for shutting down the government and slashing popular programs, cracks in the coalition began to emerge between the most committed social conservatives (including most freshmen) and more moderate conservatives who felt uneasy about some of the more drastic program cuts and felt that their own reelection chances might be hurt by continuing to insist on total victory rather than compromising with President Clinton and the Democrats.

As leader of the "revolution," Gingrich was acutely sensitive to these potential fissures in the ranks of the Republicans. And as Speaker of the House he had come to realize that Clinton's political will and constitutional position was going to keep the Republicans from achieving all of their goals and that they would have to make some compromises. The crunch came at the end of the first government shutdown, when Clinton wanted a continuing resolution to keep the government open as budget negotiations continued. The Republicans were frustrated that Clinton would not agree to a specific plan to balance the budget or concede to their priorities. On December 15 the CR ran out. Majority Leader Dole and the Senate leadership favored a short-term continuing resolution, realizing that the Republicans would be blamed for shutting down the government again.

---

[64]See the analysis by Paul Pierson, "The Deficit and the Politics of Domestic Reform," in *New Democrats and Anti-Federalists: The Politics of Social Policy Making in the 1990s*, ed. Margaret Weir (Washington, D.C.: Brookings and the Russell Sage Foundation, 1998).

[65]See Norman J. Ornstein and Amy L. Schenkenberg, "The 1995 Congress: The First Hundred Days and Beyond," *Political Science Quarterly* 110, no. 2 (Summer 1995): 183-206.

Gingrich realized that they were probably right and broached the subject at a meeting with House Republicans. The answer of the House rank and file, especially the freshmen, was unequivocal: no CR. They felt that they had to keep pressure on the president by keeping the government shut down and that Clinton would finally accede to their demands.[66] Again on December 16 Gingrich brought up the issue of a CR with the Speaker's Advisory Group and was unanimously rebuffed. In Majority Whip Tom DeLay's words, "We made history today," by refusing to compromise with the White House.[67]

Finally, in January, when Republican moderates were losing their patience with the tactics of the freshmen and threatening to break from the coalition over the shutdown issue, Gingrich was forced to impose his solution on the House and demand a continuing resolution. As he lectured the Republican caucus, he made the issue a vote of confidence in his leadership. "I realize that many of you believe you have a better approach, and that if you were Speaker, you'd do it differently," but if "You don't like the job I'm doing as Speaker, run against me."[68]

As Gingrich led the Republicans to demand that President Clinton give in to all of their policy priorities, not merely a balanced budget, he also came to appreciate that the American political system divides power and that the House Republican priorities would not be implemented without Senate and presidential participation. A necessary aspect of political leadership is realizing the limits of power and when it must be shared with other powerful forces in a polity. The 1994 electoral victories and success with pushing the Contract through the House had raised the expectations of the Republicans about what they could achieve. Gingrich, in taking the responsibility for his role in governing the nation, recognized that the aspirations of the House freshmen would have to be limited by the different priorities of the Senate and the opposition of the president. But the radical freshmen class that he had created and their unrealistic expectations, which he had helped to foster, would not allow him to make the necessary

---

[66]See the analysis in Maraniss and Weisskopf, *Tell Newt to Shut Up*, 164-68.

[67]Maraniss and Weisskopf, *Tell Newt to Shut Up*, 169.

[68]Jason DeParle, "Listen, Learn, Help, Lead," *New York Times Magazine* (January 28, 1996), 36; Drew, *Showdown*, 367.

compromises when it became apparent (to Gingrich) that they had gone as far as they were able.

Thus the overreaching of the House Republicans in 1995 can be blamed in part on Gingrich because of his primary role in creating the freshmen class and raising their expectations about what could be accomplished. But it must also be admitted that he recognized earlier than they the institutional power of the Senate and the presidency. His backbenchers, however, would not allow him to make the necessary compromises until much damage to their cause had been done.

CONCLUSION

Some of the factors that Ranney cites that make responsible party government impossible in the U.S.—the supermajority demands of the president's veto power and the threat of filibuster in the Senate—came to limit the Republicans' aspirations in 1995. The intraparty cohesion necessary for conditional party government broke down as some Republicans came to see the shutdown as self defeating. The explanation of why these realities did not become apparent to the Republicans in the fall of 1995 can be attributed to several factors. From the rational to the irrational, from individual to institutional.

Each of the factors outlined above explain part of the Republicans' behavior, and of course, not all Republicans had the same motivations. In 1994 the Republicans, led by Newt Gingrich, had created an unusual set of circumstances, and it was not irrational for them to aim higher than they were likely to achieve in the wake of their historic electoral victory. But in pursuing their policy goals they let hubris veil the political and institutional realities of the situation. In rejecting the first two years of the Clinton administration, the voters in 1994 had not given the Republicans carte blanche to enact their policy preferences. And when the Republicans pushed policy change well beyond a balanced budget and the Contract, the voters reacted against their seemingly extreme proposals and political intransigence.

The Republicans, with their lack of governing experience, also forgot the antimajoritarian nature of the U.S. Constitution. The House majority expected the momentum of the election and the 100-days victories to carry their program through the Senate and to convince the president not to exercise his veto power. In addition to the deeper institutional conditions that allowed the Republicans to win so heavily in 1994 and which limited the extent of their victories in 1995, the talents and limits of Newt Gingrich played an important role. It was his brilliance that allowed the Republicans to win control of the Congress, and it was his inability to rein in the freshmen in the fall that gave Clinton his opening to exploit the Republicans' vulnerability.

In the final analysis it was the inability of the Republicans to recognize the political and institutional limits to their electoral victories that led them to turn their impressive policy accomplishments into the resurrection of Bill Clinton as a viable and successful candidate for reelection.

III. Popular Opinion and Voting

CHAPTER 7

Class Voting in the Industrial Democracies

Robert W. Jackman
University of California, Davis

CLASS VOTING IN THE INDUSTRIAL DEMOCRACIES

Research on the social bases of partisan choice has long been at the core of electoral studies. Perhaps the most durable component of this tradition hinges on the role of class, broadly conceived. Political competition is seen as centering on the distribution of material goods, a distribution that typically favors a minority at the expense of the lower-income majority. Assuming that voters are income-maximizers, elections provide a mechanism for the lower-income majority to increase its share of material goods. In this sense, elections are often taken to represent a democratic class struggle.

The argument is hardly novel. After all, Aristotle (1962, 237) declared the poor to have more sovereign power than men of property, given their majority status and the principle of majority rule. In the nineteenth century, Marx (1852) anticipated that universal suffrage would propel the working class to political supremacy. To prevent the possibility of the "narrow" class legislation that this would generate, on the other hand, Mill (1862) urged that, although universal suffrage was intrinsically desirable, votes

---

This paper continues a line of inquiry I began in my doctoral dissertation at the University of Wisconsin, under the supervision of Austin Ranney, along with Charles Cnudde, Murray Edelman, Leon Epstein, and David Featherman. It is a genuine pleasure to have this opportunity to acknowledge again an ongoing set of intellectual debts. A revised version of the dissertation appeared as Jackman (1975).

should be weighted according to the wisdom (by which, as it turned out, he meant the education) of voters.

Lipset's (1960) interpretation of elections helped place the class struggle thesis in the mainstream of political sociology, where it remains today. Indeed, with universal adult suffrage now the norm, the argument is almost a commonplace. It forms the baseline against which analysts have attempted to gauge whether political life has recently become realigned around newer sets of issues not rooted in social class distinctions. It also forms the baseline against which pundits ponder whether Labour truly won with Tony Blair's victory in the British general election of 1997 or whether, in 1992, Bill Clinton the "New Democrat" bore any resemblance to real Democrats.

My purpose is to suggest that the democratic class struggle view of elections has always been substantially overstated because it hinges on two broad sets of implicit but misleading assumptions about political competition. First, the argument tacitly presumes that majoritarian political institutions are common in the established democracies. A second premise of the argument is that parties are programmatic with distinctive platforms and that competition is fundamentally motivated by policy. Both of these assumptions are at best substantially exaggerated, and the class struggle interpretation that motivates most studies of class voting thus constitutes a flawed approach to electoral competition.

THE CLASS STRUGGLE VIEW OF ELECTIONS

Political Man laid the groundwork for subsequent work in political sociology. In his major synthesis, Lipset devoted two chapters to "Elections: the Expression of the Democratic Class Struggle."[1] He argued that in democracies political parties reflect conflict between different social groups. Although they typically play down appeals to class divisions, parties essentially reflect the "interests of different classes." Of course, Lipset recognized country differences in this pattern stemming from group memberships based on other social divisions, including religion, gender, ethnicity, and region. He recognized that such differences could lead to

---

[1]Seymour Martin Lipset, *Political Man: The Social Bases of Politics* (New York: Doubleday, 1960).

fluctuations in the strength of the class-vote relationship both across countries, and within countries over time. Bearing this in mind, he concluded that

> The principal generalization which can be made is that parties are primarily based on either the lower classes or the middle and upper classes. This generalization even holds true for the American parties, which have traditionally been considered an exception to the class-cleavage patterns of Europe (Lipset 1960, 230).

Lipset accounted for this pattern in terms of simple economic self-interest. Political competition fundamentally occurs over a left-right dimension. Parties on the left generate support from lower-income groups by promising to reduce material inequalities. Parties on the right maintain their support by undertaking to protect the interests of higher-income voters. Thus, elections serve as the vehicle for a democratic class struggle.

This pattern of competition emerged in the early part of the twentieth century with the introduction of adult suffrage. Adult suffrage, in fact, provided parties on the left with the base they needed to develop a significant electoral presence in many countries. Once established, the social bases of political competition became "frozen." Thus, party systems of the 1960s reflected the social cleavages of the 1920s, and were even then much older than most voters (Lipset and Rokkan 1967).

Following on Lipset's heels, Lenski (1966) offered a "conflict" theory of social stratification, which specifies a strong linkage between democratic politics and redistribution. He stressed the following three features of liberal democracies: their emphasis on universal suffrage, their protection of the right to organized political opposition, and their extension to disadvantaged groups of the right to organize and engage in collective action to advance their own interests. Lenski's conflict approach concluded that lower-income groups have effectively used these rights to promote their economic interests through their support of labor unions and parties of the left. The programs of the latter, in turn, have created more egalitarian societies. Political conflict between income classes has thus helped shape the distribution of material rewards in the industrial societies.

Although generated independently of each other, Lipset's and Lenski's arguments clearly have much in common. Observe further that each also drew directly on earlier theorists but significantly elaborated on those theorists by paying more explicit attention to political parties as the institutions that mobilize, organize, and represent class interests.

In subsequent years, the argument became central to analyses of the "new political economy" of the advanced industrial democracies (Hollingsworth and Hanneman 1982). For example, Korpi's *The Democratic Class Struggle* (1983) concluded that, in the most fundamental sense, political conflict and competition hinge on the distinction between capital and labor. Where labor is strong, both organizationally and politically, labor's interests are more likely to be accommodated by the state. Korpi's empirical analyses draw largely on the Swedish experience, but also include materials from other established democracies. In his framework, elections are cast as the mechanism driving the class struggle between capital and labor, and the parallels with Lipset-Lenski are striking.[2]

The theme has repeatedly been echoed by others, using a variety of closely related labels. Thus, Stephens and Stephens (1982) made the case for a "political class struggle school" of analysis, Shalev (1983) referred to the argument as the "social democratic model" of politics, and Weir and Skocpol (1985) called it the "working class strength approach." The argument remains at the core of current empirical analyses of the welfare state (see, e.g., Hicks and Misra 1993, Stephens, Ragin, and Stephens 1993).

Over the past decade, debate about the social bases of partisanship that is at the core of the class-struggle thesis has also taken Lipset's (1960) analysis as the basic point of departure, along with Alford's (1963) companion study of class voting. With few exceptions, analysts are agreed that class voting was important in the first two decades after the Second World War.[3] Given this, most of the debate has centered on whether class voting has since been in decline or whether it persists.

---

[2] For a more complete discussion of Korpi's analysis, see Jackman (1986).

[3] One of the exceptions is Dogan (1995), who argues that religion has been more important than social class during the last half-century in most of western Europe, and who notes that most of the class-voting arguments reflect the experience of countries that are predominantly Protestant. He further argues that even religion is now losing its significance, as the links between social groups and electoral behavior are weakening. For a survey and more extensive bibliography of studies of class voting, see Manza, Hout, and Brooks (1995).

Until recently, the most common answer was that class voting has been on the wane. A number of analysts have computed and then compared simple Alford indices of class voting from sample surveys over a series of elections in a number of countries to support this claim.[4] Others have reported more complete regression analyses to make the same point (e.g., Franklin, Mackie, and Valen 1992). A variety of explanations has been offered to account for the reported decline.

Some have suggested that the postwar increase in levels of education has produced a more sophisticated set of voters less tied to the constraints of class and traditional parties and more capable of reaching political decisions independently. The result is said to be a trend toward partisan dealignment, in which, among other things, the link between social class and party choice has become attenuated (see, e.g., Dalton, Flanagan, and Beck 1984; Franklin, Mackie, and Valen 1992). Others have pushed the argument further to suggest that there has been a substantial value shift among western publics that has undermined the significance of older class distinctions. Perhaps the best-known statement along these lines is associated with Inglehart and his colleagues, who have claimed that increasing affluence has produced new cohorts of voters who attach much more significance to "postmaterialist" priorities and much less weight to the "materialist" concerns that were so central to their predecessors (e.g., Abramson and Inglehart 1995; Inglehart 1997). As a result, political competition centers on a new policy dimension that is largely independent of the traditional left-right dimension.

Not all are agreed, however, that class voting has been in decline. Some scholars have maintained that the simple manual-nonmanual distinction on which most of the above studies rely does not adequately capture the critical class distinctions. In a parallel manner, they have pointed to the difficulties of forcing multiparty systems into a dichotomous framework. They have further noted the statistical deficiencies of Alford's measure of class voting, and have proposed more sophisticated procedures for gauging the links between class and vote choice. With these issues

---

[4]Alford's measure defines class voting as the difference between the percentage of "persons in manual occupations voting for Left parties [and] . . . the percentage of persons in nonmanual occupations voting for Left parties" (Alford 1963, 79-80).

addressed and remedied, these analysts have reported little or no discernible and systematic decline in class voting in recent years. Instead, patterns over the postwar years are taken to reflect "trendless fluctuations" (see, e.g., Hout, Brooks, and Manza 1995; Weakliem 1995).

Whether or not analysts conclude that class voting is on the wane, it is noteworthy that even the most current treatments share Lipset's and Lenski's basic description of what is involved in class voting.

- Adult suffrage within the industrial democracies substantially reduced political inequalities by enfranchising lower-income voters, who comprise a majority of voters.[5]

- These voters disproportionately support parties of the left, parties that commit to redistribute income to lower-income voters, and that do so when in office.[6]

- Programmatic parties of the left compete with programmatic parties of the right, which draw the bulk of their support from higher-income voters, and therefore protect the interests of those supporters when in office.

- Failure of a party in government to pursue the economic interests of its constituents results in a loss of electoral support for that party.

Clearly, the primary emphasis of the argument is on the will of popular majorities. Little attention is paid in any of these discussions to identifying the institutional mechanisms that might translate the preferences of popular majorities into policy outcomes. The impression is instead left that majorities everywhere simply make their will known, and policy directly falls into place. Thus, even the most sophisticated analyses center on refining analyses of survey data but ignore the variety of different national sets of institutional arrangements that structure voters' choices.[7]

---

[5]Lower-income voters are a majority because the distribution of national income within all industrial democracies is positively skewed.

[6]I take parties of the left to refer to those of the noncommunist left, including socialist, social democratic, and labor parties. For surveys of classifications of parties along a left-right policy space, see Laver and Schofield (1990, Appendix B) and Castles and Mair (1997).

[7]To the extent that studies of class voting have disproportionately employed data from Britain, they have, of course, held institutional arrangements constant. By the same token, however, studies restricted to one or two countries impede our ability to make useful comparative generalizations.

Political parties are of course central to the argument, but the nature of the competition in which they engage is not addressed head on. Parties are cast as motivated primarily by policy concerns, but this casting is no more than implicit. The interests of different classes are simply presumed to be aggregated into coherent sets of preferences, in which process parties everywhere play a similar role. In other words, preferences are translated largely reflexively into public policy in a Lockean sense, almost "independently of any institutional midwifery of any kind."[8]

This impression is misleading. We have known for some time that individual preferences do not spontaneously aggregate themselves into coherent collective choices (Arrow 1963). Although its proponents may not acknowledge the fact, the class-struggle interpretation of elections instead hinges critically on a set of assumptions about the nature of political competition and the electoral process. That they are implicit makes them no less central to the interpretation. Most notably, the class-struggle thesis assumes that the institutional features of the industrial democracies are typically majoritarian, and that the veto capacity of minorities is limited. Absent this assumption, the fact that a majority of voters is lower income in any country becomes moot. The majoritarian assumption in turn implies that a responsible-parties form of competition is the modal form, in which parties are fundamentally driven by policy concerns. The substance of party competition centers on the left-right continuum and the economic interests that distinguish lower- from higher-income voters. Parties are electorally rewarded or punished according to the success with which they implement class-based programs over which they have control.

There are strong reasons for rejecting these working assumptions, and the class-struggle thesis is seriously wanting.

THE MAJORITARIAN ASSUMPTION

The majoritarianism presupposed by the democratic class struggle argument hinges on the existence of a set of institutions that resembles Dahl's (1956) description of populistic democracy. Yet we know that such a model is at odds with political institutions in the United States, where checks and balances were designed specifically to restrain majorities and

---

[8]The phrase is from Kendall (1941, 128-29).

protect minorities. Further, requirements of extraordinary majorities (such as a two-thirds majority) for constitutional amendments and selected policy issues obviously introduce a minority veto that frustrates majority rule. In fact, they were designed with this express goal in mind.

Many believe that this is a peculiarly American aberration, and indeed there is a large literature on American "exceptionalism" (see, e.g., Lipset 1996). Behind such beliefs is a presumption that parliamentary systems in particular are different and attach more weight to majority rule. However, as Lijphart pointed out over a decade ago in his comparison of majoritarian and consensus forms of democracy, this is simply not the case. His analysis remains instructive.

In its pure form, Lijphart (1984) defined majoritarian democracy (also known as the Westminster model) as comprising the following eight overlapping components:

- *Executive power is concentrated in single-party, bare-majority cabinets* so that a small majority exercises substantial political power while the (typically large) minority is consigned to the opposition benches.
- *Cabinets control the legislature.*
- Where the legislature has two chambers (as in Great Britain), *bicameralism is asymmetric*, with almost all power concentrated in the popularly elected lower house. The asymmetry is so pronounced that it is difficult to distinguish from the unicameralism of the New Zealand parliament.
- *The party system is fundamentally a two-party arrangement.*
- The two parties compete primarily on a *unidimensional left-right continuum.*
- The electoral formula is based on a *plurality, single-member district system of elections*, which typically magnifies legislative majorities and reduces the effective number of political parties (Rae 1971a; Lijphart 1994; Cox 1997).
- *Government is unitary and centralized.* That is, there are no geographic or functional restrictions on cabinet power.
- There is an *unwritten constitution and parliamentary sovereignty.* Since the legislature can change even basic constitutional laws by simple majority, there are no formal checks on the majority party in the lower house.

Taken as a whole, Lijphart's description of the ideal-typical majoritarian system makes explicit the institutional arrangements that are implicit in the democratic class struggle argument. That the type is majoritarian is self-evident.

The form of consensus democracy defined by Lijphart lies at the other end of each of these continua. It typically involves executive power-sharing, with grand coalitions of all the major political parties. It emphasizes the separation of powers, both formally and informally. The legislature is bicameral, and the relation between both houses is balanced or symmetric in a way that provides for minority representation. The consensus model is characterized by a multiparty system within which competition occurs on a variety of dimensions, not just along socioeconomic lines. At the same time, electoral systems are based on some variant of proportional representation (PR), which helps generate multipartyism and gives expression to minority interests. In contrast to the Westminster model, consensus democracy rests on a federal, decentralized apparatus. Finally, it includes a written constitution, with provisions for minority veto. Lijphart concludes that, in all, consensus democracy restrains majoritarianism by encouraging "the *sharing of power* between the majority and the minority . . . , the *dispersal of power* . . . , a *fair distribution of power* . . . , the *delegation of power* . . . , and a *formal limit on power*" (1984, 30, emphasis in original).

Lijphart's empirical analysis of the established democracies indicates, first, that the majoritarian/consensual contrast is two-dimensional. One cluster of traits centers on the effective number of political parties, and also includes bare-majority cabinets, executive dominance, the number of issue dimensions, and the degree of electoral disproportionality. The other cluster reflects the degree of federalism, as indexed by the degree of unicameralism, centralization, and constitutional flexibility.

Second, when democratic regimes are classified on these two dimensions, we obtain the pattern shown in Table 1, which reproduces Lijphart's Table 13.3 (1984, 219). The most striking feature of this table is that of the 22 democratic regimes as of the early 1980s discussed by Lijphart, only two (New Zealand and Great Britain) can unambiguously be classified as majoritarian (and only one—Switzerland—is manifestly consensual). Less than one quarter of the cases are majoritarian on one dimension and occupy an intermediate or majoritarian position on the other: New Zealand, Great Britain, Iceland, Luxembourg, and Ireland (and four of these countries have

Table 1. *Democracies Classified by the Effective Number of Political Parties and Degree of Federalism, Early 1980s*

		Degree of Federalism		
		Majoritarian	Intermediate	Consensual
	Majoritarian	New Zealand Great Britain	Ireland	Australia Austria Canada Germany U.S.A.
Number of Parties	Intermediate	Ireland Luxembourg	France V Norway Sweden	Italy Japan
	Consensual	Denmark Israel	Belgium Finland France IV Netherlands	Switzerland

Source: Lijphart 1984 (Table 13.3, p. 219). The Fourth and Fifth French Republics are identified as France IV and V, respectively.

small populations). Moreover, while New Zealand and Great Britain are located in the northwest cell of the table, they cannot be said to fit the majoritarian model exactly. Rather, New Zealand and, to a lesser extent, Great Britain can only be described as approximating that model reasonably well as of the early 1980s (see also Epstein 1980).

Other evidence reinforces the view that majoritarian systems are rare. Consider Cox's (1997) more recent analysis of voting rules, one of the major components of Lijphart's classification. Of the 52 countries that might be considered democracies as of 1992 with populations greater than one million, Cox reports that only seven employed single-member districts and plurality rule: Bangladesh, Canada, Great Britain, Nepal, New Zealand, the United States, and Zambia (1997, 28).

Since 1992, this list has shrunk further. In 1993, New Zealand voters approved significant electoral reforms in a referendum. The new system, labelled "mixed member proportional," retains the principle of territorial representation but supplements it with a proportional mechanism that draws on party lists (Temple 1995; Vowles 1997). Of the 120 parliamentary seats, 65 reflect constituency voting, and 55 are elected from national party lists. Voters cast two ballots, and the new system was first employed in the 1996 general election. These changes are noteworthy given Lijphart's (1984) earlier classification of New Zealand as closer to the Westminster model than Westminster itself. Even in Britain, the new Labour government is committed to creating an electoral commission to propose a proportional alternative to the current system and then choosing between the two in a national referendum. Majoritarian institutional arrangements as heretofore exemplified by the Westminster model may be close to assuming endangered species status.[9]

The idea that majoritarianism is unexceptional is further eroded by the incidence of minority governments, that is, governments formed by parties that collectively control fewer than one half of the seats in the national legislature, or in the lower house in bicameral settings. Strom's (1990) analysis of such governments in 15 western democracies from 1945 to 1987 indicates that they are far from uncommon. Over one third of all governments in these cases were based on minority cabinets, which averages out to about two minority governments per decade per year. This last figure, of course, conceals considerable variation across countries in the incidence of such governments. Of special interest to the elections-as-class-struggle perspective given the class-based politics often ascribed to the area is the fact that such cabinets have been especially common in Scandinavia. More than half the cabinets in Norway and Sweden and 88 percent of all cabinets in Denmark have in fact relied for their support on parliamentary *minorities* (Strom 1990, 58).

Finally, the recognition that two-party majoritarian systems are uncommon has another implication for class voting. As I noted in the preceding section, the class struggle interpretation of elections assumes that

---

[9]Recent proposals for electoral reform in Great Britain are discussed in Bagehot, "Last gasp for first past the post?" *The Economist* (May 31, 1997): 56. It is worth remembering, however, that such proposals have a long history in Britain, in the face of which current electoral arrangements have been remarkably resilient (Norris 1995).

voters punish or reward parties for their success in implementing class-based policies. This, in turn, requires that elections are decisive in the process of government formation. However, complete electoral decisiveness in this sense is common only in two-party, single-member district plurality systems (see, e.g., Rae 1971b; Duverger 1984). In the more proportional, multiparty systems associated with Lijphart's consensus democracy, coalition governments are the norm (see, e.g., Laver and Schofield 1990, 204-11). Under these circumstances, voters do not directly elect governments at all. Instead, as Downs clearly recognized (1957, Ch. 9), voters elect a legislature, the members of which *in turn* choose a government. This fact considerably weakens the link between elections and government formation, and the former become much less decisive for the latter.

There are many examples of this phenomenon, of course, but a particularly clear instance occurred with the most recent New Zealand general election of 1996, the first to be held using the new mixed-member proportional system. Under the previous single-member district, plurality system, new governments had typically been formed within 24 hours of an election. After the 1996 election, however, the process dragged out a full two months and occasioned considerable uncertainty, until a coalition agreement was finally signed between the National and New Zealand First parties. This outcome is noteworthy given that National had campaigned hard against New Zealand First prior to the election, and many voters believed they had been misled by New Zealand First about its coalition intentions (Vowles 1997). The first postreform election was clearly much less decisive in government formation than had been its predecessors.

The implications of these patterns for the class voting account of elections are straightforward. That majoritarian institutional arrangements are far from the norm in the established democracies poses a major problem for that account. All of the available evidence has indicated for some time that most democracies deviate from majoritarianism, typically in substantial ways. Of course, the class voting account does not hinge on an explicitly specified set of institutional mechanisms. It is instead quite mute on the general subject, as I have emphasized. But this does not obviate the fact that the argument is implicitly predicated on the existence of majoritarian institutions that clearly link elections to government formation. Were it not, the fact that lower-income voters everywhere constitute a majority of voters—a cornerstone of the argument since Aristotle, Marx, and

Mill—would be of no consequence. Thus, the common deviations from majoritarian political institutions I have discussed constitute a major challenge for arguments about class voting and the broader class-struggle view of elections.

RESPONSIBLE PARTIES AND POLITICAL COMPETITION

Along with its implicit assumptions about majoritarian political institutions, the class struggle interpretation of elections is predicated on a responsible-parties model of political competition. Two-party competition is optimal, according to this model, and the parties are unified and disciplined so that party members holding elective office are collectively responsible to voters. Thus, each party forms a team. Each assumes a distinct policy position that includes a program made known to voters before elections in the form of a manifesto. The emphasis on policy distinctiveness is indeed at the core of the responsible parties model: programmatic concerns are seen as the fundamental motivator of political parties and the competition in which they are engaged. Ranney summarizes the perspective well:

> In a system of [responsible] party government the parties seek power, not as an end in itself, but in order that they may put their programs into governmental action. They therefore conceive of their job as having two aspects: winning elections in order to get power and using the power they win to carry out their programs. Thus each party organizes its forces with the unity and discipline necessary *before* elections in the campaigning activities necessary to win power and after elections in the governmental activities necessary to put their programs into law (Ranney 1954, 20-21, emphasis in original).

This model clearly depends on majoritarian political institutions; indeed, proponents of responsible parties have always looked to the Westminster model for inspiration. They move beyond that model, however, in their insistence on the *programmatic* basis for political activity. Policy differences provide the basis for political competition. The class struggle argument adds the further proviso that this political competition occurs on a left-right dimension, with one party adopting a distinctively left-of-center position, and the other an equally distinctive right-of-center position.

How reasonable is this general set of assumptions? It is obvious that the responsible-parties perspective accepts the Westminster model as the modal democratic institutional arrangement, since coalition governments, decentralization, checks and balances, and provision for minority veto are inhospitable to responsible parties. From my discussion to this point, it is evident that responsible-party behavior is likely to be the exception rather than the rule. But let us ignore this for the moment and assume, counterfactually, that most democracies are relatively centralized, with most political competition occurring along a single dimension that distinguishes two major political parties.

That is the rather idealized world within which Downs developed his spatial model of electoral competition. He further assumed that party leaders and voters are utility maximizers.[10] He defined a political party as a team that "seeks to control the governing apparatus by gaining office in a duly contested election"; by team, he meant "a coalition whose members agree on all their goals instead of on just part of them." From these assumptions, Downs generated his fundamental hypothesis: "Parties formulate policies in order to win elections, rather than win elections in order to formulate policies" (Downs 1957, 25, 28). In other words, parties are primarily motivated by the goal of maximizing their political support. If they hold office, they seek reelection; if they are out of office, they seek to displace the governing party.

This approach clearly turns the responsible-parties argument on its head by denying that programmatic concerns are the principal end of political parties. Policy is instead relegated to the role of a means toward

---

[10]This is, of course, a more general assumption than the view of voters as income maximizers implied by the class-voting argument, since utility is not conceived in narrowly economic terms. Note further that some of the more interesting implications of arguments like Downs's center on maximizing or optimizing under uncertainty. For a discussion of the assumption of procedural rationality in politics, see Jackman (1993). An important recent analysis addresses the ways in which voters can make reasoned judgments with limited information (Lupia and McCubbins 1998).

the end of maximizing political support.[11] Moreover, Downs proposed that this occurs under the institutional conditions that *most favor* the responsible-parties model—where there is two-party competition along a left-right spectrum with majoritarian institutions.[12] Is this a realistic description of party behavior?

Schlesinger (1991, Ch. 1) concludes that it is. He compared the character of parties *as organizations* with business firms, interest groups, and public bureaus, to show that parties are a unique organizational form. First, like firms, parties maintain themselves through market exchange; interest groups and bureaus do not. Second, like interest groups and bureaus, parties produce collective goods; business firms do not. Third, like interest groups, parties compensate their participants indirectly; firms and bureaus do not. In view of this distinctive organizational configuration, the electoral test is the *only* criterion for party success, which is why parties attempt to maximize their electoral support.

Acceptance of this hypothesis is damaging to class voting arguments in several ways. First, those arguments assume that parties are programmatic representatives of class interests. Downs's thesis directly and explicitly challenges this assumption: "In our model, political parties are not agents of specific social groups or classes; rather, they are autonomous teams

---

[11]Since the point is repeatedly misconstrued, it bears emphasis that to relegate policy to the status of a means to the end rather than the fundamental end of political parties is not to trivialize policy. We know that the bottom line for business firms is maximizing profits. But this of course simply means that successful, competitive firms are able to market a product (goods or services) effectively. That goods and products are means to the end does not make them inconsequential. In a parallel manner, "so long as policy is relevant for voters, activists, and other electorally relevant groups, politicians will be impelled by the incentives of party competition . . . to heed the policy priorities of voters" (Laver and Shepsle 1996, 8). Thus, in the original formulations by Black and Downs, even though they are motivated by office-seeking concerns, parties compete *over policy* in a unidimensional space.

[12]Indeed, Downs was repeatedly criticized by more empirically minded students of political party systems for his single-dimensional spatial model and for his primary emphasis on two-party systems. See, e.g., Sartori (1976, Ch. 10).

seeking office *per se* and using group support to attain that end" (Downs 1957, 97).[13]

Second, the argument that parties seek to maximize their electoral support implies, in two-party systems, a process of *policy convergence* between the parties. This process is an outcome of Black's (1958) famous median-voter theorem which states that in a unidimensional policy space, the ideal point of the median voter is the only point that is preferred by a majority of voters over any other point on that dimension. The implication of Black's theorem is that when two parties are competing for majority support, each will approach the ideal point of the median voter. Even if they do not converge on the identical point, this obviously introduces a major centripetal force into electoral competition.

As originally formulated, the convergence argument depended on a variety of additional assumptions, including a (symmetric) unimodal distribution of voter preferences and perfect information among candidates. Subsequent work, however, has indicated that convergence occurs even when these assumptions are relaxed. For example, Riker and Ordeshook (1973) concluded that convergence is likely even when the distribution of voter preferences is bimodal. Calvert (1985) has shown that there are centripetal pressures on candidates to converge in their platforms *even when those candidates are policy motivated,* and even when they lack perfect information about the electoral impact of their programs. Further, there is interesting experimental evidence pointing to convergence (see., e.g., Collier, Ordeshook, and Williams 1989; Williams 1991).[14]

Consider now a three-party system with unidimensional policy space where the center party is small. British politics approximate this reasonably well, if the Liberal Democrats are taken as the center (national) party. Schofield (1997, 278-83) has suggested that under these conditions, the Westminster plurality arrangement may generate less convergence than PR. With plurality elections, the two parties typically have seats-to-votes ratios

---

[13]This approach to parties is not unique to Downs. For example, Epstein defines a party as "any group, however loosely organized, seeking to elect governmental office holders under a given label . . . is the crucial defining element" (1967, 9).

[14]For a current survey of research on spatial models of voting, see Ordeshook (1977).

greater than one, while the minor center party does not.[15] Consequently, voters at the center become electorally less important to the major parties who can target their appeals to their core constituencies. However, this suggestion overlooks the fact that in such a three-party plurality system, the voters most likely to make a difference *at the margin* to the election outcome for either major party are located near the center. Further, in such a system, each major party will assert to voters at the center that they should vote for it in part to avoid wasting their votes, a credible claim because it is true. Thus, even in this three-party, plurality arrangement, convergence toward the center by the two major parties is likely to remain substantial.

Recall that the class-struggle argument postulates that parties reflect class interests, that they are fundamentally programmatic, and that their programs are distinctive. The above considerations suggest that these conditions are unlikely to be met, even in the two-party majoritarian systems most favorable to class voting. This, of course, does not mean that party programs converge completely. Remember that even office-seeking parties compete with each other over policy space. In this setting, all major parties have a history, and any party that seeks to be an ongoing and credible electoral competitor needs to surround its product with some aura of continuing policy distinctiveness that helps differentiate it from its rivals and preserve its own policy niche (see, e.g., Budge and Robertson 1987). Further, the fact that particular policy positions may often be important for electorally significant groups such as party activists and contributors discourages complete convergence (see, e.g., Aldrich 1983). But the argument does imply strong centripetal pressures toward policy convergence.

This conclusion assumes the majoritarian set of institutions most hospitable to class voting. While multiparty systems may offer a more distinctive set of party platforms from which voters can choose, recall from the previous section that, in such systems, elections are less decisive in generating governments. As Downs noted, "Voters in multiparty systems are indeed faced with definite and well-integrated policy sets, but none of these sets will in fact govern them. Only coalitions can govern, and ambiguity and compromise are introduced on a secondary level whenever

---

[15]The 1997 British general election reminds us that this is not always the case: only Labour received a seats-to-votes ratio larger than one in this election.

coalitions are formed" (1957, 155). It is nonetheless noteworthy that recent work on this "secondary level" generalizes Black's median voter argument to government formation in multidimensional, multiparty systems as well (Austen-Smith and Banks 1990; Laver and Shepsle 1996). Thus, the centripetal tendencies that generate policy convergence are not the exclusive hallmark of two-party majoritarian democracies, although these remain the systems with the only institutional arrangements even potentially receptive to class voting.

The policy convergence predicated on the proposition that it is the parties' and candidates' primary goal to maximize their electoral support implies that the policy positions they do endorse are likely to be *ambiguous*. Even with unlimited time and resources, candidates would have little incentive to become too specific on issues, especially on those that are potentially divisive. For one thing, such specificity exposes candidates to the risk of criticism that can readily consign them to a defensive strategy, thus making it more difficult to project a positive image. Perhaps more important, specificity on divisive issues is not a productive vote generator because *any* particular policy position will offend *some* set of voters. The better strategy is to concentrate primarily on consensual appeals that are general in their focus (see, e.g., Downs 1957, Ch. 8; Page 1976).

Candidates therefore play down (and seek to avoid) discussion of the details in domestic policy areas like taxation, income maintenance, and health care, but devote considerable energy and time to convincing voters of their commitment to fairness, growth, and even the elimination of poverty. To the extent that candidates and parties do adopt different positions in competitive elections, these differences are most typically revealed through the emphasis of different but broadly defined themes (presumably those themes they believe show them to comparative advantage). However, policy differences are seldom manifested through the adoption by competitive parties of conflictual positions on the same issue (see, e.g., Budge and Robertson 1987).

Some seem to believe that this phenomenon is a recent product of the electronic media, with its emphasis on soundbites. The litany is familiar: with recent patterns of dealignment, along with the exigencies of the mass media, campaigns have come to hinge more on political personalities than on issues. Thus, *The Economist* was moved to ask of Tony Blair after his election, "Now Reveal Yourself" (May 3, 1997, 15). A year later, the same journal was still reporting difficulty in discerning distinct, concrete, and consistent elements in announced Labour government positions:

> By the time you have got through the controversial "responsibilities and rights are the equal elements of citizenship" to the arresting "policy must modernize as fast as society changes," you see the virtue of judging New Labour by its deeds rather than its words (*The Economist*, May 2, 1998, 19).

But were earlier campaigns really more issue-oriented? Recall the emphasis of the British Labour party in its 1964 campaign on slogans like "Let's go with Labour and we'll get things done," and "Labour believes that the good life enjoyed by a few rich people must give way to a fuller life for us all" (Butler and King 1965). Who could beg to differ?

The optimal strategy, of concentrating on symbolic appeals to shared goals is in fact far from new. This strategy has always helped project a positive stance and minimize conflict. It also serves to simplify complex policy options and tradeoffs whose implications are often unclear even to specialists, not to mention the candidates themselves (Edelman 1964). Such simplification is essential as voters process (and reduce) political information into a form that can be translated into a vote for a single candidate or simple preference ordering (or abstention)—which is, after all, a rather restricted range of alternatives. This does not preclude candidates and parties from projecting distinctive images. As in 1964, the Labour party's slogans of 1997 were, in fact, a little more populist in tone than those of the Conservatives. But the differences tend to be of degree rather than of kind and offer little in the way of concrete policy alternatives.

Symbolic appeals are of special significance to the redistributive politics with which class voting arguments and the class-struggle interpretation of elections are concerned. Further, few candidates or parties ever reap electoral rewards from explicitly favoring *in*equality. The idea of equality is complex and enjoys a wide variety of sometimes incompatible meanings (see, e.g., Rae et al. 1981). It follows that promises to "reduce inequalities" can assume a multitude of contradictory forms and yet be characterized as "democratic." The most notable distinction for our purposes is that between equality of opportunity and equality of results. The former refers to the process by which rewards are allocated (merit versus social background); the latter refers to the shape of the distribution of the rewards themselves.

And meritocracy, with its emphasis on individual rights, is perfectly compatible with a highly unequal size distribution of, say, income (see, e.g., Schaar 1967; Dorn 1979). In this connection, symbolic appeals are very effective. Egalitarian impulses can be declared by parties and their candidates in a way that is highly consensual and ambiguous, and the issue is further obscured by the common conflation of equality with justice, or equity.[16]

Electoral convergence and policy ambiguity, along with the use of symbolic appeals, have consequences for voter preferences. Those preferences, after all, do not emerge in a political vacuum, as implied by discussions of class voting with their implicitly populist view of democracy. They instead mold *and are molded by* the policy stances and activities of parties and their candidates. This, indeed, is the major insight to be derived from Black's median voter theorem and from Downs's model. The general approach obliges us to consider the incentives facing parties and their candidates for office along with the ways in which those incentives structure the responses of voters. It thereby gives substance to Key's (1966) intuition about the "echo chamber" within which voters, parties, and their candidates interact.

The Downsian framework suggests that candidates have strong incentives to adopt centrist, ambiguous, and symbolic appeals, both during and between election campaigns. In so doing, candidates have a major impact on the political agenda, because their rhetoric and activities help determine which issues belong on that agenda, and which do not. Further, on those issues that do appear on the agenda, candidates help determine the *range* of appropriate positions, so that on various issues some positions are defined as more fruitful than others because they offer more potential for electoral reward. This is not to assert that candidates completely dominate the political agenda, but it is to suggest that they have a major hand in shaping it. Given pressures for convergence and ambiguity in political debate, that hand substantially favors the status quo by placing primary emphasis on centrist, consensual positions.

Finally, the status-quo bias is compounded by an inherent inequality of political power in capitalist democracies. Downs concluded that this inequality stems from the existence of uncertainty and the division of

---

[16]For an excellent discussion on this point, see Bronfenbrenner (1973).

political labor. The disparity of influence is one that benefits producers at the expense of consumers, despite the fact that governments formulate policies to maximize votes and that consumers vastly outnumber producers (Downs 1957, Ch. 13). Downs's distinction has a direct parallel in Olson's argument that while smaller groups may be relatively coherent and effective, larger groups will fall far short of providing themselves with meaningful collective goods (Olson 1965, Chs. 1 and 2). Starting from quite different premises, Edelman similarly distinguished two broad types of political groups. The first is relatively small, well-organized, well-informed, and has specific and clearly identified goals; the second is the polar opposite. Groups of the first type receive a disproportionate amount of the tangible rewards, while those of the second type receive rewards that are primarily symbolic (Edelman 1964, Ch. 2). Lindblom's discussion of "constrained volitions" in capitalist democracies underscores the same point. Although there are limits on the extent to which the public agenda and public demands can be manipulated, large corporate interests can and do mold the volitions of citizens in a centrist manner on the "grand issues" (Lindblom 1977, Ch. 15).

Dahl has suggested that this form of political inequality is perhaps inescapable given the existence (and promotion) of independent organizations in pluralist democracies:

> Organized pluralism is a stabilizing force that is highly conservative in the face of demands for innovative structural change. Each of the major organized forces in a country prevents the others from making changes that might seriously damage its perceived interests. As a consequence, structural reforms that would significantly and rapidly redistribute control, status, income, wealth, and other resources are impossible to achieve— unless, ironically, they are made at the expense of the unorganized (Dahl 1982, 43).

This conclusion rests on two reasonable premises. First, it is always easier to thwart new policy efforts than it is to initiate them, especially since most democracies deviate significantly from majoritarianism. This introduces an inertia that clearly favors the status quo. Second, groups that benefit from the status quo (i.e., those with interests to protect) occupy the best strategic positions from which to engage in obstructive tactics. Dahl (1982, Ch. 3) concluded that, beyond the political inequalities they perpetuate, independent organizations deform civic consciousness, distort the public agenda, and alienate final control.

In all, then, the conservative effects of electorally induced party convergence and policy ambiguity coincide with and are reinforced by the status quo bias of political inequalities that seem endemic to political democracy. Again, the overall pattern is at variance with the class-struggle interpretation of elections, with its emphasis on the role of leftist political parties as the programmatic and responsive representatives of the economic interests of low-income voters.

This general conclusion is hardly new. Although originating from a radically different intellectual tradition, Michels's famous iron "law" of oligarchy implies that, for organizational reasons, the primary goal of political parties becomes the attainment of office. In their nascent stages, parties rely on ideology to help develop an organizational infrastructure, and this initially gives them a programmatic flavor. As the organization develops, however, the program is diluted and assigned a secondary role because the party acts to moderate its appeal to enhance its odds of electoral success. This pattern of convergence to the center continues as the party comes closer to electoral victory and is completed with that victory: "The socialists might conquer, but not socialism, which would perish in the moment of its adherents' triumph" (Michels 1958, 391; see also Michels 1927). Michels thus concluded that far from being a struggle between economic classes, political history is a struggle between contending political elites—that is, between competing office-seekers.

CONCLUSIONS

Evaluated in light of a variety of studies of political competition, arguments about class voting and the democratic class-struggle interpretation of elections are difficult to sustain because they are predicated on seriously deficient assumptions. First, few democracies are organized along the majoritarian lines of the Westminster model. Most have instead adopted (in varying degrees) constitutional procedures designed to restrict majorities and to protect the rights of minorities, procedures that additionally loosen the connection between elections and the formation of governments. Second, the responsible-parties model of political competition is also wanting, even among the small (and shrinking?) subset of democracies with majoritarian institutions. There is little reason to believe that parties are primarily motivated by programmatic concerns, with one party staking out a distinctively left-of-center position representing the economic interests of lower-income voters, and the other adopting an equally distinctive right-wing position. Parties are instead primarily concerned with electoral concerns as they seek to gain (or maintain) office. Parties and their candidates therefore have strong incentives to adopt positions close to the center of policy space. These incentives to converge place a premium on ambiguous electoral appeals that contain substantial doses of symbolism, doses that are especially pronounced in the area of domestic redistributive politics.

I reiterate that this conclusion about the class-struggle argument is not meant to deny potential significance to specific policy choices. Such choices can matter, of course, and my claim is more modest. Given the incentives for parties to converge toward the policy center, there is little reason to believe that different parties will consistently offer *distinctive* sets of *specific* policy alternatives. For the reasons I have already discussed, this does not imply either that policy is irrelevant or that parties will converge on the same point. After all, even office-seeking parties compete over policy. It does suggest, however, that clear-cut policy choices between parties will not be the norm.

Nor am I asserting that voters are incapable of responding to changes in economic conditions. There is much evidence to indicate that voters are sensitive to such changes (among other things), especially when they involve real disposable income. These responses, however, typically take the form of retrospective voting, which is quite incidental to any class-struggle interpretation of elections.[17] Retrospective voting instead leads more directly to the median voter argument, where voters at the center are again electorally decisive because they are the ones most available for defection in a two-party system. They are therefore the voters for whose support parties compete most actively.

---

[17]Again, Downs provides one of the earliest and clearest discussions of the role of retrospective judgments in voters' formation of party differentials (see, especially, Ch. 3, "The Basic Logic of Voting"). Given his treatment, the common distinction between retrospective and prospective voting becomes a little difficult to sustain. For a recent evaluation of the relevant issues, see Fiorina (1997).

This conclusion has several implications for the meaning we attach to elections. First, it is often suggested that to deny the class-struggle interpretation of elections, with its emphasis on the role of programmatic parties, is to propose that politics does not matter. Some have gone further to suggest that the only alternative to this "conflict" interpretation of elections is a functionalist view in which the shape of the social structure responds primarily to changes in the technological order in a consensual manner (see, e.g., Castles and McKinlay 1979; Orloff and Skocpol 1984). Such assertions are misplaced. The constitutional arrangements of capitalist democracies that typically restrain popular majorities and protect minorities did not somehow emerge by themselves. Instead, they have been politically crafted, and, like all institutions, these arrangements were designed, in good part, by those with interests to protect (see, e.g., Knight 1992). Similarly, far from denying the relevance of politics, the argument that office-seeking considerations motivate politicians is fundamentally political (see, e.g., Schlesinger 1991). It is more reasonable to conclude that the class-struggle interpretation of elections is misleading precisely because it has *always* glossed over the more fundamental *political* processes that underlie institutional arrangements and the nature of democratic political competition.

Second, this analysis has a rather obvious bearing on the much-discussed issue of American "exceptionalism." For those who regard the majority-restraining constitutional arrangements of the United States as unique, the comparative evidence provides a useful corrective. No established democracy allows the unfettered expression of popular majorities. Instead, arrangements that restrain majorities in varying degrees are closer to the norm, hardly an exception. Beyond this, when politicians are viewed in office-seeking terms, American politics becomes less unusual, and elected officials in other countries (including Ramsay MacDonald, Willy Brandt, François Mitter, Felipe Gonzalez, and Tony Blair) become more explicable. Indeed, the idea that labor has gained control of the state when a party of the left wins an election sounds a little grandiose when we contemplate actual cases in both the recent and more distant historical record.

Third, some analysts have claimed that the nature of political competition has changed in the last half century. According to this view, although elections did reflect a class struggle in the decade or more after World War II, they no longer do so. Perhaps the best-known version of this argument has been offered by Inglehart and his colleagues (e.g., Abramson and Inglehart 1995; Inglehart 1997), who claim that increasing affluence and associated changes in the shape of the occupational structural manifested in all capitalist economies have generated a major shift in voter preferences. Specifically, the proportion of national labor forces in blue-collar jobs has declined, the proportion in the service sector has increased, and prosperity has become more widespread. This has led to a lessened interest in material issues and therefore a major decline in voting by class, along with a corresponding increase in the prevalence of noneconomic, "postmaterialist" values. Elections have therefore decreasingly reflected a class struggle.

Such observations perhaps reflect the ever-present temptation to divine a trend from the most current election or two. For example, there are those who cite contemporary political leaders like Tony Blair as evidence that the class-struggle interpretation of elections has lost the force it once had. The problem, then, is to account for the awkward fact that Ramsay MacDonald, the *first* Labour prime minister of Great Britain in 1924 and from 1926 to 1931 was a centrist *par excellence*.[18] Similarly, the idea that unprecedented affluence has generated a new postmaterialist set of values seems very much a product of the "golden age" of economic performance from about 1950 to the early 1970s (see, e.g., Maddison 1991). The claimed widespread endorsement of postmaterialist values fits poorly with the chronically high levels of unemployment that have plagued most of Europe in the last decade or so (see, e.g., Layard, Nickell, and Jackman 1991). Indeed, the recent electoral successes of parties of the extreme right in several European countries are quite at odds with the social changes that were supposed to have accompanied widespread postmaterialism and are instead reminiscent of an earlier period in this century (see, e.g., Jackman and Volpert 1996).

In my view, the conclusion that elections were ever part of a class struggle is substantially overstated because it neglects the institutional and political contexts within which voter preferences and behaviors are expressed. Most notably, the institutional procedures that inhibit class voting in most democracies have been in place throughout the period. Further, the empirical deficiencies of the responsible-parties model of

---

[18]In August 1931, MacDonald dissolved the cabinet and then formed a new national coalition cabinet that lasted until 1935. He was expelled from the Labour party in September 1931. On these events, see, e.g., Pelling (1961).

political competition that I have discussed are not new problems that have arisen over the last two decades or so. There have always been temporal oscillations in the class-vote relationship within the established democracies (the "trendless fluctuations" observed by Manza, Hout, and Brooks 1995), but these have little intrinsic bearing on the general interpretation of elections. Despite implicit claims to the contrary, the meaning of electoral outcomes cannot be evaluated independently of the mechanisms that help generate both voter preferences and party strategies. The failure to consider such mechanisms is, indeed, the principal weakness of most studies of class voting and of the broader class-struggle interpretation of elections.

REFERENCES

Abramson, Paul R., and Ronald Inglehart. 1995. *Value Change in Global Perspective*. Ann Arbor: University of Michigan Press.

Aldrich, John H. 1983. "A Downsian Spatial Model with Party Activism." *American Political Science Review* 77: 974-90.

Alford, Robert R. 1963. *Party and Society: The Anglo-American Democracies*. Chicago: Rand McNally.

Anderson, Dewey, and Percy Davidson. 1943. *Ballots and the Democratic Class Struggle*. Stanford: Stanford University Press.

Aristotle. 1962. *The Politics*. Translated by T. A. Sinclair. Harmondsworth, U.K.: Penguin.

Arrow, Kenneth. 1963. *Social Choice and Individual Values*, 2d ed. New Haven: Yale University Press.

Austen-Smith, David, and Jeffrey Banks. 1990. "Stable Portfolio Allocations." *American Political Science Review* 84: 891-906.

Black, Duncan. 1958. *The Theory of Committees and Elections*. Cambridge: Cambridge University Press.

Bronfenbrenner, Martin. 1973. "Equality and Equity." *The Annals* 409: 9-23.

Budge, Ian, and David Robertson. 1987. "Do Parties Differ, and How?" In *Ideology, Strategy and Party Change: Spatial Analyses of Post-War Election Programmes in 19 Democracies,* ed. Ian Budge, David Robertson, and Derek Hearl. Cambridge: Cambridge University Press, 387-416.

Butler, David, and Anthony King. 1965. *The British General Election of 1964*. London: Macmillan.

Calvert, Randall L. 1985. "Robustness of the Multidimensional Voting Model: Candidate Motivations, Uncertainty, and Convergence." *American Journal of Political Science* 29: 69-95.

Castles, Francis C., and Peter Mair. 1997. "Revisiting Expert Judgements." *European Journal of Political Research* 31: 150-57.

Castles, Francis G., and R. D. McKinlay. 1979. "Public Welfare Provision, Scandinavia, and the Sheer Futility of the Sociological Approach to Politics." *British Journal of Political Science* 9: 151-71.

Collier, Kenneth E., Peter C. Ordeshook, and Kenneth C. Williams. 1989. "The Rationally Uninformed Electorate: Some Empirical Evidence." *Public Choice* 60: 3-29.

Cox, Gary W. 1997. *Making Votes Count: Strategic Coordination in the World's Electoral Systems.* New York: Cambridge University Press.

Dahl, Robert A. 1956. *A Preface to Democratic Theory.* Chicago: University of Chicago Press.

_____. 1982. *Dilemmas of Pluralist Democracy.* New Haven: Yale University Press.

Dalton, Russell J., Scott C. Flanagan, and Paul A. Beck. 1984. *Electoral Change in Advanced Industrial Democracies.* Princeton: Princeton University Press.

Dogan, Mattei. 1995. "Erosion of Class Voting and of the Religious Vote in Western Europe." *International Social Science Journal* 146: 525-38.

Dorn Edwin. 1979. *Rules and Racial Equality.* New Haven: Yale University Press.

Downs, Anthony. 1957. *An Economic Theory of Democracy.* New York: Harper and Row.

Duverger, Maurice. 1984. "Which is the Best Electoral System?" In *Choosing an Electoral System,* ed. Arend Lijphart and Bernard Grofman. New York: Praeger, 31-39.

Edelman, Murray. 1964. *The Symbolic Uses of Politics.* Urbana: University of Illinois Press.

_____. 1967. *Political Parties in Western Democracies.* New York: Praeger.

_____. 1980. "What Happened to the British Party Model?" *American Political Science Review* 74: 9-30.

Fiorina, Morris P. 1997. "Voting Behavior." In *Perspectives on Public Choice,* ed. Dennis C. Mueller. New York: Cambridge University Press, 391-414.

Franklin, Mark N., Thomas T. Mackie, and Henry Valen. 1992. *Electoral Change: Responses to Evolving Social and Attitudinal Structures in Western Countries.* New York: Cambridge University Press.

Hicks, Alexander, and Joya Misra. 1993. "Political Resources and the Growth of Welfare in Affluent Capitalist Democracies, 1960-1982." *American Journal of Sociology* 99: 668-710.

Hollingsworth, Rogers, and Robert Hanneman. 1982. "Working-Class Power and the Political Economy of Western Industrial States." In *Comparative Social Research,* vol. 5, ed. Richard F. Tomasson. Greenwich, Conn.: JAI Press, 61-82.

Hout, Michael, Clem Brooks, and Jeff Manza. 1995. "The Democratic Class Struggle in the United States, 1948-1992." *American Sociological Review* 60: 805-28.

Inglehart, Ronald. 1997. *Modernization and Postmodernization: Cultural, Economic, and Political Change in 43 Societies*. Princeton: Princeton University Press.

Jackman, Robert W. 1975. *Politics and Social Equality: A Comparative Analysis*. New York: Wiley-Interscience.

_____. 1986. "Elections and the Democratic Class Struggle." *World Politics* 34: 123-46.

_____. 1993. "Rationality and Political Participation." *American Journal of Political Science* 37: 279-90.

Jackman, Robert W., and Karin Volpert. 1996. "Conditions Favouring Parties of the Extreme Right in Western Europe." *British Journal of Political Science* 26: 501-21.

Kendall, Willmoore. 1941. *John Locke and the Doctrine of Majority Rule*. Urbana: University of Illinois Press.

Key, V. O., Jr. 1966. *The Responsible Electorate*. Cambridge: Harvard University Press.

Knight, Jack. 1992. *Institutions and Social Conflict*. New York: Cambridge University Press.

Korpi, Walter. 1983. *The Democratic Class Struggle*. London: Routledge.

Laver, Michael, and Norman Schofield. 1990. *Multiparty Government: The Politics of Coalition in Europe*. Oxford: Oxford University Press.

Laver, Michael, and Kenneth A. Shepsle. 1996. *Making and Breaking Governments: Cabinets and Legislatures in Parliamentary Democracies*. New York: Cambridge University Press.

Layard, Richard, Steven Nickell, and Richard Jackman. 1991. *Unemployment: Macroeconomic Performance and the Labour Market*. Oxford: Oxford University Press.

Lenski, Gerhard. 1966. *Power and Privilege: A Theory of Social Stratification*. New York: McGraw-Hill.

Lijphart, Arend. 1984. *Democracies: Patterns of Majoritarian and Consensus Government in Twenty-One Countries*. New Haven: Yale University Press.

_____. 1994. *Electoral Systems and Party Systems: A Study of Twenty-Seven Democracies*. Oxford: Oxford University Press.

Lindblom, Charles E. 1977. *Politics and Markets: The World's Political-Economic Systems.* New York: Basic Books.

Lipset, Seymour Martin. 1960. *Political Man: The Social Bases of Politics.* New York: Doubleday.

_____. 1996. *American Exceptionalism: A Double-Edged Sword.* New York: Norton.

Lipset, Seymour Martin, and Stein Rokkan, eds. 1967. *Party Systems and Voter Alignments: Cross-National Perspectives.* New York: Free Press.

Lupia, Arthur, and Mathew D. McCubbins. 1998. *The Democratic Dilemma: Can Citizens Learn What They Need to Know?* New York: Cambridge University Press.

Maddison, Angus. 1991. *Dynamic Forces in Capitalist Development: A Long-Run Comparative View.* Oxford: Oxford University Press.

Manza, Jeff, Michael Hout, and Clem Brooks. 1995. "Class Voting in Capitalist Democracies Since World War II: Dealignment, Realignment, or Trendless Fluctuation?" *Annual Review of Sociology* 21: 137-62.

Marx, Karl. 1852. "The Chartists." *New York Daily Tribune,* August 25.

Michels, Robert. 1927. "Some Reflections on the Sociological Character of Political Parties." *American Political Science Review* 21: 753-72.

_____. 1958. *Political Parties: A Sociological Study of the Oligarchical Tendencies of Modern Democracy.* New York: Dover Books.

Mill, John Stuart. 1862. *Considerations on Representative Government.* New York: Harper and Brothers.

Norris, Pippa. 1995. "The Politics of Electoral Reform in Britain." *International Political Science Review* 16: 65-78.

Olson, Mancur. 1965. *The Logic of Collective Action: Public Goods and the Theory of Groups.* Cambridge: Harvard University Press.

Ordeshook, Peter C. 1997. "The Spatial Analysis of Elections and Committees: Four Decades of Research." In *Perspectives on Public Choice,* ed. Dennis C. Mueller. New York: Cambridge University Press, 247-70.

Orloff, Ann Shola, and Theda Skocpol. 1984. "Why Not Equal Protection?" *American Sociological Review* 49: 726-50.

Page, Benjamin I. 1976. "A Theory of Political Ambiguity." *American Political Science Review* 70: 742-52.

Pelling, Henry. 1961. *A Short History of the British Labour Party*. London: Macmillan.

Rae, Douglas W. 1971a. *The Political Consequences of Electoral Laws*, 2d ed. New Haven: Yale University Press.

_____. 1971b. "An Estimate for the Decisiveness of Election Outcomes." In *Social Choice*, ed. Bernhardt Lieberman. New York: Gordon and Breach, 379-92.

Rae, Douglas W., et al. 1981. *Equalities*. Cambridge: Harvard University Press.

Ranney, Austin. 1954. *The Doctrine of Responsible Party Government: Its Origins and Present State*. Urbana: University of Illinois Press.

Riker, William H., and Peter C. Ordeshook. 1973. *An Introduction to Positive Political Theory*. Englewood Cliffs, N.J.: Prentice-Hall.

Sartori, Giovanni. 1976. *Parties and Party Systems: A Framework for Analysis*. New York: Cambridge University Press.

Schaar, John H. 1967. "Equality of Opportunity and Beyond," In *Equality*, ed. J. Roland Pennock and John W. Chapman. NOMOS IX. New York: Atherton Press, 228-49.

Schlesinger, Joseph A. 1991. *Political Parties and the Winning of Office*. Ann Arbor: University of Michigan Press.

Schofield, Norman. 1997. "Multiparty Electoral Politics." In *Perspectives on Public Choice*, ed. Dennis C. Mueller. New York: Cambridge University Press, 271-95.

Shalev, Michael. 1983. "The Social Democratic Model and Beyond: Two Generations of Comparative Research on the Welfare State." In *Comparative Social Research*, vol. 6, ed. Richard F. Tomasson. Greenwich, Conn.: JAI Press, 315-52.

Stephens, Evelyne Huber, Charles Ragin, and John D. Stephens. 1993. "Social Democracy, Christian Democracy, Constitutional Structure, and the Welfare State." *American Journal of Sociology* 99: 711-49.

Stephens, Evelyne Huber, and John D. Stephens. 1982. "The Labor Movement, Political Power, and Worker's Participation in Western Europe." In *Political Power and Social Theory*, vol. 3, ed. Maurice Zeitlin. Greenwich, Conn.: JAI Press, 214-49.

Strom, Kaare. 1990. *Minority Government and Majority Rule*. New York: Cambridge University Press.

Temple, Philip. 1995. "Changing the Rules in New Zealand: the Electoral Reform Referenda of 1992 and 1993." *The Political Quarterly* 66: 234-38.

Vowles, Jack. 1997. "The New Zealand General Election of 1996." *Electoral Studies* 16: 258-62.

Weakliem, David L. 1995. "Two Models of Class Voting." *British Journal of Political Science* 25: 254-70.

Weir, Margaret, and Theda Skocpol. 1985. "State Structures and the Possibilities for 'Keynesian' Responses to the Great Depression in Sweden, Britain, and the United States." In *Bringing the State Back In,* ed. Peter Evans, Dietrich Rueschemeyer, and Theda Skocpol. New York: Cambridge University Press, 107-63.

Williams, Kenneth C. 1991. "Candidate Convergence and Information Costs in Spatial Elections: an Experimental Analysis." In *Laboratory Research in Political Economy*, ed. Thomas R. Palfrey. Ann Arbor: University of Michigan Press, 113-35.

CHAPTER 8

Policy Innovations and Policy Reversals

William Keech

University of Wisconsin, Madison

THE 1932 AND 1980 U.S. PRESIDENTIAL
ELECTION CAMPAIGNS

The 1932 presidential election is widely interpreted as a repudiation of the incumbent, Herbert Hoover. As Sundquist has observed, it "probably did not matter what kind of campaign Roosevelt conducted, cautious or otherwise. When unemployment stands at 24 percent, as it did in 1932, an incumbent president is not reelected" (1983, 210; see also Leuchtenburg 1963, 3). Historical treatments do not question that the election was a negative judgment on Hoover, his resistance to government activism, and the performance of the economy.

Franklin Roosevelt, then governor of New York, did not provide a very clear alternative. He campaigned without many specific proposals or promises of policy changes, though his identity as a progressive Democrat was secure, given his record as governor of New York and his previous activities in national politics. Roosevelt's campaign gave little hint of the flood of innovations that were to come in the New Deal.

Leuchtenburg observes that in retrospect, "a fair amount of the New Deal had been foreshadowed during the campaign. . . . Yet what is striking in light of later developments is what he did not mention in 1932" (1963, 11-12). Even the progressive signals were garbled by oscillations and

---

I would like to acknowledge the research assistance and advice of Gabriel Ondetti, and the helpful suggestions of audiences at UCLA, the University of South Carolina, the University of North Carolina at Chapel Hill, and the University of Michigan.

vacillation. Roosevelt criticized the Hoover administration for spending too much, for too many agencies, and suggested that he would *reduce* federal spending. Marriner Eccles later observed that "Given later developments, the campaign speeches often read like a giant misprint, in which Roosevelt and Hoover speak each other's lines" (1951, 95).

What Roosevelt was able to do in his campaign was to articulate "strongly and clearly the basic objective that he sought—a revitalization of prosperity—and in outlining only enigmatically the course of action by which he hoped to achieve it. . . . Only one factor seemed certain as Walter Lippmann pointed out in the aftermath of the election, 'The people have willed the end without willing the means to that end'" (Freidel 1973, 16). Lippmann's observation is congruent with the theoretical point being argued here: preferences for prosperity are given, i.e., exogenous, but preferences for policies are open, pragmatic, and subject to experience, i.e., endogenous.

The 1980 election was, like 1932, more of a repudiation of an incumbent president than a positive choice of an alternative. Ronald Reagan himself helped to make this so by his well-known appeal to retrospective voting in his debate with Carter: "ask yourself, are you better off than you were four years ago?" (quoted in Abramson, et al. 1982, 45). Candidate Reagan emphasized the poor record of the Carter administration on inflation, which had reached double digit levels during the election year.

In contrast with some of the conventional wisdom of the time, the Reagan campaign suggested that a painful recession would not be necessary to bring down inflation. Rather, a program of tax cuts, expenditure cuts (in areas other than defense), balancing the budget, and regulatory reform would bring a painless return to prosperity and growth with low inflation. As Herbert Stein points out, Reagan had earlier held the traditional Republican position that austerity was necessary for economic progress, but by 1978 he was moving in the direction of "the economics of joy" and of painless improvements, which came to characterize his stance during the 1980 campaign (Stein 1994, Ch. 7).

We know that candidate Reagan did not give any hint of the deep recession in 1981 and 1982 that would accompany the successful reduction of inflation that took place during his administration. Unemployment rose above 10 percent in the deepest recession since the Great Depression. But by the 1984 election it was falling, and inflation had dropped from 13 percent in the final year of the Carter administration to the four percent range in the final two years of the first Reagan administration.

RETROSPECTIVE AND PROSPECTIVE VOTING AND THE INNOVATIONS OF THE ROOSEVELT AND REAGAN ADMINISTRATIONS

My interpretation of the 1932 and 1980 elections is that they hinged basically on negative retrospective evaluations of the incumbent presidents. Insofar as they were positive choices of the winning candidate, they were more or less leaps in the dark that were subsequently approved by the voters in the next election. A first bit of evidence for this view is provided by Hibbs (1987, Ch. 6) and Erikson (1989), who find that a purely retrospective measure of aggregate national income growth in the previous four years does a good job of predicting the vote shares of the incumbents in the 1980 and 1984 elections. That is, these elections are predictable on the basis of an assessment of the economic performance under Carter in 1980, and under Reagan in 1984. Specifically, a regression of two party vote shares on a discounted measure of national income growth over the previous administration predicts defeat for the incumbent president in 1980 and victory for the incumbent in 1984, which is exactly what happened.

An important feature of this measure is that performance over the four year periods is discounted so as to weight most recent quarters most heavily, and earlier quarters at geometrically declining weights chosen to maximize goodness of fit. This means that the relatively good performance of the early years of the Carter administration was outweighed *politically* by the poorer performance of the later years. This is perhaps unfair to Carter, but it made possible a painful austerity program under Reagan that probably would not have been endorsed prospectively by the voters in 1980, but which yielded results that were endorsed retrospectively in 1984.

In the regressions of vote shares on past economic performance, the pre-election quarter is given full weight, but the performance of a quarter two years before that is weighted at about a fifth of the full value. This fact made it possible for the Reagan administration to induce a recession that brought down inflation by the 1984 election but to pay a very small political price for the painful investment in a low-inflation future. Note that this is a different interpretation of the incentives and possibilities provided by voters' discounting or forgetting the past from that offered by Nordhaus

(1975). Nordhaus's presidents would exploit voters' forgetfulness to engineer vote-maximizing but unsustainable macro-economic outcomes by election time. The Reagan policies took an undesirable economic situation inherited from the Carter administration and took advantage of short voter memories to create improved and *sustainable* levels of inflation, unemployment and growth (see Keech 1995, 84-85).

The message of the aggregate data is borne out by analyses of sample surveys of voter opinion. Miller and Wattenberg (1985) code survey responses regarding retrospective and prospective evaluations of performance and policy for eight elections between 1952 and 1980. While the mix of these judgments, those of candidate attributes, and of party identification varies from election to election and regarding incumbents and challengers, there is clear support for my interpretation of 1980. The retrospective performance judgment of Carter was more negative than that of any other incumbent in this period. Furthermore, in a regression analysis of the importance of short-term factors in determining the election outcome, retrospective performance had a much larger coefficient than other performance and policy measures, and it was somewhat larger than that on candidate attributes (1985, 368-70). An analysis of survey responses for the 1984 election shows that retrospective judgments of economic performance were again dominant, but that this time they were basically positive, leading to support of the incumbent, President Reagan (Abramson, et al. 1986, Ch. 7).

There is of course no survey analysis for the 1932 and 1936 election pairs, but we do have an aggregate data-based regression of vote shares on economic performance under the incumbent party. Fair (1978) analyzes the impact of economic performance on a long time series of presidential elections, including 1932 and 1936, and finds that economic growth is a significant positive influence on outcomes. Lynch (1995) analyzes an even longer time series (1872-1992), and he has kindly provided residuals for the 1932 and 1936 elections. His regression results also provide strong support for the hypothesis that incumbent support is related to past economic performance, especially economic growth and inflation. Lynch's analysis shows that the economic performance of the Hoover administration predicts 39 percent for the incumbent, which is almost exactly what Hoover received in that election. Moreover, the model predicts 59 percent for the 1936 incumbent, which is just below the 60 percent that Roosevelt received. As is well known, the first Roosevelt administration did not end the Great

Depression, but economic growth was positive from 1934 through 1936, and was 13 percent in the election year of 1936.

In sum, the experience with Roosevelt's and Reagan's first administrations are consistent with the view that voters value results, but are pragmatic about policy. Voters did not choose the New Deal, but approved it in hindsight by their reelection of Roosevelt. Similarly, voters did not actively choose the policies of the Reagan administration, and especially not the deep recession of 1981-1982, but in hindsight they approved it by re-electing Reagan. This is consistent with the view that voter preferences for prosperity are exogenous, whereas their preferences for policies are endogenous and pragmatic.

VOTING THROUGH THE LOOKING GLASS

Although I have argued that there are important developments in the administrations of Roosevelt and Reagan that could not have been anticipated on the basis of information available before the election, the nature of the innovations was not strongly at odds with the new president's previous policy identity. FDR's advances were harder to anticipate than Reagan's, but neither involved major reversals of previously defined identities.

There is another whole class of policy innovations that is so unique it deserves another name: "policy reversals." Robert Goodin (1983) tries to show that it is "rational" for voters to expect some policy reversals, like that of Nixon on China, de Gaulle on Algeria, Begin on peace with Egypt, etc., and rational for them to vote accordingly. His argument is that candidates articulate ambiguous positions and that voters are uncertain about what they will do. He represents the choice facing voters as an overlapping distribution of probable positions of ambiguous candidates.

However, according to Goodin, there are limitations on what the rest of the political system would allow these candidates to put into practice. These limitations prevent left-wing candidates from going too far to the left, and right-wing candidates from going too far to the right, according to Goodin, leading to probability distributions that are truncated. If the truncations are sharp enough and the candidates' mean positions are close enough, this implies that the expected position of the left candidate can be to the right of the expected position of the right candidate. Therefore, according to Goodin, it may be rational for voters to choose candidates who seem least likely to do what their policy identity implies that they will do.

Rivers (1984) criticizes Goodin's use of probability theory and the validity of his assumptions and dismisses the argument that "rational voters should occasionally vote perversely," as Goodin suggested. Goodin's model may be flawed, but his article is an excellent discussion of the importance of policy reversals as something that deserves analysis and explanation. And Rivers's critique does not explain the admittedly rare, but still significant phenomenon of policy reversals.

Cukierman and Tommasi (1998) give a more satisfying explanation of policy reversals in terms of asymmetric information about the mapping of policy instruments into policy outcomes. Their framework is consistent with that of this paper in considering voter preferences for outcomes as exogenous, but their preference for policies endogenous to information. Their model depends on incumbents having superior information to that of the public about the consequences of policies. Specifically, incumbents observe a stochastic parameter mapping policies into outcomes that the public does not observe. Cukierman and Tommasi present a unidimensional spatial model in which different regions of the line provide different probabilities of two parties (left and right) taking given positions. In a central region, the "conventional result" obtains, such that policies to the left are more likely to be carried out by the left wing party, and vice versa. In regions to the left (right) of this central one, policies are more likely to be taken by the right (left) wing party and vice versa. In the most extreme left (right) region, *only* the right (left) party can take action.

Using this framework, I will argue in the remainder of this paper that voter preferences for grand scale outcomes, such as prosperity and peace, are indeed exogenous and not very flexible. In contrast, voter preferences for policies are endogenous to experience and to ideology (see Gerber and Jackson 1993). After a preliminary discussion of the Nixon and China case, I will elaborate the argument regarding President Menem of Argentina and his stabilization program.

William Keech

POLICY REVERSALS AS AN OPPORTUNITY FOR CREDIBLE PRESIDENTIAL LEADERSHIP

I begin with a recollection of the most widely discussed and acknowledged policy reversal of all, that of President Richard Nixon regarding relations with communist China. Nixon's political identity had been built on being an opponent of communism. He had been especially prominent as an enemy of the Peoples' Republic of China, and as a friend of Nationalist China, which he saw as the true and legitimate government of that nation.

As of 1971, the isolation of the Peoples' Republic by the U.S. was an increasingly unrealistic and self-defeating position. Yet as of 1971, for any American president to open the road to normal relations with it would still have been a dramatic and daring step. For Richard Nixon, "the world's number one anti-communist for two decades," to make this move was stunning.

But as Stephen Ambrose has put it, Nixon was uniquely qualified to make this change:

> First, as he often pointed out, he was the one, the only one, who could pull it off. It was not just that his anti-communist credentials were impeccable; it was that he did not have to deal with Nixon. That is, had anyone but Nixon tried to promote detente, Nixon would have been the leading, and devastating, critic who would have rallied the right wing to kill the initiative (1989, 440).

Richard Nixon had helped to create a climate of opinion in which most politicians would not dare to risk opening relations with the Peoples' Republic, but this very fact made it more possible for him to change the policy than anyone else. Instead of undermining his credibility, Richard Nixon could *make use* of his credibility as an anti-Communist to bring about a new policy direction, and to reverse a policy that was dated. In Cukierman and Tommasi's terms, detente with China was so far from the current mainstream that only someone like Nixon could have changed it.

MENEM AND ORTHODOX STABILIZATION
IN ARGENTINA

The first administration of Argentine President Carlos Menem is an example of a policy reversal like that of Richard Nixon on China. Menem is a member of the Justicialista party, which is the party of President Juan Peron, and which had been in office from 1946 through 1955 and 1973 through 1976. The Peronist program had been a unique brand of populism that involved import substitution industrialization that was implemented with high protective tariffs, nationalization of private industry and extensive public-sector employment, extensive government intervention in the economy, and downward redistribution of income to the working classes, implemented through a form of corporatism for the labor movement.

This program was controversial, but popular. Although the Peronists had held the presidency for only 12 of the 36 years between 1946 and 1982, they had won every presidential election in which they were allowed to run. In the remaining 24 years they had been out of power because of military coups against them in 1955 and 1976, or because they had not been allowed to run in elections held in 1958 and 1963. The Partido Justicialista (PJ) had a broad base of popular support that gave it a reputation of electoral invincibility. Yet when the military dictatorship that had taken over in 1976 gave up its power in 1983 in elections that followed its disastrous performance in the Malvinas (Falklands) war, the Peronists lost a presidential election for the first time. The winner was the Radical party, and the new president was Raul Alfonsin, who defeated the Peronist candidate with 52 percent of the vote against 40 percent.

The Alfonsin government was oriented to the restoration of democracy and human rights. It did have two major economic stabilization plans (the Austral and the Primavera plans as well as a few minor plans), but both failed to correct an increasingly unsatisfactory economic performance. By the time the next presidential election took place in 1989, the economy was in a recession, and the annual rate of inflation was in three and four digits.

It is my view that the Radicals lost to the Peronists in 1989 at least in substantial part because of negative retrospective voting on the economic performance of the incumbents. That is, I will argue that the defeat of the Radicals was comparable to the defeat of Hoover in 1932 and Carter in 1980. President Alfonsin was not able to succeed himself, and Eduardo Angeloz was the Radical candidate. Angeloz campaigned on a program of free markets, privatization of nationalized industry, balanced budgets, central bank autonomy, and breaking the power of the labor movement.

The Peronist candidate was Carlos Saul Menem, governor of the province of La Rioja. His record as governor raised no questions about his Peronist credentials. And his campaign was a mixture of traditional Peronist promises and vague appeals:

> During his presidential campaign, Menem pledged that if elected he would faithfully adhere to the Peronist creed of economic nationalism, strong state regulation of the economy, economic growth through government financing . . . and social justice in the form of income redistribution in favor of salary and wage earners (Manzetti 1993, 64).

Menem campaigned as a charismatic figure in a white suit and long sideburns and said things like:

> For the hunger of poor children, for the sadness of rich children, for the young and the old, with the flag of God, which is faith, and the flag of the people, which is the fatherland, for God, I ask you: follow me. I will not deceive you. (quoted in *Economist,* November 26, 1994)

POLICY REVERSAL AND RE-ELECTION

Menem easily defeated Angeloz in the 1989 election, as might have been expected based on several grounds: the retrospective voting argument that I have articulated, on the basis of the general popularity of Peronist appeals, or on the fact that the alternatives articulated by Angeloz seemed to promise pain and austerity. The election was not a surprise so much as the program that Menem introduced as president. Manzetti calls it a "stunning policy reversal" that

> Menem came to the conclusion that the recipe for turning around the economy no longer rested on the old populist, nationalistic, redistributive approach, but in the reestablishment of a free-market economy through a sweeping market-oriented reform worthy of Thatcher and Reagan. Oddly enough, it took a Peronist president to undo most of Peron's reform policies of the 1940's (Manzetti 1993, 66).

There were multiple stages to Menem's reforms. The first phase involved placing economic policy in the hands of a Bunge y Born, a major business conglomerate that was far from a predictable Peronist ally. The reforms that took hold and succeeded began in 1991, when Domingo Cavallo, a Harvard-trained economist, moved from the foreign ministry to the ministry of finance. The Cavallo program included many of the things that Eduardo Angeloz, the Radical candidate that Menem had defeated, had proposed: extensive privatization of publicly owned firms (many of which were originally nationalized by Peron himself in the 1940s); bringing the national government's budget into balance with expenditure cuts, tax increases, and tax reform, and with the proceeds from the sale of the public firms; trade liberalization and the reduction of tariffs; deregulation; and a currency board that maintained a one-to-one exchange rate between the peso and the U.S. dollar. Cavallo himself was not only a technocrat, but also a person of remarkable political skill and acumen (see Corrales 1997).

The results have been a dramatic reduction of inflation from hyperinflation levels to single digits, and a return to economic growth. By most standards of retrospective voting, President Menem earned re-election. In the 1989 election, Menem won a second term as president with nearly 50 percent of the vote against 13 other candidates. The Radical candidate, Horacio Massaccesi, ran third, marking the first time since 1912 that this historic party did not run first or second in a presidential election.

Menem succeeded in carrying out an orthodox, neoliberal stabilization program that was in many respects the very opposite of what Peronism had historically stood for. I will suggest that Menem was uniquely qualified to do this in a way that is similar to Richard Nixon's qualifications to bring about a detente with China. Menem succeeded where Alfonsin, who was *ex ante* much more likely to try such a program, had failed. According the de la Balze, Alfonsin had been unable to carry out the painful changes needed to establish stability. His government "either did not think it was strong enough or lacked the conviction to overcome the iron opposition of various groups blocking change" (1995, 69).

With Cavallo's guidance, Menem did have the will, the conviction, and the ability to carry out painful adjustment. Just as it took a Nixon to open U.S. relations with China, it may have taken a Peronist to carry out a successful structural adjustment. There are two features of this logic.

First, by being "least likely" to do what they did, Nixon and Menem co-opted the most likely and effective opponent of what they were doing.

To adapt the Ambrose quote regarding Nixon, it was not just that his (Peronist) credentials were impeccable, it was that he did not have to deal with (Menem). That is, had anyone but (a Peronist) tried to carry out (a neoliberal structural adjustment, Menem) would have been the leading, and devastating critic who would have rallied the (labor movement) to kill the initiative.

Second, by having credibility with the part of the population most likely to oppose the innovation, Nixon and Menem were uniquely qualified to sell their new programs to their erstwhile supporters. He argued that "Current Peronism is a totally updated Peronism. . . . If the world changes, the political parties must change. I would be a fool or a slow-witted person if I wanted to practice in 1991 the Peronism practiced in the 1940s" (Manzetti 1993, 74-75).

POLICY INNOVATIONS AND REVERSALS
IN THE CONTEXT OF PRESIDENTIAL
LEADERSHIP AND REPRESENTATIVE GOVERNMENT

Not everybody approves of policy reversals. For example Mainwaring and Scully observe that

> [d]issatisfied with the performance of their governments, voters have punished the parties in power. But they have frequently not gotten what they voted for. For example, in Bolivia, Brazil, Peru, and also Argentina, popularly elected presidents implemented orthodox shock programs that violated fundamental campaign promises and party platforms. Under these circumstances, the relationship between a citizen's policy predilec-tions and his/her vote becomes more opaque than is desirable, further undermining party system institutionalization" (1995, 25).

I contend that democracy does not depend on voters having rational expectations, or being bankers rather than peasants. If it did, it would be much more conservative and less adaptable than it is. V. O. Key meant to elevate the status of voters from the low status to which survey research had consigned them when he said that "they are not likely to be attracted in great numbers by promises of the novel or the unknown." Had Menem (or Roosevelt or Reagan) campaigned on the basis of promises to carry out the controversial innovative features of their programs that I have identified, they may well have been elected anyway. However, I believe that promising to do what they did would have worked against them, would have distracted from the negative retrospective judgments of the incumbent parties they defeated, and would have made their victories less likely. But to return to the words of Key, "once innovation has occurred, they may embrace it, even though they would have, earlier, hesitated to venture forth to welcome it" (1966, 61).

While I will sidestep the issue of the desirability of the New Deal, I will comment on the desirability of the Reagan and Menem *stabilization* programs. The reduction of inflation was a prominent achievement of the Reagan administration, though critics asserted that it was at the expense of the deepest recession since the Great Depression. Economic wisdom at the time had moved beyond a stable short run tradeoff between inflation and unemployment towards a long run Phillips curve that presumed a "natural rate of unemployment" that was thought to be compatible with any rate of inflation. There was disagreement between adaptive expectations and rational expectations views about whether or not inflation could be brought down without a recession. (This disagreement parallels that between adherents of retrospective and prospective voting.)

For whatever reason, the U.S. inflation rate dropped from over 13 percent in the final year of the Carter administration to just over four in 1984. I have argued elsewhere that by at least one standard, this was a constructive change even if the costs of the recession are confronted. Keech (1995, 84-85) shows that the value of an unweighted misery index (the sum of the rates of inflation and unemployment) declined steadily over the course of the first Reagan administration. One would have to weight unemployment more heavily than inflation in this "social welfare function" in order to conclude that, by this standard, the Reagan stabilization program was not desirable. Even if the index weighted unemployment more heavily than inflation, it would be a question of time preference, since unemployment had dropped below the lowest level of the Carter administration by the end of the second Reagan term.

Although Argentina's decline from being one of the world's rich nations began much earlier, Peronist programs are seen as solidifying and increasing the kinds of policies that were responsible for its long decline. It is ironic in the extreme that a Peronist president created the reversal of these programs. To what extent is the policy reversal of the Menem administration desirable?

The Menem-Cavallo reforms are a variant of a package of neo-liberal reforms that is part of a "new Latin American consensus." This "Washington consensus" replaces an earlier Latin American consensus for a quite opposite pattern of policies: high tariffs to protect import substitution industrialization and heavy government intervention into the economy (see Edwards 1995, Ch. 3; Love 1994). The new consensus is not unchallenged. Adam Przeworski calls it "the greatest experiment since the forced Stalinist industrialization of 1929. . . . [I] is based on a belief about the virtues of markets . . . that is not justifiable in the light of contemporary economic theory. . . . This model is but a conjecture" (1995, viii).

While the evidence is not in on the long term consequences of reforms inspired by the Washington consensus for economic growth and prosperity, there is little doubt that these reforms have been successful in Argentina in ending hyperinflation and bringing remarkable price stability to a country with perhaps the worst inflation performance in the post-World War II world. The fact that this non-Peronist program was carried out by a Peronist president who did not give his supporters "what they voted for" (in Mainwaring and Scully's phrase) is something that enhances the possibility that democracy can adapt to many conditions and problems.

Menem may not have known what he was going to do, but if he had campaigned on a program that accurately predicted his policies, it would surely have undermined his prospects of winning and carrying out a successful stabilization program. This experience is good news for democracy in that it shows that successful stabilizations can be implemented by popularly elected governments as in Argentina, as well as by military dictatorships that seize power from popularly elected governments as in Chile. (See Stokes 1997 for a slightly different perspective on neo-liberal reforms in Latin American that is quite congruent with that put forward here.)

It involves no disrespect of voters to consider them as risk averse discounters of campaign rhetoric who make their decisions substantially on the basis of concrete information available to them. And it involves no disrespect of democracy to argue that it does not depend on voters making positive, forward looking choices among clearly delineated alternatives.

REFERENCES

Abramson, Paul R., John H. Aldrich, and David W. Rohde. 1982. *Change and Continuity in the 1980 Elections.* Washington: Congressional Quarterly Press.

_____. 1986. *Change and Continuity in the 1980 Elections.* Washington: Congressional Quarterly Press.

Ambrose, Stephen E. 1989. *Nixon.* New York: Simon and Schuster.

Bresser-Pereira, Luiz Carlos, Jose Luis Maravall, and Adam Przeworski. 1993. *Economic Reforms in New Democracies: A Social-Democratic Approach.* New York: Cambridge University Press.

Bruno, Michael. 1993. *Crisis, Stabilization, and Economic Reform: Therapy by Consensus.* Oxford: Clarendon Press.

Catterberg, Edgardo. 1991. *Argentina Confronts Politics: Political Culture and Public Opinion in the Argentine Transition to Democracy.* Boulder: Lynne Rienner Publishers.

Chappell, Henry W., Jr., and William R. Keech. 1985. "A New View of Political Accountability for Economic Performance." *American Political Science Review* 79: 10-27.

Corrales, Javier. 1997. "Why Argentines Followed Cavallo: A Technopol Between Democracy and Economic Reform." In *Technopols: Freeing Politics and Markets in Latin America in the 1990s*, ed. Jorge Dominguez. University Park, Penn.: The Pennsylvania State University Press.

Cowen, Tyler, and Daniel Sutter. 1995. Why Only Nixon Could Go to China. Paper presented at the 1995 Public Choice Society Meetings.

Cukierman, Alex, and Mariano Tommasi. 1998. "When Does It Take a Nixon to Go to China?" *American Economic Review* 88: 180-97.

de la Balze, Felipe A. M. 1995. *Remaking the Argentine Economy.* New York: Council of Foreign Relations Press.

Eccles, Marriner. 1951. *Beckoning Frontiers: Public and Personal Recollections.* New York: Knopf.

Echegaray, Fabian. 1995. "Economic Voting or Political Referendum: The Determinants of Presidential Election Outcomes in Latin America, 1982-1994." Manuscript. Department of Political Science, University of Connecticut.

Edwards, Sebastian. 1995. *Crisis and Reform in Latin America: From Despair to Hope.* New York: Oxford University Press.

Erikson, Robert S. 1989. "Economic Conditions and the Presidential Vote." *American Political Science Review* 83: 567-73.

Fair, Ray C. 1978. "The Effect of Economic Events on Votes for President." *Review of Economics and Statistics* 60: 159-73.

Freidel, Frank. 1973. *Franklin D. Roosevelt: Launching the New Deal.* Boston: Little, Brown.

Gerber, Elisabeth R., and John E. Jackson. 1993. "Endogenous Preferences and the Study of Institutions." *American Political Science Review* 87: 639-56.

Goodin, Robert E. 1983. "Voting through the Looking Glass." *American Political Science Review* 77: 420-34.

Hibbs, Douglas A. 1987. *The American Political Economy.* Cambridge: Harvard University Press.

Keech, William R. 1995. *Economic Politics: The Costs of Democracy.* New York: Cambridge University Press.

Key, V. O., Jr. 1966. *The Responsible Electorate: Rationality in Presidential Voting 1936-1960.* Cambridge: Harvard University Press.

Kiguel, Miguel A., and Nissan Liviatan. 1995. "Stopping Three Big Inflations: Argentina, Brazil, and Peru." In *Reform, Recovery and Growth: Latin America and the Middle East,* ed. Rudiger Dornbusch and Sebastian Edwards. Chicago: University of Chicago Press.

Leuchtenburg, William E. 1963. *Franklin D. Roosevelt and the New Deal.* New York: Harper and Row.

Love, Joseph L. 1994. "Economic Ideas and Ideologies in Latin America Since 1930." In *The Cambridge History of Latin America,* vol. 6, part 1, ed. Leslie Bethell. New York: Cambridge University Press.

Lynch, G. Patrick. 1995. "Economic Fluctuations and Presidential Elections from 1872-1992: The Impact of Changes in Government Authority over the Economy." Manuscript. Georgetown University.

MacKuen, Michael B., Robert S. Erikson, and James A. Stimson. 1992. "Peasants or Bankers? The American Electorate and the U.S. Economy." *American Political Science Review* 86: 597-611.

Mainwaring, Scott, and Timothy R. Scully, eds. 1995. *Building Democratic Institutions: Party Systems in Latin America.* Stanford: Stanford University Press.

Manzetti, Luigi. 1993. *Institutions, Parties, and Coalitions in Argentine Politics.* Pittsburgh: University of Pittsburgh Press.

Miller, Arthur, and Martin P. Wattenberg. 1985. "Throwing the Rascals Out: Policy and Performance Evaluations of Presidential Candidates, 1952-1980." *American Political Science Review* 79: 359-72.

Nordhaus, William. 1975. "The Political Business Cycle." *Review of Economic Studies* 42: 169-90.

Przeworski, Adam, et al. 1995. *Sustainable Democracy*. New York: Cambridge University Press.

Rivers, R. Douglas. 1984. "Comment on Goodin." *American Political Science Review* 78: 502-04.

Sargent, Thomas. 1986. "The Ends of Four Big Inflations." In *Rational Expectations and Inflation*. New York: Harper and Row.

Stein, Herbert. 1994. *Presidential Economics: The Making of Economic Policy from Roosevelt to Clinton*. Washington: American Enterprise Institute.

Stigler, George J., and Gary S. Becker. 1977. "De Gustibus Non Est Disputandum." *American Economic Review* 67: 76-90.

Stokes, Susan C. 1997. "Constituency Influence and Representation." Paper presented at the Memorial Panel for Donald E. Stokes, American Political Science Association annual meeting, Washington, D.C.

Sundquist, James L. 1983. *Dynamics of the Party System*, rev. ed. Washington, D.C.: The Brookings Institution.

Wintrobe, Ronald. 1993. "Fourteen Ways to Credibly Escape a Credible Commitment (and Still Get Re-elected)." In *Preferences and Democracy: Villa Colombella Papers*, ed. Albert Breton, et al. Dordrecht: Kluwer Academic Publishers.

CHAPTER 9

Ideological Cohesion in
The American Two-Party System

Nelson W. Polsby
University of California, Berkeley
William G. Mayer
Northeastern University

Th' dimmycratic party ain't on speakin' terms with itsilf. Whin ye see two men with white neckties go into a sthreet car an' set in opposite corners while wan mutthers "Thraiter" an' th' other hisses "Miscreent" ye can bet they're two dimmycratic leaders thryin' to reunite th' gran' ol' party.

> Finley Peter Dunne, 1901

The folklore of American politics, at least since the turn of the twentieth century, is rich with stories and one-liners about fractious, combative, bickering Democrats. Perhaps the most visible single arena in which the divisions and disagreements within the Democratic party are expressed is the national party nominating convention. If the Democrats' 1996 convention seemed tranquil and harmonious, it was a striking exception to the historical pattern. Clinton's easy renomination marked the first time in 60 years that a Democratic presidential candidate had been nominated without significant opposition. More typically, Democratic conventions end with a spate of news stories claiming that one group of Democrats or another is so deeply dissatisfied that there is serious doubt about whether all of the party's disparate factions will be able to unite behind the ticket in the fall.

Although the image of the Democrats as a divided, discordant party—and specifically as a party more internally divided than the Republicans—is firmly established in American political folklore, the implications of this difference are rarely taken seriously by academic analysts. The difference is not mentioned in most of the standard textbooks on American political parties[1] and receives only fleeting attention even in most major works on voting behavior.[2] The purpose of this essay is to document the extent to which the Democrats are less ideologically cohesive than the Republicans and to explore what this difference in the structure of the two major party coalitions implies for the conduct of American elections and political institutions.

Our argument proceeds in three stages. First, we define more precisely what we mean by "ideological cohesion" and indicate how this concept can be measured. Second, we present a variety of indicators of ideological

---

[1]See, for example, L. Sandy Maisel, *Parties and Elections in America: The Electoral Process* (New York: Random House, 1987); Paul Allen Beck and Frank J. Sorauf, *Party Politics in America*, 7th ed. (New York: Harper Collins, 1992); and John F. Bibby, *Politics, Parties, and Elections in America* (Chicago: Nelson-Hall, 1992).

[2]See, for example, Angus Campbell, Philip E. Converse, Warren E. Miller, and Donald E. Stokes, *The American Voter* (New York: Wiley, 1960); V. O. Key, Jr., *The Responsible Electorate* (Cambridge: Harvard University Press, 1966); Gerald M. Pomper, *Voters' Choice: Varieties of American Electoral Behavior* (New York: Dodd, Mead, 1975); William H. Flanigan and Nancy H. Zingale, *Political Behavior of the American Electorate*, 6th ed. (Boston: Allyn and Bacon, 1987); and Herbert B. Asher, *Presidential Elections and American Politics*, 5th ed. (Pacific Grove, Calif.: Brooks/Cole, 1992). Among the few works that do pay some attention to this difference are Everett Carll Ladd, *Where Have All the Voters Gone? The Fracturing of America's Political Parties* (New York: Norton, 1978), Ch. 2; Norman H. Nie, Sidney Verba, and John R. Petrocik, *The Changing American Voter* (Cambridge: Harvard University Press, 1976), Ch. 12; Nelson W. Polsby and Aaron Wildavsky, *Presidential Elections: Strategies and Structures in American Electoral Politics*, 9th ed. (Chatham, N.J.: Chatham House, 1996), 36ff; and Gary C. Jacobson, *The Electoral Origins of Divided Government: Competition in U.S. House Elections, 1946-1988* (Boulder, Colo.: Westview Press, 1990), 130-33. Also see McClosky, Hoffmann, and O'Hara's classic 1960 article, which tries to measure "homogeneity of support" as a way of comparing leaders and followers within the same party. McClosky et al. make no attempt, however, to compare the homogeneity of Democrats vs. Republicans. See Herbert McClosky, Paul J. Hoffmann, and Rosemary O'Hara, "Issue Conflict and Consensus Among Party Leaders and Followers," *American Political Science Review* 54 (June 1960): 406-27.

cohesion, drawn from the years 1968 through 1996, which provide remarkably strong evidence for the claim that the Democratic party is, indeed, substantially more divided than the Republican party. Finally, we talk about the implications of these findings for American politics and the two-party system.

MEASURING IDEOLOGICAL COHESION

In speaking of the "ideological cohesion" of a political party, we mean the extent to which its members are or are not united in their opinions about important political and policy questions. A party whose members are drawn mostly from one part of the political spectrum, or who all feel alike about the issues, would thus be ideologically cohesive. And conversely: a party whose members are drawn from many parts of the spectrum, or who are sharply polarized over one or more issues, would be ideologically divided.

On those occasions when journalists or political commentators have tried to compare the internal divisions within the two major parties, they have usually referred to findings generated in the following manner. A national sample of party identifiers is asked a survey question in which respondents are given a choice between two possible answers: approve or disapprove, favor or oppose, should or should not. A party's ideological cohesion is then measured by the extent to which its identifiers line up on one side of the question.

The problem with this method is that the results depend very heavily on the particular survey questions that are used. By changing the way a question is worded, or by altering the set of circumstances asked about, one can arrive at widely differing conclusions about ideological cohesion. Consider, as an example, the question of U.S. policy toward Central America. Which party was more divided on this issue during the mid-1980s? As the four items in Table 1 indicate, the answer depended very much on which particular question one chose to examine. In the first two questions, it appears that the Republicans are more cohesive; but if either of the next two questions is selected, the Democrats look more unified.

A better method for measuring ideological cohesion begins by representing public attitudes on an issue by the familiar device of a horizontal scale, as shown in Figure 1. Each point on such a scale is taken

Table 1. *How Question Selection Can Influence Conclusions About Which Party is More Cohesive*

1. Gallup (May 1985): "Do you approve or disapprove of the embargo on trade with Nicaragua?"

	All	Republicans	Democrats	More Cohesive Party
Approve	46	65	26	
Disapprove	37	16	58	Republicans

2. CBS (April 1986): "Do you think it's important to the security of the United States to eliminate Communism from Latin America, or can Communist governments exist in Latin America without threatening U.S. security?"

Eliminate Communism	50	59	47	
No threat	30	29	30	Republicans

3. CBS (April 1986): "Do you think the U.S. government should give $100 million in military and other aid to the Contras trying to overthrow the government in Nicaragua?"

Yes	25	36	16	
No	62	51	74	Democrats

4. Gallup (February 1984): "Do you approve or disapprove of the way Reagan is handling the situation in Central America?"

Approve	29	44	22	
Disapprove	48	34	58	Democrats

Figure 1

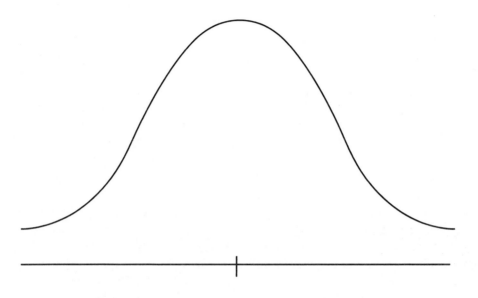

Figure 2

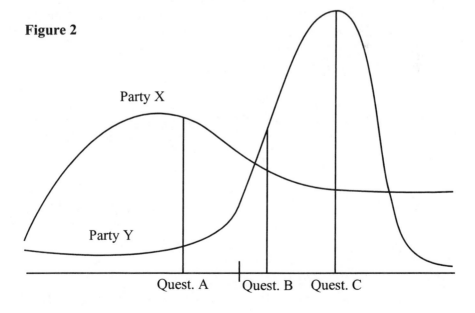

to represent a particular position on some kind of policy issue, while the curve above it shows the distribution along that scale of the population being studied. If we were asking about government's role in the economy, for example, a point at the far right side might represent opposition to all forms of government intervention. At the other extreme would be those who want an economy that is closely managed or even owned by government. Middle points represent more moderate or ambivalent positions.

Without introducing any important new assumptions, one can also think of this scale as having been generated by a set of different survey questions, which together form a cumulative or Guttman scale.[3] In this case, each point on the scale can then be thought of as representing a *specific question*, rank ordered according to the percentage of the respondents who choose the pro-intervention answer. At one end of the scale, we might have a particularly stringent test of pro-intervention attitudes. The other end would involve a form of intervention that only the most libertarian respondent would reject.

Figure 2 shows such a scale, along with two curves that show the distribution along that scale of the members of two political parties. If a researcher tries to measure ideological cohesion by examining a survey question that is close to one end of the scale, such as question C, it appears that party Y is sharply, almost evenly divided on the issue, whereas party X is very cohesive. If one chooses question A, on the other hand, party Y is united, and party X is divided. One could also choose question B, which would make the two parties look more equal, though with some advantage to party Y.

The problem with this method, as Figure 2 makes clear, is that it attempts to measure the shape of the entire distribution on the basis of only one observation. Any one question, no matter where along the distribution it is located, only tells us what percentage of the respondents are situated on either side of a single cut-point.

This analysis has two important implications for how we ought to measure ideological cohesion. In the first place, it suggests that we ought to steer away from questions that force people to choose between two possible responses, and look instead for questions that allow for a variety

---

[3]On the general properties of Guttman scales, see James A. Black and Dean J. Champion, *Methods and Issues in Social Research* (New York: Wiley, 1976).

of possible answers, ranging from responses of fairly extreme support or opposition through more qualified approval to moderate or middle positions.

Second, analyzing such questions clearly requires a better way of measuring cohesion than simply looking at what percentage of each party's members happen to choose a particular response or set of responses. Trying to measure the spread or dispersion of a variable is a common endeavor in descriptive statistics, and is discussed in every elementary statistics text.[4] No text we have consulted suggests that one can measure the dispersion of an interval variable by selecting an essentially arbitrary value somewhere along its range, and then determining what percentage of the observations are located on either side of it. What these texts do recommend as the most important and commonly used measure of dispersion—which we will use here—is the *standard deviation*. As is well known, the standard deviation measures the extent to which the values of a variable are clustered or dispersed around its mean. It thus provides an excellent measure of the underlying concept of ideological cohesion as we have defined it. High standard deviations indicate considerable disagreement among party members; lower standard deviations show greater unity and cohesion.

DATA

Following these criteria, we have inspected two types of survey questions, both drawn from the CPS American National Election Studies (ANES), in examining the ideological cohesion of the Democratic and Republican parties over the last three decades.

1. Seven-point scale questions, first used in the election studies in 1968, have been a principal means for assessing public positions on important election issues since 1970. These scales allow respondents to locate themselves at any one of seven points along a continuum, with the end points usually phrased so as to express relatively extreme positions.

2. "Feeling thermometers," in which respondents are asked to indicate how "favorable and warm" they feel toward some group or political actor

---

[4]See, for example, William Mendenhall, *Introduction to Probability and Statistics*, 7th ed. (Boston: PWS-Kent, 1987); and Herbert F. Weisberg, *Central Tendency and Variability* (Newbury Park, Calif: Sage, 1992).

by locating it along a scale ranging from 0 to 100 degrees. The feeling thermometers do not ask specifically about policy issues. But they do assess public attitudes toward a variety of important and controversial groups that have played a major role in contemporary political disputes. Not surprisingly, studies have often found such ratings to be very good measures of how respondents perceive the political universe, and to be highly correlated with other important political variables such as voting behavior and ideological self-identification.[5]

Once we started to take a closer look at these thermometer ratings, however, it quickly became apparent that not all of the rated groups were appropriate for our purposes. Many of the groups that respondents were asked to rate represent significant and controversial political actors: "black militants"; "anti-abortionists"; "big business"; "gays and lesbians." But others were simply demographic groups, whose activities in American political life are neither very salient nor divisive. Examples in this category include: "Protestants"; "whites"; "older people"; "working men"; and "middle-class people." Since our argument is that Democrats are more divided about important political issues, and not that they are simply more cantankerous and disagreeable people, we offer no prediction that Democrats will be less cohesive in evaluating largely nonpolitical or politically neutral stimuli.

After these politically neutral stimuli were excluded, we were left with about 10 groups in each ANES survey that fit our criteria of being politically significant and controversial. Together, such groups embody some of the most important cleavages in recent American politics: liberals vs. conservatives; business vs. labor; radical students and protesting ministers vs. policemen and the military; evangelicals and anti-abortionists vs. gays and lesbians and the women's liberation movement.

---

[5]See, among others, Herbert F. Weisberg and Jerrold G. Rusk, "Dimensions of Candidate Evaluation," *American Political Science Review* 64 (December 1970): 1167-85; Pamela Johnston Conover and Stanley Feldman, "The Origins and Meaning of Liberal/Conservative Self-Identifications," *American Journal of Political Science* 25 (November 1981): 617-45; and Arthur H. Miller, Anne Hildreth, and Christopher Wlezien, "Social Group Dynamics of Political Evaluations," paper delivered at the annual meeting of the Midwestern Political Science Association, Chicago, 1988.

Having identified a large battery of survey questions, we measured ideological cohesion by dividing the full ANES sample into Democratic and Republican party identifiers[6] and then computing the standard deviation of the responses provided by each party's members. All "don't know" and "no answer" responses were excluded from these calculations. For comparison purposes, we also present the standard deviation of responses for the entire population.

As our references to the ANES should indicate, our concern here is with ideological cohesion within the *mass public*: within what V. O. Key has called the "party in the electorate." Which party has a more cohesive organizational apparatus, or a more ideologically cohesive set of governmental officeholders, are quite different questions, which would require us to examine a different body of data. They might also require us to speculate about the relative effects and significance of, for example, the underlying

---

[6]There is some disagreement within the political science community as to the best way to define "party identifiers." Traditionally, most election scholars have used the term to include all respondents who indicate an affiliation with one of the two major parties in the initial ANES party identification question ("Generally speaking, do you usually think of yourself as a Republican, a Democrat, an Independent, or what?"). More recently, however, a group of scholars affiliated with the University of California, Berkeley, have argued that the "independent" category marked out by this question actually includes a substantial number of "closet partisans," and that most respondents who initially call themselves independents will, when asked, admit that they feel closer to one of the two major parties. These so-called "independent leaners" were actually found to behave more like traditional party identifiers than like "pure independents." See Bruce E. Keith, David B. Magleby, Candice J. Nelson, Elizabeth Orr, Mark C. Westlye, and Raymond E. Wolfinger, *The Myth of the Independent Voter* (Berkeley: University of California Press, 1992).

The choice of definition is, in this case, purely a cosmetic one: We have run all of the data presented in this essay using both definitions and have not found a single important difference. See, in particular, note 7 below.

In the end, we are convinced by Keith et al.'s analysis; hence, unless otherwise indicated, we use the expanded definition of party identification, in which Democratic identifiers consist of strong Democrats, weak Democrats, and Democratic-leaning independents, and similarly for Republicans. Using the expanded definition also provides us with a somewhat larger number of cases for analysis.

attitudes of elected officials (so far as these can be measured), versus the incentives and sanctions each party can use to enhance intraparty unity.

RESULTS

Using the methods described above, we examined the ideological cohesion of Democratic and Republican party identifiers in every one of the ANES fall surveys conducted between 1968 and 1996. To conserve space, we present detailed results in Table 2 only for the years 1972, 1980, 1988, and 1994. A summary of the results for all years can be found in Table 3.

Although we expected the data to provide a general confirmation of the view that the Democrats are more ideologically divided than the Republicans, in fact, they support it overwhelmingly. Across a wide variety of policy issues and politically relevant groups, with a vast range of underlying frequency distributions, the Democrats emerge as decisively less cohesive than the Republicans. Democratic identifiers have a higher standard deviation than Republicans identifiers for:

— 115 of 127 seven-point-scale questions (91 percent);

— and 105 of 138 thermometer ratings (76 percent).[7]

Indeed, in a large number of cases, Democrats are actually more divided than the American adult population as a whole, a population that includes both Democrats and Republicans as well as independents. If a political party is in any sense expected to rally its members behind a common program and a common slate of candidates, the very minimum we ought to anticipate is that its adherents should be selectively drawn from the entire population in such a way that they are at least somewhat more unified than the full population on the most important political issues of the day. But not the Democrats. Democratic identifiers have a higher standard deviation than the entire population for 77 of 127 seven-point-scale questions (61 percent). (There were also two ties.) By way of comparison, the Republi-

---

[7]If independent leaners are removed—i.e., if we use the more restricted definition of party identification that includes only strong and weak identifiers—the totals are almost exactly the same. The Democrats are more divided than the Republicans on:

—115 of 127 seven-point-scale questions;

—and 106 of 138 thermometer ratings.

Table 2. *Ideological Cohesion among Democratic and Republican Party Identifiers, 1972-1994*

	Stnd. Dev. for American Population	Stnd. Dev. for Democrats	Stnd. Dev. for Republicans	Difference (Dems - Reps)
1972 SEVEN-POINT SCALES				
Busing	1.66	1.89	1.20	0.69
Student unrest	1.86	1.98	1.60	0.38
Aid to minorities	1.97	2.08	1.75	0.33
Marijuana	2.16	2.25	1.99	0.26
Guaranteed jobs	2.01	2.06	1.82	0.24
Rights of accused	2.12	2.17	2.01	0.16
Tax rate	2.33	2.39	2.23	0.16
Health insurance	2.43	2.44	2.29	0.15
Ideology	1.28	1.28	1.13	0.15
Urban unrest	2.09	2.14	1.99	0.15
Vietnam	1.94	1.92	1.80	0.12
Role of women	2.27	2.29	2.23	0.06
Inflation	1.54	1.55	1.49	0.06
Pollution	1.91	1.92	1.88	0.04
1972 FEELING THERMOMETERS				
Ministers who protest	29.25	31.16	25.61	5.55
Black militants	22.23	23.90	18.48	5.42
People who riot	18.42	20.04	15.01	5.03
The military	23.40	25.13	20.19	4.94
Civil rights leaders	29.53	31.19	26.28	4.91
Radical students	22.92	24.02	20.16	3.86
Marijuana users	25.09	26.42	22.60	3.82
Policemen	19.02	19.96	16.86	3.10
Big business	20.52	21.20	18.94	2.26
Conservatives	18.96	19.64	17.39	2.25
Women's liberation	27.64	27.97	26.46	1.51
Liberals	20.47	20.48	19.40	1.08
Labor unions	22.15	21.32	22.27	-0.95

Table 2.   *Continued*

	Stnd. Dev. for American Population	Stnd. Dev. for Democrats	Stnd. Dev. for Republicans	Difference (Dems - Reps)
1980 SEVEN-POINT SCALES				
Busing	1.60	1.83	1.08	0.75
Preferential treatment for women	1.21	1.36	0.90	0.46
Aid to minorities	1.59	1.69	1.32	0.37
Defense spending	1.50	1.60	1.27	0.33
Ideology	1.39	1.41	1.12	0.29
Guaranteed jobs	1.88	1.88	1.62	0.26
Role of women	1.93	1.94	1.88	0.06
Getting along with Russia	1.83	1.83	1.82	0.01
Services vs. spending	1.89	1.77	1.78	-0.01
Inflation vs. unemployment	1.50	1.46	1.47	-0.01
1980 FEELING THERMOMETERS				
Black militants	24.97	26.04	22.64	3.40
The military	22.21	22.96	20.01	2.95
Conservatives	18.64	18.79	16.93	1.86
Radical students	22.49	23.04	21.51	1.53
Big business	22.46	22.70	21.35	1.35
Civil rights leaders	23.79	23.48	22.78	0.70
People on welfare	23.13	22.78	22.21	0.57
Labor unions	23.36	22.76	22.25	0.51
Women's liberation	25.90	25.93	25.42	0.51
Evangelical groups in politics	25.56	25.62	25.69	-0.07
Environmentalists	21.50	20.56	22.43	-1.87
Liberals	21.05	18.60	20.90	-2.30

Table 2. *Continued*

	Stnd. Dev. for American Population	Stnd. Dev. for Democrats	Stnd. Dev. for Republicans	Difference (Dems - Reps)
1988 SEVEN-POINT SCALES				
Aid to blacks	1.83	1.99	1.54	0.45
Aid to minorities	1.87	1.94	1.64	0.30
Guaranteed jobs	1.85	1.88	1.61	0.27
Defense spending	1.59	1.62	1.41	0.21
Ideology	1.38	1.36	1.18	0.18
Cooperation with Russia	1.79	1.86	1.70	0.16
Spending vs. services	1.60	1.53	1.49	0.04
Role of women	1.84	1.85	1.84	0.01
Health insurance	2.02	1.92	1.96	-0.04
1988 FEELING THERMOMETERS				
The military	20.71	21.74	18.24	3.50
Illegal aliens	24.30	25.22	21.96	3.27
Gays and lesbians	26.39	27.34	24.55	2.79
Civil rights leaders	22.86	23.39	20.70	2.69
Big business	21.20	22.16	19.63	2.53
People on welfare	21.30	21.80	20.15	1.65
Christian fundamentalists	25.05	25.46	24.19	1.27
Conservatives	19.34	19.06	18.06	1.00
Evangelical groups in politics	24.82	25.10	24.12	0.98
Feminists	22.33	22.14	21.27	0.87
Labor unions	24.54	23.76	22.96	0.80
Opponents of abortion	29.77	29.78	29.14	0.64
Environmentalists	19.60	19.33	19.76	-0.43
Liberals	20.03	18.70	19.56	-0.86

Table 2.   *Continued*

	Stnd. Dev. for American Population	Stnd. Dev. for Democrats	Stnd. Dev. for Republicans	Difference (Dems - Reps)
1994 SEVEN-POINT SCALES				
Aid to blacks	1.69	1.78	1.44	0.34
Ideology	1.36	1.30	1.10	0.20
Defense spending	1.48	1.51	1.31	0.20
Guaranteed jobs	1.79	1.76	1.61	0.15
Health insurance	2.01	1.89	1.82	0.07
Role of women	1.74	1.76	1.71	0.05
Services vs. spending	1.60	1.50	1.51	-0.01
1994 FEELING THERMOMETERS				
Gays and lesbians	29.37	30.80	26.35	4.45
Big business	21.13	22.80	18.61	4.19
Christian fundamentalists	27.16	28.70	24.87	3.83
Wealthy people	20.01	21.21	18.12	3.09
Illegal immigrants	26.16	26.95	23.94	3.01
People on welfare	23.60	23.46	22.32	1.14
Conservatives	20.63	20.24	19.41	0.83
Labor unions	24.14	22.23	23.49	-1.26
Liberals	23.08	19.44	22.16	-2.72
Environmentalists	22.99	20.59	23.60	-3.01
Women's movement	24.61	21.04	25.48	-4.44

Table 3. *Ideological Cohesion among Democratic and Republican Party Identifiers: A Summary*

Year	Number of questions in which the Democratic standard deviation exceeded the Republican standard deviation	Number of questions in which the Republican standard deviation exceeded the Democratic standard deviation
SEVEN-POINT SCALES		
1968	2	0
1970	7	1 *
1972	14	0 ***
1974	6	1
1976	11	0 ***
1978	6	0 *
1980	8	2
1982	7	0 **
1984	10	1 **
1986	8	0 **
1988	8	1 *
1990	8	0 **
1992	6	2
1994	6	1
1996	8	3
TOTALS	115	12 ***

Table 3. *Continued.*

Year	Number of questions in which the Democratic standard deviation exceeded the Republican standard deviation	Number of questions in which the Republican standard deviation exceeded the Democratic standard deviation

THERMOMETER RATINGS

Year		
1968	--	--
1970	12	1**
1972	12	1**
1974	10	1*
1976	11	1**
1978	--	--
1980	9	3
1982	1	1
1984	10	2*
1986	4	2
1988	12	2**
1990	4	4
1992	7	6
1994	7	4
1996	6	5
TOTALS	105	33***

  * p < .05
 ** p < .01
*** p < .001

Note: Statistical significance figures have been computed separately for each year (and for the totals), and indicate that the number of questions for which the Democrats have a larger standard deviations exceeds what one would expect if the two parties were equally cohesive (i.e., if $P[s_{Dem} > s_{Rep}] = .5$).

can standard deviation exceeds that of the entire population on only four of 127 scale questions (three percent). The same result appears in the thermometer ratings. The standard deviation for Democratic identifiers exceeds that of the whole population in 80 of 138 cases (58 percent); Republicans are more divided than the population on only 18 of 138 cases (13 percent).

Clearly, the Democrats are a more divided, less cohesive party than the Republicans. Still, one might ask, are differences of the kind shown in Table 2 large or small? What does it really mean, in practical terms, to say that when attitudes about student unrest are measured on a seven-point scale, the Democratic responses have a standard deviation of 1.98 while the Republicans have a standard deviation of only 1.60?

To answer these questions, it is worth taking a closer look at some of the data that lie behind Tables 2 and 3. In Table 4, we present the actual distribution of Democratic and Republican identifiers for five of the seven-point-scale questions from the 1984 and 1988 ANES surveys. Although the hundreds of questions we have analyzed produce a wide variety of underlying frequency distributions, several patterns show up again and again in the data.

One such pattern is illustrated by the first three items in Table 4, which record public attitudes on aid to minorities, guaranteed jobs, and general ideology in 1988. In all three cases, the Republicans present the outside world with a fairly united front, whose center of gravity is clearly on the conservative side of the issue. To be sure, some Republicans gave liberal responses to these questions—but not many. The Democrats, on the other hand, were considerably more divided on these three issues. A plurality of Democrats was, not unexpectedly, on the liberal side of the scales; but in each case, there was also a sizable contingent of Democratic conservatives. In two of three issues, in fact, the number of Democratic conservatives was almost as large as the number of Democratic liberals. When asked to classify themselves ideologically, for example, 65 percent of the Republicans in 1988 said they were at least slightly conservative; only 10 percent described themselves as liberals. The Democratic party, in contrast, was split almost in thirds: 38 percent said they were liberals, 34 percent moderates, 27 percent conservatives.

Not every question, of course, finds Democrats congregating on the liberal side of the issue. The fourth item in Table 4, a question on school busing from the 1984 survey, shows a strong majority of both Democrats

Table 4. *Ideological Divisions within the Democratic and Republican Parties: Five Examples*

		Democrats		Republicans	
IDEOLOGY, 1988					
Liberal	1	4%		1%	
	2	14	38%	2	10%
	3	20		7	
	4	34		25	
	5	15		28	
	6	10	27	31	65
Conservative	7	2		6	
		s=1.36		s=1.18	
GUARANTEED JOB, 1988					
Government should	1	16%		4%	
guarantee	2	10	40%	4	16%
	3	14		7	
	4	22		19	
	5	16		22	
	6	10	38	24	65
Each person on their own	7	11		20	
		s=1.88		s=1.61	
AID TO MINORITIES, 1988					
Government help	1	16%		6%	
minorities	2	9	40%	3	19%
	3	15		11	
	4	24		24	
	5	10		22	
	6	11	35	16	57
Minorities help themselves	7	14		19	
		s=1.94		s=1.64	

BUSING, 1984

Bus to achieve	1	6%		1%	
integration	2	2	11%	2	4%
	3	4		1	
	4	9		6	
	5	11		10	
	6	20		24	
Keep children in	7	48		56	
neighborhood					
schools		s=1.73		s=1.23	

DEFENSE SPENDING, 1984

Greatly decrease	1	16		3	
	2	14		5	
	3	15		10	
	4	29	44%	36	
	5	14		24	60%
	6	7		13	
Greatly increase	7	6		9	
		s=1.68		s=1.38	

Source: 1988 and 1984 ANES.

and Republicans opposed to busing. Where the parties clearly differ, however, is in the proportion of their members who dissent from this majority position. Only four percent of Republicans expressed positive feelings toward busing; almost three times as many Democrats did so.

Consider finally the question on defense spending in 1984. After the large increases in the military budget of the late 1970s and early 1980s, most rank-and-file party members took centrist positions on this issue. But the Republicans were discernibly more centrist than the Democrats. Where 44 percent of Democrats were located within half a scale point of the party mean (i.e., points three and four on the scale), 60 percent of Republicans were within a half point of their party's average response. And while 30 percent of Democrats wanted to pull their party further to the left—to make much deeper cuts in the defense budget—only 22 percent of Republicans advocated larger increases in military spending.

THE MAGNITUDE OF THE DIFFERENCES

Granting the general point that the Democrats are more ideologically divided than the Republicans, there are nonetheless some important variations in the magnitude of these differences across issues. On some issues, the Democrats are much less cohesive than the Republicans. On others, the difference in standard deviations is considerably smaller. In a very few cases, the Republicans are actually more divided than the Democrats. As the data in Table 2 indicate, the magnitude of the differences varies from survey to survey, but a number of important generalizations can be made.

1.   Social and cultural issues, especially race and crime, are clearly among the leading causes of disharmony within the Democratic coalition.[8] When the seven-point-scales are rank-ordered by the size of the difference in standard deviations, as they are in Table 2, questions on busing and aid to minorities almost always come out near the top. In the 1970s, questions on student unrest, marijuana, and the rights of the accused also showed large differences in the parties' relative cohesion. (Unfortunately, none of these questions was asked in the National Election Studies after 1978.) Similarly, in the thermometer ratings, such groups as "black militants," "civil rights leaders," "radical students," "gays and lesbians," and "policemen" elicited significantly more disagreement among Democrats than they did among Republicans.

2.   Questions about military and defense issues were also a great source of disunion for the Democratic party. The seven-point-scale

---

[8]For other discussions of how social issues have affected the Democratic party, see Richard M. Scammon and Ben J. Wattenberg, *The Real Majority* (New York: Coward-McCann, 1970); Everett Carll Ladd, Jr., and Charles D. Hadley, *Transformations of the American Party System: Political Coalitions from the New Deal to the 1970s* (New York: Norton, 1975); Thomas Byrne Edsall and Mary D. Edsall, *Chain Reaction: The Impact of Race, Rights, and Taxes on American Politics* (New York: Norton, 1991); and William G. Mayer, *The Changing American Mind: How and Why American Public Opinion Changed Between 1960 and 1988* (Ann Arbor: University of Michigan Press, 1992).

question on defense spending, first used in 1980, stands out in almost every survey as producing a large difference in standard deviations. The same is true for thermometer ratings of the military. Questions that dealt with policy toward the Soviet Union show more variation across surveys. Seven-point-scale questions about getting along with Russia or trading with the Soviets elicited very narrow differences in 1980 and 1982, much larger differences in 1984, 1986, and 1988.

3. It is less easy to generalize about the consequences of economic issues for Democratic and Republican party unity. Since the modern Democratic party was originally brought together in the Great Depression around economic issues,[9] one might have expected the Democrats to be relatively more united on economic questions than on social or foreign policy concerns. In general, this does seem to be the case. The scale questions about inflation, national health insurance, and services versus spending usually produce higher standard deviations for the Democrats than for the Republicans, but the differences are fairly small, especially when compared to issues like defense spending or aid to minorities. In a number of cases (the inflation scale in 1970, the services vs. spending question in 1980, 1992, 1994, and 1996, the health insurance scale in 1988 and 1992), the Democrats are actually *less* divided than the Republicans. Similarly, in thermometer ratings for "labor unions," the Democrats were less divided in their assessment of unions in five surveys (1972 and 1990 through 1996), very slightly more divided in six other years.

There are some important exceptions to this pattern, however. The guaranteed jobs question, in particular, is often among those producing the largest difference in standard deviations between the two parties. Perhaps because this question requires government to guarantee "a good standard of living" and not just a job, and thus brings in issues connected with welfare, the guaranteed jobs question was a generally divisive one for the Democrats, considerably more consensual for Republicans. And if the Democrats were sometimes more united than Republicans in their attitude toward "labor unions," this was not the case for "big business." Thermometer ratings of business always produced larger standard deviations for the

---

[9]On the centrality of economic issues to the New Deal coalition, see Mayer, *Changing American Mind*, Ch. 12.

Democrats than for the Republicans, though the difference was usually modest.

4. Aside from the economic questions just mentioned, two issues stand out as especially disunifying for the Republican party: the role of women and environmental protection. In the seven-point-scale question about equal rights for women, Republicans were more divided than Democrats in 1974, 1984, and 1996; in other years, Democrats had a slightly larger standard deviation, but the difference was exceedingly small (in no year did the difference exceed 0.1). Similarly, in the thermometer ratings, "the women's liberation movement" (later changed to "the women's movement") was more divisive for Republicans than for Democrats in 1984, 1986, 1990, 1992, 1994, and 1996. The Republicans had the advantage in other years, but except in 1970, these differences were also very small.

Some caution is in order in interpreting these results. A vast range of policies and concerns are sometimes lumped together under the heading "women's issues," and the evidence does not suggest that all such issues are potential sources of harmony for Democrats. In 1980, for example, the ANES survey included a seven-point-scale question asking whether "women should be given preferential treatment when applying for jobs and promotions." In this case, Republicans were quite united in rejecting such a policy, while Democrats were more divided about the issue (though a majority of Democratic identifiers also opposed it). The difference in standard deviations (0.46) was the second largest of 10 issues in the 1980 survey.

Over the last several years, much has also been written about the potentially divisive nature of the abortion issue for the Republican party.[10] The evidence on this point from the ANES surveys is not extensive, but taken as a whole, it suggests that the abortion issue is highly divisive for both parties, but somewhat *less* so for the Republicans. On a small number of occasions, the National Election Studies have asked respondents to provide thermometer ratings for "anti-abortionists" (in 1984), "opponents of abortion" (in 1988 and 1990), and "supporters of abortion" (in 1990). The extraordinarily controversial character of this issue is shown by the fact

---

[10]For example, William Schneider, "Trouble for the GOP," *Public Opinion* 12 (May/June 1989): 2; and Michele McKeegan, *Abortion Politics: Mutiny in the Ranks of the Right* (New York: Free Press, 1992).

that the thermometer ratings for these groups had higher standard deviations than those for any other group assessed in these three surveys.[11] In all four cases, however, the standard deviation for Democrats was higher than that for Republicans, though the differences were never especially large. Unfortunately for our purposes, the ANES surveys do not measure attitudes about abortion policy on a seven-point scale. The standard ANES question, introduced in 1972 and slightly revised in 1980, asks respondents to choose from among four specific policy options, ranging from making all abortions illegal to making them all legal. Since these alternatives constitute an ordinal, rather than an interval, scale, it is risky to use the standard deviation as a measure of dispersion for this question. But if one is willing to take such a risk, the Democrats were more divided on 12 of the 13 occasions when the question was asked. Again, the differences are fairly small.

Environmental issues have not been measured regularly in the National Election Studies; but when suitable questions on this issue have been included, they indicate that this issue is also more unsettling for Republicans than for Democrats. In three different surveys (1980, 1988, and 1990), respondents were asked to provide a thermometer rating for "people seeking to protect the environment"; the 1992, 1994, and 1996 surveys sought the public's opinion of "environmentalists." On all six occasions, the Democrats had a lower standard deviation than the Republicans. Through most of the period we are examining, the only seven-point-scale question on this topic was an item included in the 1970 and 1972 surveys, asking whether "government should force private industry to stop its pollution." In both instances, the Republicans were less divided than the Democrats, but only by a very narrow margin. Finally, in 1996, two more seven-point-scale questions on the environment were added to the National Election Study survey. One posed the issue as a tradeoff between jobs and the environment and found that the Democrats were the more divided party. The other asked more narrowly about whether greater efforts were needed

---

[11]Normally, groups rated on the thermometer scale receive either a sizable number of zero ratings or a sizable number of 100 ratings, but not both. In 1990, however, 18 percent of the sample gave "opponents of abortion" a rating of 100, while 12 percent put them at zero. "Supporters of abortion" got 100 ratings from 10 percent of the sample, zero ratings from 24 percent.

to preserve the environment and showed the Republicans to be more divided.

5. One other point is worth noting about the ordering of differences in intraparty cohesion, though its practical significance is unclear. As we have seen in Table 3, of the 138 thermometer rating questions that we analyzed, there were 33 instances in which the Republican standard deviation exceeded the Democratic standard deviation. Ten of these cases involved ratings for the group "liberals." Republicans were more divided in their reaction to liberals in 1974, 1976, 1980, and all of the surveys between 1984 and 1996. Republicans betrayed no such ambivalence, however, in their feelings about "conservatives": In 11 out of 13 surveys that inquired about this group, it was the Democrats who had the higher standard deviation.

How to interpret this pattern? It may indicate that the liberal label (as distinct from liberal policies) is not an especially troubling one for Democrats, and that when Democratic presidential candidates are accused of being liberals, they suffer little net loss by conceding the point.[12] Alternatively, it may simply indicate that large percentages of the population aren't really sure what the term means, and therefore find it difficult to have a coherent opinion on the subject.[13]

---

[12]Further support for this view can perhaps be gleaned from the 1988 presidential campaign. After spending several months ducking the question of whether or not he was a liberal, on October 30, 1988, Michael Dukakis finally announced that, "I am a liberal in the tradition of Franklin Roosevelt and Harry Truman and John Kennedy" (see *New York Times*, October 31, 1988, A1). There is no indication that he suffered for this admission. His standing in the polls increased slightly over the next week, and Bush and the GOP campaign seem to have stopped talking about the matter shortly thereafter.

[13]On the problems of interpreting ideological self-identifications, see, among others, Philip E. Converse, "The Nature of Belief Systems in Mass Publics," in *Ideology and Discontent*, ed. David E. Apter (New York: Free Press, 1964), 206-61; Lloyd A. Free and Hadley Cantril, *The Political Beliefs of Americans: A Study of Public Opinion* (New Brunswick, N.J.: Rutgers University Press, 1967), Ch. 4; and Teresa E. Levitin and Warren E. Miller, "Ideological Interpretations of Presidential Elections," *American Political Science Review* 73 (September 1979): 751-71.

Nelson W. Polsby and William G. Mayer

CHANGES OVER TIME

Has the pattern of greater Democratic divisiveness changed significantly over the last three decades? There are good reasons to expect so.
Considerable evidence shows that the party coalitions were rearranged
during the 1960s and early 1970s, in ways that might have made both
parties less ideologically diverse. Gerald Pomper, for example, found that
the correlation between party identification and policy attitudes increased
significantly across an important range of issues between 1956 and 1968,
and that during the same years, both parties developed more distinct policy
images. Voters in 1956 often saw no difference between the parties in their
stands on major issues. Where they did perceive differences, they usually
disagreed about which party was the more liberal and which the more
conservative. By 1968 most voters clearly recognized that Democrats stood
to the left of Republicans.[14] Others have traced the defections from the
Democratic party that occurred in the mid-1960s among white southerners,
the one group that was most out of step with the party's generally progressive cast.[15] More recently, a number of scholars have argued that partisan
differences among political activists and officeholders increased during the
years of Ronald Reagan's presidency.[16] Taken together, these developments might lead to the conclusion that the Republicans' advantage over the
Democrats in intraparty cohesion declined significantly between 1968 and
1990.

Another development that might have produced the same result is the
increase in Republican party identifiers that took place between 1980 and
1988. Through most of the Reagan presidency, political reporters and party
strategists often talked about the Republican party's search for new
members among such groups as white southerners, Christian fundamental-

---

[14]Gerald M. Pomper, "From Confusion to Clarity: Issues and American Voters,
1956-1968," *American Political Science Review* 66 (June 1972): 415-28.

[15]See especially Nie, Verba, and Petrocik, *Changing American Voter*; and
Philip E. Converse, *Dynamics of Party Support: Cohort-Analyzing Party
Identification* (Beverly Hills, Calif.: Sage, 1976).

[16]See, for example, Walter J. Stone, Ronald B. Rapoport, and Alan I.
Abramowitz, "The Reagan Revolution and Party Polarization in the 1980s," in *The
Parties Respond: Changes in the American Party System*, ed. L. Sandy Maisel
(Boulder, Colo.: Westview, 1990).

ists, the white working class, and yuppies. To the extent that any of these efforts bore fruit, the new and larger Republican party might have been expected to become more diverse and internally divided.

The measurement technique developed here, along with the ANES surveys, can provide us with a remarkably rich and detailed portrait depicting whether and how each party's level of ideological cohesion has changed since 1968. Thirteen of the seven-point-scale questions were asked, with the same wording[17] in at least three different ANES surveys. These results are shown in Table 5. A large number of the thermometer ratings have also been used on a regular basis. Though the data are reported elsewhere,[18] the following analysis takes account of those results as well.

One point that is immediately clear from these data is that the standard deviation figures—for the entire population and for both parties—fluctuate a fair amount from year to year, perhaps owing to sampling error, perhaps owing to real (but possibly temporary) changes in public opinion and/or the party coalitions. Normally, one would use statistical significance tests to help distinguish random variations from real and systematic changes. Unfortunately, the calculation of confidence intervals for standard deviations requires assumptions that do not hold for the seven-point-scale questions.[19]

Granting this difficulty, these results provide surprisingly weak evidence for the proposition that the Democrats have become a more ideologically unified party at the grass roots over the last three decades. There are a number of cases—aid to minorities, equal role for women, busing—in which the Democratic standard deviations have declined somewhat, but so have standard deviations for Republicans, principally, it appears, because these issues have become less divisive for the entire pop-

---

[17]We emphasize the need to have the same question wording. The ANES surveys have sometimes changed the wording of the scale questions in ways that make over-time comparisons suspect. This explains why we have excluded from Table 5 the aid to minorities and services vs. spending questions from the 1980 survey and distinguished two different versions of the health insurance question.

[18]See William G. Mayer, *The Divided Democrats: Ideological Unity, Party Reform, and Presidential Elections* (Boulder, Colo.: Westview, 1996), 107-22. Chapters 4 and 5 of this book were written by both present authors.

[19]*Ibid.*

Table 5. *Trends in Ideological Cohesion: Seven-Point-Scale Questions*

Year	Stnd. Dev. For American Population	Stnd. Dev. for Democrats	Stnd. Dev. for Republicans	Difference (Dems - Reps)
URBAN UNREST				
1968	1.93	2.00	1.73	0.27
1970	2.03	2.08	1.89	0.19
1972	2.09	2.14	1.99	0.15
1974	2.04	2.01	1.96	0.05
1976	1.91	1.90	1.84	0.06
1992	1.88	1.87	1.75	0.12
VIETNAM				
1968	1.97	1.98	1.89	0.09
1970	2.12	2.15	1.98	0.17
1972	1.94	1.92	1.80	0.12
AID TO MINORITIES[a]				
1970	2.03	2.11	1.81	0.30
1972	1.97	2.08	1.75	0.33
1974	2.01	2.11	1.70	0.41
1976	2.00	2.09	1.84	0.25
1978	1.90	2.03	1.60	0.43
1982	1.68	1.75	1.43	0.32
1984	1.64	1.65	1.45	0.20
1986	1.65	1.70	1.43	0.27
1988	1.87	1.94	1.64	0.30

Table 5. *Continued.*

Year	Stnd. Dev. For American Population	Stnd. Dev. for Democrats	Stnd. Dev. for Republicans	Difference (Dems - Reps)
AID TO BLACKS				
1986	1.68	1.77	1.50	0.27
1988	1.83	1.99	1.54	0.45
1990	1.80	1.85	1.60	0.25
1992	1.76	1.82	1.52	0.30
1994	1.69	1.78	1.44	0.34
1996	1.64	1.71	1.33	0.38
RIGHTS OF THE ACCUSED				
1970	2.17	2.27	1.97	0.30
1972	2.12	2.17	2.01	0.16
1974	2.14	2.16	1.90	0.26
1976	2.13	2.20	1.98	0.22
1978	2.00	2.09	1.78	0.31
HEALTH INSURANCE (version 1)[b]				
1970	2.37	2.33	2.25	0.08
1972	2.43	2.44	2.29	0.15
1976	2.38	2.37	2.23	0.14
1978	2.34	2.30	2.18	0.12
HEALTH INSURANCE (version 2)[b]				
1984	1.94	1.90	1.88	0.02
1988	2.02	1.92	1.96	-0.04
1992	1.90	1.76	1.88	-0.12
1994	2.01	1.89	1.82	0.07
1996	1.88	1.76	1.75	0.01

Table 5. *Continued.*

Year	Stnd. Dev. For American Population	Stnd. Dev. for Democrats	Stnd. Dev. for Republicans	Difference (Dems - Reps)
GUARANTEED JOB				
1972	2.01	2.06	1.82	0.24
1974	1.97	2.01	1.75	0.26
1976	2.02	2.08	1.80	0.28
1978	1.80	1.86	1.46	0.40
1980	1.88	1.88	1.62	0.26
1982	1.83	1.80	1.62	0.18
1984	1.80	1.77	1.64	0.13
1986	1.88	1.91	1.64	0.27
1988	1.85	1.88	1.61	0.27
1990	1.88	1.89	1.72	0.17
1992	1.80	1.74	1.65	0.09
1994	1.79	1.76	1.61	0.15
1996	1.75	1.70	1.53	0.17
ROLE OF WOMEN				
1972	2.27	2.29	2.23	0.06
1974	2.17	2.09	2.14	-0.05
1976	2.07	2.09	2.04	0.05
1978	2.08	2.10	2.07	0.03
1980	1.93	1.94	1.88	0.06
1982	1.96	1.95	1.91	0.04
1984	1.82	1.78	1.83	-0.05
1988	1.84	1.85	1.84	0.01
1990	1.89	1.86	1.85	0.01
1992	1.71	1.70	1.69	0.01
1994	1.74	1.76	1.71	0.05
1996	1.67	1.62	1.68	-0.06

Table 5. *Continued.*

Year	Stnd. Dev. For American Population	Stnd. Dev. for Democrats	Stnd. Dev. for Republicans	Difference (Dems - Reps)
IDEOLOGY				
1972	1.28	1.28	1.13	0.15
1974	1.40	1.37	1.18	0.19
1976	1.34	1.33	1.17	0.16
1978	1.35	1.29	1.18	0.11
1980	1.39	1.41	1.12	0.29
1982	1.36	1.32	1.12	0.20
1984	1.36	1.30	1.18	0.12
1986	1.26	1.24	1.13	0.11
1988	1.38	1.36	1.18	0.18
1990	1.33	1.33	1.17	0.16
1992	1.42	1.41	1.12	0.29
1994	1.36	1.30	1.10	0.20
1996	1.39	1.26	1.06	0.20
BUSING				
1972	1.66	1.89	1.20	0.69
1974	1.63	1.88	1.15	0.73
1976	1.71	1.92	1.41	0.51
1980	1.60	1.83	1.08	0.75
1984	1.55	1.73	1.23	0.50

Table 5. *Continued.*

Year	Stnd. Dev. For American Population	Stnd. Dev. for Democrats	Stnd. Dev. for Republicans	Difference (Dems - Reps)
DEFENSE SPENDING				
1980	1.50	1.60	1.27	0.33
1982	1.57	1.64	1.33	0.31
1984	1.63	1.68	1.38	0.30
1986	1.59	1.63	1.38	0.25
1988	1.59	1.62	1.41	0.21
1990	1.55	1.62	1.37	0.25
1992	1.41	1.47	1.23	0.24
1994	1.48	1.51	1.31	0.20
1996	1.42	1.48	1.26	0.22
SERVICES vs. SPENDING[c]				
1982	1.70	1.65	1.45	0.20
1984	1.59	1.49	1.48	0.01
1986	1.62	1.55	1.54	0.01
1988	1.60	1.53	1.49	0.04
1990	1.63	1.60	1.52	0.08
1992	1.57	1.45	1.53	-0.08
1994	1.60	1.50	1.51	-0.01
1996	1.52	1.37	1.42	-0.05

[a]A question on this topic was also asked in 1980, but with a different wording.
[b]The wording of this question was altered slightly between 1978 and 1984, in a way that seems to have encouraged more moderate answers.
[c]A question on this topic was also asked in 1980, but with a different wording.

ulation. The magnitude of the *difference* between Democratic and Republican cohesion, however, seems to have stayed fairly constant for these questions. In the end, only three of 13 questions show detectable gains for the Democrats: guaranteed jobs (after 1980); services vs. spending (after 1982), and defense spending (after 1984).

The thermometer ratings provide somewhat more evidence of growing Democratic cohesion. In particular, beginning in 1990 there emerged a solid core of four groups—labor unions, liberals, environmentalists, and the women's movement—on which the Republicans are consistently more divided than the Democrats. In all other cases, however, the general pattern continues to be one of greater Republican cohesion, with surprisingly little indication of a clear trend in the opposite direction.

It may also be that a substantial increase in Democratic cohesion occurred just *before* the years we discussed in this essay. The literature referred to above, especially the works of Pomper and Nie, Verba, and Petrocik, describe changes that generally took place prior to 1968, with 1964 an especially crucial point in the transformation. Since our own data begin in 1968, it may be that we have just missed an important change in intraparty cohesion; and that the modern-day Democratic party, even with all of its numerous divisions and disagreements, is nevertheless a substantially more unified party now than it was in 1932 or 1952.

Unfortunately, we know of no data series that would allow a careful test of this conjecture. As is well known, the ANES significantly changed their issue-question formats between 1960 and 1964, and again in the late 1960s. Seven-point-scale questions were not used until 1968 (and there were only two that year); and the major difference between the new and old question formats is precisely in the number of alternative positions that respondents were offered. The thermometer ratings were used in the 1964, 1966, and 1968 surveys, but the coding procedures were changed between 1968 and 1970 in a way that makes any comparisons of partisan cohesion extremely suspect.[20]

---

[20]From 1964 to 1968, respondents who said they could not rate a group or were not sure where to place them were assigned a score of 50. Starting in 1970, such responses were put into a separate, "don't know" category. The former procedure, in our view, makes the standard deviation a questionable measure of dispersion—and certainly complicates any comparisons with later surveys.

Whatever the history of the two parties before 1968, however, the data in Tables 2 and 3 leave no doubt about the fact that the Democrats were much more divided than the Republicans in that year—and in every year since then for which survey data are available. The latter point is worth stressing: At a minimum, the data do *not* show that the Republicans are now—or ever have been—*more* divided than the Democrats. The strongest inference one could draw from these results is that the once-substantial Republican advantage in ideological cohesion has diminished somewhat and that the Democrats are now only slightly less united than the Republicans.

SOME IMPLICATIONS

The findings in this essay have a number of important implications for the study of American politics and the two-party system. At their most basic level, they suggest that, all other things being equal, party unity will be a greater problem for Democrats than for Republicans. This conclusion has ramifications for the conduct of election campaigns, the parties' behavior in Congress, their relative abilities to formulate, enact, and implement a program, and their capacity to control the executive branch.

In the remainder of this paper, we develop only one of these implications, but it is an important one. For these data suggest a partial answer to the question of why the Democrats, who have been the larger of the two parties for the entire postwar period, have nevertheless managed to lose most of the presidential elections held over the last 50 years. It appears that the Democratic party's edge in party identifiers is, from the perspective of presidential voting, somewhat misleading. Although there are more Democrats than Republicans, Democrats are less likely to maintain partisan unity. Given the internal divisions reported here, it is reasonable to suppose that Democrats would be much more likely to defect to an opposition candidate (Republican or third party) than Republicans.

As Table 6 shows, across the 12 presidential elections between 1952 and 1996, an *average* of about one out of every five self-identified Democrats has decided not to vote for their party's presidential candidate. The Republicans have suffered defections too, of course, but at a far lower

Table 6. *Party Loyalty in Presidential Elections, 1952-1996*

	Percentage of Republican identifiers who voted for the Republican presidential candidate		Percentage of Democratic identifiers who voted for the Democratic presidential candidate	
	Gallup	CPS	Gallup	CPS
1952	92%	96%	77%	70%
1956	96	96	85	74
1960	95	93	84	80
1964	80	72	87	89
1968	86	88	74	71
1972	95	93	67	58
1976	91	85	82	81
1980	86	88	69	72
1984	96	95	79	78
1988	93	92	85	82
1992	77	73	82	82
1996	85	82	90	90
Average, 1952-1996	89%	88%	80%	77%

Source: Gallup data taken from *Gallup Poll Monthly*, no. 374 (November 1996): 17-20. CPS data are calculated from the American National Election Studies.

rate: about one in every 10 party identifiers. Democrats broke ranks more often than Republicans in eight of 11 elections—even in 1960 and 1976, when the Democratic candidate won the election.

It seems logical that larger political parties, encompassing many groups and many interests, ought to win elections over smaller parties if internal disagreements can be suppressed long enough to mobilize their big battalions and bring them to the polls. But it is of little advantage to enroll large numbers of voters if in key elections they defect to the other side. In general, therefore, we can say that conditions favor the Democrats when elections are structured so as to mitigate the effects of intraparty disagreement, and they favor the Republicans when little or nothing is done in the election process to mute these internal divisions.

Thus, findings that Democrats and Republicans differ markedly in their capacities to hold the loyalties of their voters in presidential elections because of differences in their internal composition lend strength to the argument proffered some years ago that attempted to show why reforms of the electoral process seemed to affect the two major parties differently.[21] The argument, reduced to its bare essentials, is that the net effect of reforms in the nomination process in the late 1960s and early 1970s was to drive state parties and their leaders out of the process, and to change the goals of prospective presidential nominees away from coalition building among state parties and toward the mobilization of intraparty factions, each faction consisting of primary voters attaching to one and only one candidate for the presidential nomination. The seven-month-long exercise in intraparty mayhem that these changes promoted tended to weaken the candidacy of the eventual nominee of the party. Republicans retained a substantial residual capacity to rally around the flag of internal ideological agreement—but this option was generally denied to the more numerous but more fractious Democrats.

The result has been the extraordinary anomaly of modern American electoral politics, in which most presidential elections have been won by the minority party. In party identifications, party registrations, and electoral success at all other levels of government where partisan elections are held, Democratic majorities have prevailed most of the time. In the grand aggregation of voters necessary to elect a president, however, Democrats have found themselves at a notable disadvantage, especially since the

---

[21]See Nelson W. Polsby, *Consequences of Party Reform* (New York: Oxford University Press, 1983).

enactment of party reforms distinctively enabling the expression of intra-party disagreement in the presidential nominating process.

Of course, as Bill Clinton's victories in 1992 and 1996 indicate, this obstacle is not a total bar to Democratic victory. A bad economy and/or a particularly weak Republican candidate may allow the Democrats to put aside their internal disagreements for a while, and induce in them a higher than usual measure of partisan unity at the polls. In 1996, the unusually rigid and combative posture assumed by the Republican Congress permitted Clinton and his fellow partisans to unite around their opposition to the Republican agenda, without being very specific about what kinds of policies they favored.

But at the very least, the data presented here suggest caution to anyone who thinks that Clinton's victories spell an end to the Democrats' recent difficulties in presidential elections. Whether or not Clinton is a "new Democrat" is a matter of some dispute; but even if he himself is one, this hardly means that he can easily remake the Democratic party in his own image. When Clinton announced in his 1995 State of the Union address that "the era of big government is over," for example, it is likely that at least 40 percent of his own party disagreed with him. If our analysis is correct, such divisions are still common in the Democratic party and will require continuous effort at coalition building for the Democrats to achieve electoral success commensurate with their numbers.

IV. Party Decline?

CHAPTER 10

If "The Party's in Decline," Then What's That Filling the News Columns?

Marjorie Randon Hershey
Indiana University

Political observers have long debated whether, and in what ways, the American political parties are in a state of decline. Some researchers contend that the parties have slipped steadily into a condition of weakness from which they are unlikely to recover. For example, in his foreword to Martin Wattenberg's *The Decline of American Political Parties 1952-1988*, Walter Dean Burnham cites "the rapid decline of American political parties over the past generation, from the levels of revitalized activity and effectiveness they had achieved in and just after the New Deal period" (Wattenberg 1990, x). The parties are fading out of public consciousness, Burnham argues, and the consequences are dire. "As the salience of party-in-the-electorate decays, the media coverage of elections shifts heavily from many references to party toward preoccupations with candidates—one is tempted to say, American politics as understood and reported by *People* magazine" (Burnham in Wattenberg 1990, xii).

Those who contend that the parties are in decline focus primarily on "party in the electorate"—citizens' party attachments (Sorauf 1964, 7-8). It is widely acknowledged that beginning in the mid-1960s, a smaller proportion of U.S. survey respondents were willing to identify themselves as Republicans or Democrats, a smaller proportion called themselves *strong* party identifiers, and a considerably smaller proportion voted the straight party ticket than had done so in the 1950s (Beck 1997, 136, 158). Although party identification appears to remain the most stable of political attitudes, the party-decline school suggests that it is no longer the most central, and that because of expansion of the mass media and candidate-centered campaigns, partisanship means less to voters, and has less impact on voters than it did formerly (see Wattenberg 1990, 35, Ch. 4).

Another school of thought grants that the parties slid into decline in the 1960s, but argues that the decline was reversed two decades later. This school looks at a second aspect of parties—party organization and activists—as well as party in the electorate. By the 1960s and 1970s, researchers note (see Ceaser 1990, 87-88), both party organizations had lost the power to nominate candidates for most offices and had suffered a reduced role in campaigns. But by the 1980s, the national and state party organizations had begun to adapt to the changes that once seemed likely to doom them: for example, by using the electronic media and campaign consultants, and making these technologies available to selected candidates (Ceaser 1990, 136). Thus, more candidates could find value in partisanship, as many did in the 1994 congressional elections. So party organizations had developed greater strength, even without a recovery of their nominating power, and the incidence of party identification was again on the rise.

This would seem to be a straightforward empirical question. If we can agree on a definition of party strength that encompasses the state of the party organization and the party in government as well as voters' attachment to parties, and on ways to measure that definition against empirical fact, then we should be able to determine what aspects of parties, if any, are in decline, and during what time period. To this point, however, many of the claims of party decline have been extended into terrain, and time periods, about which we have little empirical evidence.

The party-decline school often seems to assume, for example, that there has been a linear trend, beginning at least with the New Deal, of decline in voters' and candidates' reliance on party (at least until the mid-1970s). Yet the data needed to identify any such trend have been available mainly since the early 1950s. We have voting data prior to 1950, but little information about psychological attachments to the parties and strength of partisanship until 1952, with the advent of systematic political polling, as well as good studies of party organizations (e.g., Eldersveld 1964). Without a longer time series, we cannot be sure whether the 1950s were a point on the downward slope of psychological attachment, or an all-time high in that attachment, or something else.

In related fields we have found that it can be risky to assume the existence of long-term secular trends in politics. For instance, many studies of realignment once envisioned party change as taking the form of a dramatic, critical event that upset the existing equilibrium and produced a new, fairly stable political agenda for the next 32-36 years. Carmines and Stimson (1989) have demonstrated that party change may take a variety of different forms that vary in their durability.

The purpose of this chapter is to examine the question of party strength using a new source of data and a longer time frame. It builds on John Aldrich's reminder that parties are endogenous institutions—created by, and interactive with, ambitious political actors seeking advantage at a particular time. "Parties . . . can be understood only in relation to the polity, to the government and its institutions, and to the historical context of the times" (Aldrich 1995, 19). This raises the possibility that party strength is more variable than either of the party decline schools suggests: that although long-term forces (such as public ambivalence about parties, as well as social and technological trends) have a major impact, parties' capabilities are strongly affected by the influence of political events and actors at a particular time.

Given that parties are, according to Austin Ranney, the main forms of "institutional machinery . . . necessary to translate the popular will faithfully and effectively into government action" (Ranney 1951, 190), the extent to which parties are deteriorating as an intermediary institution is vital to our understanding of the health of our democracy. The dynamics of such a change are important as well. Our ability to affect the functioning of the parties—a major concern of Ranney's work (e.g., Ranney 1975)—depends in part on whether any such deterioration has been caused by long-term, socially-embedded forces, or whether the changes are also responsive to shorter-term (and manipulable) political conditions.

THE PARTY DECLINE THESIS

Research during the last two decades has helped flesh out a complicated story of party "strength" and "weakness." The story combines underlying institutional and behavioral forces with stimuli from the political environment at different times in our history.

Party Organization

Developing and maintaining a strong party organization has always been a challenge in the American political environment. Ranney (1962,

160-62) has reminded us that the antimajoritarian design of the U.S. constitutional system, in particular the separation of powers, impedes the development of cohesive parties like those in many parliamentary systems. The Republicans and Democrats have created and abandoned a number of organizational forms in dealing with these constraints. They began with the congressional caucus, the device used by the national parties to nominate presidential candidates in the early 1800s. Both parties later moved to a national convention, in which state parties had primacy in choosing their delegates; this both reflected and encouraged the marked decentralization of the American parties (Ranney 1975, 174-76)—weak at the national level, stronger at the state level.

For a considerable period, patterns of immigration into urban areas combined with socio-economic forces to facilitate the growth of the great urban party machines. Their strength was drawn from their ability to incorporate new groups into the local party structure and to monopolize the distribution of benefits in their urban areas, and sometimes within a state as well. These organizational forms were heavily affected by the wave of Progressive reforms, including the Australian ballot and the direct primary (see Epstein 1986), intended to weaken the power of the party "bosses" and their organizations. Ranney (1975, 121) refers to the states' adoption of the direct primary as "the most radical of all the party reforms adopted in the whole course of American history," directed as it is at weakening party leaders' and activists' hold on the most important function of the parties, that of nominating candidates.

It is unlikely that primary laws would have been adopted by the states if the party organizations had been strong enough to prevent it. But the direct primary did indeed cut further into party organizational strength—though many such organizations managed to keep control over nominations despite the primary laws (Epstein 1986, 139-40). Further, the decline of patronage and other environmental changes also reduced the incentives the machines had to offer to citizens, potential activists, and candidates. As a result, by the 1950s, many or most urban party organizations suffered from a declining number of party workers and more sporadic public participation.

Beginning in that same decade, however, some aspects of party organization have undergone what Ranney terms (1975, 180) "a modest but distinct revival of *national* party control" (italics added). As a result of the Dixiecrat break from the national Democratic ticket in 1948, the party's national convention in the mid-1950s affirmed that it had the right to insist that the state parties send delegates willing to support, rather than to bolt from, the party's choice of nominees. Then, first on civil rights and later more broadly, the Democratic convention in the 1960s and 1970s increased the convention's authority over the delegate selection procedures used by states.

At the same time, party organizations at the state and national levels were becoming richer and more institutionalized, with bigger, more specialized, and more professional staffs; larger budgets, more accessible headquarters, and greater activity. Gibson et al. (1983) find that the state party organizations were substantially stronger in organizational terms in the late 1970s than they were in the early 1960s. Herrnson (1995, Ch. 4) shows that party committees, especially those at the national level, have become more active particularly since the mid-1970s, with much larger staffs and much greater revenues (see also Aldrich 1995, 257-58). Local parties as well (Gibson et al. 1985) were at least as active and organized in the late 1970s as they had been in the early 1960s, at least in the opinion of party leaders.

Granted, by this time, the parties could no longer effectively monopolize the resources needed to run a winning campaign: money, workers, means of communication, information-gathering (e.g., through polling). Ambitious politicians could get access to these resources without having to turn to the party and become vulnerable to its influence (Aldrich 1995, 269). Getting access to these resources independently, however, was becoming more and more expensive. It made sense for services such as polling and media consulting to be provided by an organization that could reduce their cost to individual users. This opened a niche that could be filled by state and national party organizations—one that the national Republican party began to fill in the mid-1970s, with the national Democrats and state organizations following suit.

In short, parties have found ways to adapt to a candidate-centered politics, at least at the national level and in many states. Because candidates, and especially challengers, need funding, extensive research, and media and strategic advice, the national party committees have found a role in providing these services. In fact, services provided by the parties' congressional campaign committees are rated as at least moderately helpful by large numbers of House and Senate candidates (Herrnson 1995, 97-98). This does not suggest a pattern of decline, even from the time of the New

Deal. Rather, it suggests that continuing environmental change has elicited party organizational response.

Party in the Electorate

Richard Hofstadter points out that the mainstream of political thought in the period before the Revolution was that parties were likely to distort the expression of the public will. The necessary limits on power, he wrote, would be provided by the constitutionally established checks and balances within the governmental structure, "and not by parties, which were indeed usually thought of, when they were thought of at all, as forces likely to upset the desired constitutional balance by mobilizing too much force and passion in behalf of one limited interest" (Hofstadter 1969, 51).

Yet parties very quickly developed in the new republic in order to permit the making of policy. In fact, Hofstadter questions whether the Constitution could have been made to work without the development of parties (1969, 70-71). That leaves us, he points out, with "our central paradox of party government instituted by anti-party thinkers." (1969, 54) Ranney, similarly (1975, 22), refers to "the persistence of this combination of antiparty thought and partisan action throughout our history," and to the prevailing image of the American parties that "for many Americans then and now they have never lost their reputations as facades erected by devious men to mask secret conspiracies for selfish purposes" (Ranney 1975, 96).

This strain of thought about parties has had considerable staying power. Using data from a 1964 survey of Wisconsin adults, Dennis (1966) found that most adults have more negative than positive attitudes toward the idea of party. The modal response was that party competition is a good thing, but that parties thus create conflicts, which is not. Parties confuse the issues. It's better to vote for the person, not the party. And politicians shouldn't blindly follow their party leaders.

Yet most Americans are willing to describe themselves to pollsters as Republicans or Democrats. It is demonstrably the case that parties lost influence over individuals' voting choices between the 1950s and the 1970s. Survey research shows a drop in the percentage of strong party identifiers, a decrease in the proportion of party identifiers who vote for their party's candidates in elections, and fewer mentions of party as a reason for liking or disliking a particular candidate (see Nie, Verba, and Petrocik

1979, Ch. 4). But even at the low point of self-described partisanship in the National Election Studies surveys, 1974, fully 61 percent of the respondents were willing to term themselves strong or weak Democrats or Republicans, and another 22 percent, while calling themselves independents, admitted that they leaned toward one party or the other (Aldrich 1995, 15). These numbers have increased since that time, especially beginning with the Reagan election in 1980.

However, levels of partisanship, and the relative proportions of Republican and Democratic identifiers, do seem to be affected by major events in the political climate at the time. Aldrich (1995, 246-47) shows that when the Democratic-dominated national government took dramatic action on civil rights—the Civil Rights and Voting Rights Acts of the mid-1960s, the first of which the 1964 Republican presidential nominee failed to support—party identification among blacks changed. Democratic self-identification jumped by about 20 percent, and the proportion of apoliticals among black respondents dropped from just under 20 percent to almost zero.

Similarly, the temporary drop in partisanship in the 1960s and 1970s may well have reflected a change in the national political agenda: the movement from the economic issues of the New Deal to the questions of race, crime, and antiwar protest that began to dominate media coverage in the 1960s. At least initially, these issues did not fit cleanly within the existing party coalitions; they divided Democrat from Democrat and Republican from Republican. During this period of turmoil, it would not be surprising if the development of partisanship by new voters, in particular, were inhibited. As these issues evolved and the increasing gulf between the two parties' leaders was absorbed by the broader public, the development and transmission of party identification was probably enhanced (Carmines and Stimson 1989, Ch. 6). So political leaders and events help shape the party in the electorate as well.

Party in Government

The influence of party on government can be conceptualized and measured in a number of different ways. If we look at the degree of unity the parties display in congressional voting, we find that the number of party unity votes fell from the mid-1960s through the 1970s, but recovered beginning with the second Reagan term. The Republican party in Congress has shown impressive homogeneity since then, and the temporary drop in Democratic scores seems to have been due largely to a decline in the party voting of southern Democrats (Maisel 1993, 352-57; see also Rohde 1991). After the 1994 elections, the level of party voting among House and Senate Republicans was nothing short of remarkable, at least for a time (see Beck Ch. 13).

Another way of looking at this question is to examine the power of the party leaders in government. There have been pronounced changes, for example, in the role and powers of the Speaker of the House (Sinclair 1995), reflecting such factors as the personal skills of the officeholders, the effect of the workload of the House on its leaders, and the cohesion of the parties at the time. During this century, some Speakers have been described as "czars," while others could best be termed conciliators. Most recently, in the wake of the first Republican congressional majority in 40 years, the Speaker's power was increased relative to that of the committee chairs (Smith and Lawrence 1997).

Party has been found to have even greater influence on state legislators (Beck, 1997, Ch. 13), though there is great variation among the states. We even see differences between Democratic and Republican judges in state courts in the ways they decide some types of cases, though this seems to resemble the impact of party identification among committed partisans rather than any external party organizational influence (Beck 1997, 347).

In sum, the evidence supporting the idea of party decline is mixed. There has not been a unidirectional decline in party strength, even as it relates to party-in-the-electorate. Rather, there have been peaks and valleys in voter attachment to parties, as Americans struggle to balance their disgust with parties in principle and their need for parties in practice. Organization-ally, the parties have undergone a number of adaptations to their environ-ment in our history, ranging from the development of mass organizations beginning in the late 1820s and 1830s to the great urban machines of the late 1800s, and more recently, from organizations that ran candidates' campaigns to organizations that provide services to free-standing candidates' organizations. As Aldrich suggests, "[scholars and observers] are only beginning to recognize and understand that a new form of party emerged in the 1970s and 1980s to replace the old form destroyed in the 1960s" (Aldrich 1995, 287). And the strength of party in government has varied markedly over time.

This chapter looks at a data source not often used to examine these questions of party strength. If there has been change in the salience of the parties and/or in their roles and activities, then we ought to see the change reflected in press coverage. Prominent newspapers, read by political activists and influential among political decision-makers (see Graber 1993, 18, 109), are very likely to reflect the extent to which, and the ways in which, parties leave their mark on the political landscape at a particular time. Press coverage also offers an advantage in that it makes available a much longer time series than that provided by survey research among either citizens or party leaders.

METHOD

I examined newspaper coverage of domestic political stories in off-year congressional elections, because parties are presumed to be more salient in congressional than in presidential elections. I selected the first off-year election of each decade beginning with 1930, and ending in 1990. News stories, editorials, columns, and letters to the editor were coded in two time periods in each of these years: 10 days around the congressional election (from five days prior to the election through the fourth day afterward), and the first 10 days in May of that year. The May time period normally included coverage of some congressional and gubernatorial primaries, but tended to center on nonelectoral politics to a much greater extent than the November time period.

Two newspapers were chosen for analysis. The *New York Times* was selected because it was one of the premier national newspapers throughout these years, widely read by elected officials and political activists; thus its coverage should be a good indicator of the salience of various political institutions. But because it is published in a city that had long been dominated by a party machine, I also analyzed coverage in the *Los Angeles Times*, a comparable-sized paper in a weak-party area, and one of the nation's primary political sources in the latter half of this time period.[1]

Domestic political news was defined as coverage of elections at any level of government, behavior of the president, Congress, state governors, statewide elected officials and legislatures, mayors and city councils, and

---

[1] I am grateful to David Weaver for his suggestions on this point.

political parties, and the reactions to any of these by interest groups. This definition does not include court decisions or administrative activities such as reports and actions by federal, state, or local agencies and agency heads. Nonpolitical stories about public figures (e.g., the president goes fishing) were excluded as well. "Pure" foreign policy stories, such as war news, treaties, and visits by leaders of other nations, were not coded, though foreign policy stories that mentioned domestic political considerations (for example, farm groups' reactions to a tariff, student protests against the Vietnam War, or the likely impact of foreign policy developments on the political careers of elected leaders) were included. The total number of items is 7,030 (3,471 in the *Los Angeles Times* and 3,559 in the *New York Times*).

I coded all mentions of political parties in these items, other than those used to identify an individual (e.g., former Governor Bayh, a Democrat) or to vary the presentation of a name already mentioned (e.g., "The Republican candidate said that . . . "). These mentions were categorized with regard to the type of party activity or function they represented. Categories included references to candidate selection and nomination; the party's electoral functions (a party's electoral prospects or results, the normal party vote to be expected in a district, group support for parties, straight-ticket or split-ticket or cross-party voting); party campaign or strategic activities; party organizational characteristics or activity; party leadership (including bosses and machines); corruption or scandal; internal party conflict; party policies; party majorities in the legislature or executive; legislative parties and party leaders; references to partisanship or bipartisanship, the need for a two-party system or for a strong opposition party; and references to third parties and party coalitions.

Data are presented as the percentages of articles that mention party, rather than the raw totals, in order to control for the varying amounts of domestic political coverage from one year to the next. For example, domestic political coverage in the *New York Times* dropped sharply from 1930 to 1942, because so much of the "news hole" in the latter year was devoted to coverage of the Second World War. Similarly, domestic political coverage in the *New York Times* peaked in 1970 and dropped markedly in 1982 and again in 1990 (in the *Los Angeles Times* the peak occurred in 1962), presumably because of increasing publishing costs and diminishing revenues.

HYPOTHESES

If the thesis of party decline is generally accurate, and parties have become less and less relevant to U.S. politics, then mentions of parties as a proportion of total domestic political items should decrease beginning with the 1930 data. If it is the case that this trend hit bottom in the 1960s and 1970s and has since recovered, we should see a bimodal pattern. Alternatively, just as Nie, Verba, and Petrocik show that individuals' conceptualizations of politics depend in part on the content of political debate at the time (1979, Ch. 7), so might the salience of parties change in a nonlinear manner, moving between greater and lesser salience, depending on the nature of the issues and the other stimuli from the political world at the time.

We can also test for change over time in the mentions of particular party activities, as suggested by the competing theories. If the party decline model is correct, then we should see decreasing references to the parties' electoral functions and organizational activities at least until the 1962-1970 period, perhaps followed by a resurgence. If the party's role in electoral politics is changing in the manner suggested by Ceaser and Aldrich, then we should see increasing references to parties' use of consultants and provision of polling and other services.

FINDINGS

Wattenberg, looking at a slightly different question (the *relative* salience of parties and candidates from 1952-1988 in election coverage by two newspapers and three news magazines), found that as the total number of campaign-related stories declined during these years, "the number of instances in which parties were mentioned by name in the stories fell precipitously" (1990, 93).

That was not the case in these data (see Figure 1). The patterns are more subtle. In *New York Times* coverage during the years cited by Wattenberg, looking only at the November election period, there is indeed a drop in the percentage of party mentions from 1950 through 1970, though the decrease is only 13 percent—not easily described as "precipitous." But the 1950 level is almost completely restored by 1982, so the overall decline from 1950-1982 is only 3.4 percent. The trend line is better characterized,

267

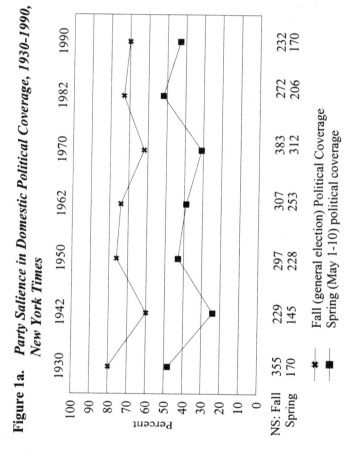

Figure 1a. *Party Salience in Domestic Political Coverage, 1930-1990, New York Times*

| NS: Fall | 355 | 229 | 297 | 307 | 383 | 272 | 232 |
| Spring | 170 | 145 | 228 | 253 | 312 | 206 | 170 |

— ✳ — Fall (general election) Political Coverage
— ■ — Spring (May 1-10) political coverage

Note: Data points are the percentage of all domestic political items (new stories, columns, editorials, and letters to the editor) in particular time period in which political parties were mentioned.

Figure 1b. *Party Salience in Domestic Political Coverage, 1930-1990, Los Angeles Times*

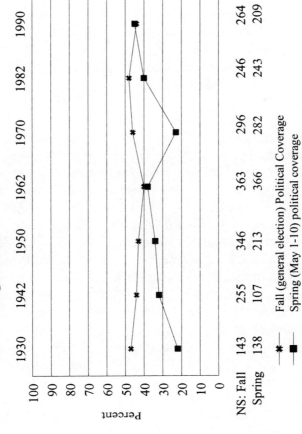

| NS: Fall | 143 | 255 | 346 | 363 | 296 | 246 | 264 |
| Spring | 138 | 107 | 213 | 366 | 282 | 243 | 209 |

✳——— Fall (general election) Political Coverage

■ Spring (May 1-10) political coverage

Note: Data points are the percentage of all domestic political items (new stories, columns, editorials, and letters to the editor) in particular time period in which political parties were mentioned.

then, as virtually constant, except for a sharp drop in party mentions in 1970.

When we expand our focus to the whole time series, again looking at the November election period, the idea of party decline becomes less plausible. The proportion of party mentions takes a big plunge from 81 percent in 1930 to 60 percent in 1942, jumps back up to 73-74 percent in the next two decades, drops again in 1970, and then largely recovers. The pattern in the May *New York Times* data, when there were some primary races but no general congressional election to focus on, closely paralleled that of the November election period. The slope of the overall decline from 1930 to 1950 and 1962 was more gentle, however, and the proportion of party mentions in the "recovery" of 1982 reached the highest levels recorded in the May time series. It would be easy to argue, then, that the trend line in these May data varies little from 1930-1990, with the exception of big drops in party mentions during 1970 and, especially, 1942.

These findings can be interpreted in two ways. If we ignore the data for 1942, the slopes look like those predicted by the decline-and-resurgence school: a drop in party mentions through 1970, followed by a partial recovery in the 1980s and 1990s. But when we consider 1942, which of course we must, then the pattern changes. Now we see a line more consistent with environmental influence, in which something—presumably stimuli from the political environment—in 1942 and 1970 dampened the levels of party mentions that were typical of the other years.

In addition, coverage in the *Los Angeles Times* (see Figure 1b) showed very little support for the party decline thesis. In the general election coverage, mentions of party declined only slightly (from 48 percent to 40 percent), though monotonically, during the 1930-1962 period, and then recovered fully in 1970 and 1982, before dropping again in 1990. The difference between the largest and the smallest proportion of party mentions among these seven time points is just nine percent. In contrast, mentions of party in the May data *increased* steadily from 1930 to 1990, with only one interruption—the big drop in 1970.

Let us briefly explore the meaning of these declines during 1942 and 1970. At the height of the Second World War, coverage in the *New York Times* in 1942 was preoccupied with war news. There was less domestic political coverage generally (374 items, compared with 525 in both 1930 and 1950), but because we are looking at percentages, that does not explain the drop in references to party. Rather, elected officials and other news sources seem to have avoided mentions of partisanship at this time in their references to domestic politics. Thus the *New York Times* on October 29, 1942, carried the text of a speech given by House Speaker Sam Rayburn. The Speaker defended Congress' record on the war. Yet although the speech was given six days before the congressional elections, and focuses on those elections, neither the Speaker nor anyone else quoted in the item made any mention of party ("'Victory' Congress" 1942, 12).

Similarly, in May of 1970, President Nixon ordered U.S. troops to invade Cambodia. Four students were killed by National Guardsmen in a subsequent protest at Kent State University, followed by nationwide student demonstrations against the invasion and the war more generally. The parties as organizations took no immediate stands on these dramatic events, and each party experienced disagreement among its elected officials. At the same time, mentions of political parties in both newspapers' coverage declined (by 10 percent in the *New York Times*, relative to the data for May 1-10, 1962, and by 15 percent in the *Los Angeles Times*). By the November election, however, Nixon had directed a nationalized Republican campaign targeted against student protesters and in favor of a particular vision of "law and order," and the Democratic National Committee had bought television time to respond on that issue. By that time, the proportion of references to parties in domestic political coverage, at least in the California paper, had bounced back up.

Is this a rally-round-the-flag phenomenon, in which journalists' political sources try to show their patriotism by eschewing partisan language in times of trouble? This may be a partial explanation, but it cannot be a complete one. The United States was in a shooting war in 1950 as well, in Korea, but mentions of parties were not comparably depressed during this time. Nor were they in November of 1962, at the height of the Cuban Missile Crisis, nor in November of 1990, at the time of the military buildup that later led to the Gulf War. And although foreign policy news, as a percentage of all front page stories, was most dominant during the 1942 coding periods, the percentage of foreign policy stories in 1970 was substantially less than in November of 1962 (the Cuban Missile Crisis), May of 1982 (the Falklands conflict), and the Cold War news of the November, 1950, election period (see Table 1).

Much of the remaining front page news in 1970, however, had to do with domestic antiwar protest and the reactions to it by the Nixon administration, college officials, and others. These stories were clearly domestic in

Table 1. *Foreign Policy Stories as a Percentage of Front Page News Items, 1930-1990*

	1930	1942	1950	1962	1970	1982	1990
May Coding Period	18%	63*	36	40	35*	49	42
n =	126	115	121	131	116	73	74
November Coding Period	21	55*	41*	53	32*	33	28
n =	122	116	115	128	106	75	72

Cell entries are the percentage of front page stories devoted primarily to foreign policy news in a given coding period.

*Front page stories during these coding periods indicated U.S. involvement in a shooting war.

but they were intimately connected with American involvement in a shooting war in Vietnam. Other studies have shown (see Hershey 1992) that political events normally have more than one possible interpretation, and that explanations are constructed for these events in a dynamic interaction among political activists and journalists. It is at least plausible, then, that the events of the Second World War in 1942 and the Cambodian invasion and subsequent domestic protests, at least in the spring of 1970, were interpreted by activists and journalists as being less appropriate for partisan definition than were other major international conflicts such as the Cold War in 1950 and the missile crisis of 1962.

The most important point, however, is that the trend lines in Figures 1a and 1b look like a portrait of party decline only if we limit our focus to the *New York Times* data during the years 1950, 1962, and 1970. When we take a broader perspective, the data do not fit the predictions of either of the party decline schools. There is no monotonic decline in the figure, and where we see a bimodal pattern, it is either in the wrong direction, as in the May *Los Angeles Times* data, or the second peak starts too soon, as in the general election items in that newspaper.

References to particular types of party activities also failed to support the party decline theories. In a one-fifth sample of the *New York Times* data, we find that references to the parties' electoral activities, always more frequent in the fall coding period than in the May data, did not decline over time. In fact, references to such activities as the parties' electoral prospects or results occurred in 35 percent of all items that mention parties in the fall of 1930, and only eight percent in the fall of 1942, but in as much as 49 percent and 44 percent of all items that mention parties in the fall of 1982 and 1990 (data not shown).

References to party organizations and organizational activities (rallies, luncheons, meetings) did decline from their earlier high levels beginning in May of 1962. But as Ceaser and Aldrich would expect, references to party strategy and consultants (pollsters, media advisers, and others), which scarcely existed before the 1950 general election period, jumped sharply (occurring in 30-40 percent of all items that refer to party) in the 1982 and 1990 coding periods.

Consistent with his argument that the parties have changed substantially since the 1960s, Aldrich (1995, 170-74) demonstrates that survey respondents see greater party differences on issues in the 1980s and 1990s than they did in the 1960s and 1970s. After the Voting Rights Act, the composition of southern Democrats changed. There was a big increase in black voters in the southern Democratic ranks. Other southern Democrats found the newly viable Republican party a more congenial outlet for their ambitions, and switched parties. The result was that southern Democrats became more liberal, and the ideological gulf widened between the Republicans and Democrats nationally.

In the current data set we can see support for this increased ideological salience. In three of the four coding periods in 1982 and 1990, at least 40 percent of all the items that referred to parties made mention of public policies in relation to the parties. That is considerably higher than the norm in earlier years (data not shown). Yet the percentage of items referring to intraparty conflict was fairly consistent throughout the coding period, most often mentioning possible coalitions of Republicans and Democrats in opposition to the president or the leadership of the majority party in Congress. So although it does appear that the two parties were perceived in more issue-oriented terms in the 1980s and 1990s, journalists and their sources continued to look for, and to find, evidence that these reshaped parties have not evolved into cohesive, unified organizations.[2]

CONCLUSION

These data suggest a different picture from that painted by either school of "party decline" analysts. There was no linear decline in party salience in the domestic political coverage of either the *New York Times* or the *Los Angeles Times* during the period 1930-1990. In fact, in the *Los Angeles Times's* May coverage, the parties became increasingly salient during this time. And in the *New York Times* coverage, we see relatively little variation (12 percent) in mentions of the parties throughout the period, with the exception of two marked drops in 1942 and 1970. In both these years, there were dramatic environmental events—the Second World War and the Nixon invasion of Cambodia—that may have been more resistant to partisan definition than events at other times. Thus the data are more consistent with the idea that the salience of party in political coverage tends to vary with changes in the stimuli provided by the political environment at the time.

If parties were becoming less prominent on the political landscape, the consequences might well be powerful. In the absence of a "standing decision" for a party, citizens could become more volatile and more easily swayed in their voting decisions (Wattenberg 1990, 130-31). Extremist groups could open up irreconcilable divisions in the public, and the balance between articulating and aggregating interests in American politics could become seriously unbalanced in favor of the former (Wattenberg 1990, 128-29). But the floodgates are not yet open. In *New York Times* general election coverage in 1982 and 1990, approximately seven in 10 stories made at least one party-related reference. Election results were generally presented in party-related terms: "a Democratic tide," "Republican gains," "the failure of the Republicans to win any . . . ," "voters substantially strengthened the Democrats' control over. . . ."

The data suggest that the parties reported in 1982 and 1990 are different kinds of organizations than were the parties reported in the 1930s and

---

[2]On the tendency for journalists to focus on conflict in political reporting, see Graber (1993, 120).

1940s; they concentrate on different activities and are seen in different terms. But with respect to their salience in the coverage of domestic politics, the American parties remain alive and well.

REFERENCES

Aldrich, John H. 1995. *Why Parties? The Origin and Transformation of Party Politics in America.* Chicago: University of Chicago Press.

Beck, Paul Allen. 1997. *Party Politics in America*, 8th ed. New York: Longman.

Carmines, Edward G., and James A. Stimson. 1989. *Issue Evolution.* Princeton: Princeton University Press.

Ceaser, James W. 1990. "Political Parties—Declining, Stabilizing, or Resurging?" In *The New American Political System*, 2d version, ed. Anthony King. Washington, D.C.: American Enterprise Institute, 87-137.

Dennis, Jack. 1966. "Support for the Party System by the Mass Public." *American Political Science Review* 60 (September): 600-15.

Eldersveld, Samuel J. 1964. *Political Parties: A Behavioral Analysis.* Chicago: Rand McNally.

Epstein, Leon D. 1986. *Political Parties in the American Mold.* Madison: University of Wisconsin Press.

Gibson, James L., Cornelius P. Cotter, John F. Bibby, and Robert J. Huckshorn. 1983. "Assessing Party Organizational Strength." *American Journal of Political Science* 27 (May): 193-222.

_____. 1985. "Whither the Local Parties? A Cross-Sectional and Longitudinal Analysis of the Strength of Party Organizations." *American Journal of Political Science* 29 (February): 139-60.

Graber, Doris A. 1993. *Mass Media and American Politics*, 4th ed. Washington, D.C.: CQ Press.

Herrnson, Paul S. 1995. *Congressional Elections.* Washington, D.C.: CQ Press.

Hershey, Marjorie R. 1992. "The Constructed Explanation: Interpreting Election Results in the 1984 Presidential Race." *Journal of Politics* 54 (November): 943-76.

Hofstadter, Richard. 1969. *The Idea of a Party System.* Berkeley: University of California Press.

Maisel, L. Sandy. 1993. *Parties and Elections in America*, 2d ed. New York: McGraw-Hill.

Nie, Norman H., Sidney Verba, and John R. Petrocik. 1979. *The Changing American Voter*, enlarged ed. Cambridge, Mass.: Harvard University Press, 1979.

Ranney, Austin. 1951. "The Reception of Political Parties into American Political Science." *Southwestern Social Science Quarterly* 32 (December): 183-91.

_____. 1962. *The Doctrine of Responsible Party Government.* Urbana: University of Illinois Press.

_____. 1975. *Curing the Mischiefs of Faction.* Berkeley: University of California Press.

Rohde, David W. 1991. *Parties and Leaders in the Post-Reform House.* Chicago: University of Chicago Press.

Sinclair, Barbara. 1995. *Legislators, Leaders and Lawmaking.* Baltimore: Johns Hopkins University Press.

Smith, Steven S., and Eric D. Lawrence. 1997. "Party Control of Committees in the Republican Congress." In *Congress Reconsidered*, 6th ed., ed. Lawrence C. Dodd and Bruce I. Oppenheimer. Washington, D.C.: CQ Press, 163-92.

Sorauf, Frank J. 1964. *Political Parties in the American System.* Boston: Little, Brown.

"'Victory' Congress Urged by Rayburn." 1942. *New York Times* (October 29), 12.

Wattenberg, Martin P. 1990. *The Decline of American Political Parties 1952-1988.* Cambridge, Mass.: Harvard University Press.

APPENDIX: ELECTION AND CODING DATES

Year	Election Date	Coding Period
1930	November 4	October 30-November 8
1942	November 3	October 29-November 7
1950	November 7	November 2-11
1962	November 6	November 1-10
1970	November 3	October 29-November 7
1982	November 2	October 28-November 6
1990	November 6	November 1-10

CHAPTER 11

The Future of the Political Party

Anthony King
University of Essex

Over the past two decades students of political parties have come increasingly to resemble delegates to an undertakers' convention. The titles of recent books and articles speak for themselves: "Political Parties in Decline," "The Party's Over," "A Crisis of Party," "Party Politics in Contemporary Europe: A Challenge to Party," "Are British Political Parties in Decline?" "The Decline of American Political Parties," and (for those with a taste for the melodramatic) "Political Parties and Democracy: A Mutual Murder?" To be sure, not all political scientists believe that parties are in decline, and the authors of several of the articles cited above answer the questions posed in their titles in the negative. Nevertheless, the prevailing view does appear to be that the political party as an institution is under threat, and Reiter (1989, 325) points to "a sizeable literature that accepts as a given that 'party decline' is a useful concept analytically and that it characterizes trends in most western industrialized nations."

Austin Ranney, in a celebrated essay on the American parties published in the 1970s, toyed with the idea that, if a national presidential primary were introduced, it might wipe out altogether the presidential party organizations. "What if it did?" he asked in his peroration (1978, 247):

The Republic would not collapse, at least not right away. The party labels would persist for a while and serve as cues for the dwindling number of voters for whom they were still meaningful. The candidate organizations, the women's caucuses, the black caucuses, the right-to-life leagues, and the like would become the only real players in the game. The mass communications media would become the sole agencies for sorting out the finalists from the original entrants and for defining the voters' choices. And the societal functions of interest-aggregation, consensus-building and civil war-prevention would presumably be left to the schools, the churches, and perhaps Common Cause and Nader's Raiders.

A national presidential primary has not been introduced, and the presidential party organizations have not been entirely wiped out; but Ranney's depiction of the future of American presidential politics, read two decades later, sounds remarkably prescient.

This essay seeks to assess the evidence for the decline of political parties in the western world over the past several decades and also to hazard some guesses about what the political parties of the future might be like. But the first question that needs to be asked concerns the nature of the alleged threats to the privileged status of political parties in western democracies. What social and political forces are supposed to be leading to parties' decline or at least to their "de-institutionalization" and "marginalization" (Panebianco 1988, 267, 268)?

FORCES THREATENING PARTIES

There seems to be general agreement among scholars that there are no fewer than five such forces at work. To put it another way, the political party as an institution is widely thought to be under attack from no fewer than five sides. The image is one of white settlers in the American West in the nineteenth century surrounded by tribes of Indians on the warpath.

The first such threat emanates from the privatization of society (see, among others, Epstein 1967, 233). Once upon a time, so the story goes, human beings obtained many of their most important satisfactions and pleasures from interacting (as the Americans say) with their fellow citizens. They went to the pub, they sang in the church choir, they chatted to their neighbors in the street, they gossiped with the butcher and baker—and so on. They still do, of course, but it is a matter of common observation (as well as sociologically documented fact) that at the end of the twentieth century more people derive more of their satisfactions from essentially private pursuits. They engage in do-it-yourself hobbies in the home (note the significance of "your self"), they tend their gardens, they watch television, they go for a drive; even going to the movies has largely been replaced by watching video cassettes at home with other members of the family. It is these trends that have caused Robert D. Putnam and others to worry about a possible decline in "social capital" throughout the western world. Putnam's most famous essay (1995) is called, poignantly, "Bowling Alone."

The consequences for political parties of this high degree of privatization of social life are obvious. In the first place, to the extent that privatization leads to a decline in civic engagement, it also leads to a decline in engagement in the political process. People no longer feel they have a degree of personal responsibility for the society in which they live and no longer feel, therefore, that they have some obligation to participate in politics. Privatized societies tend to be apolitical societies. In the second place, and much more directly, privatization and the spread of popular entertainments and other leisure activities mean that there are far more counterattractions to politics than there were in the past. Why join a party, or knock on doors on a rainy night, or drink in the local working men's club when one can stay at home and paint the deck, or weed the garden, or, better still, take the children to Disneyland?

The second threat to political parties as we have known them arises from what has been called (Finer 1984, 3) the secularization of politics, running in parallel with the secularization of society generally and the decline of religion. There was a time, lasting at least until the 1960s, when many of the political struggles in democratic countries were fought with all the fervor of religious struggles. The word "struggle" itself was apt, with democrats and fascists, Communists and Catholics, militant trade unionists and capitalist employers, not merely competing with each other in democratic elections but seeking, in effect, to destroy one another, to gain ultimate and final supremacy. Even in a relatively nonideological and peaceable country like Great Britain, a left-wing member of the postwar Labour government could describe his Conservative opponents as "lower than vermin" (Butler and Butler 1994, 270).

By contrast, the political atmosphere in most democracies at the end of the twentieth century is far less fraught. The ferocity of the political struggle has abated. The old antagonisms are muted. Questions of ideology have given way to practical policy questions. Politics in the late 1990s is far more about means than about ends. When the electoral contests in most democracies are between candidates such as Clinton and Dole, Blair and Major, and Schroder and Kohl, who can get terribly worked up? The consequences for the parties are, once again, obvious. Fewer voters identify with them, in the sense of feeling passionately about them. More and more voters come to resemble consumers in the commercial market place as they "shop around" among parties and leaders. The active memberships of the parties fall. Not enough is at stake.

The third of the threats to the position of the parties comes from the mass media, especially, but not only, television. Not only do the mass media contribute largely to the privatization of society; they also make it possible for political elites to communicate with voters and citizens without the intermediation of party workers. Just as radio and television advertising have largely killed off the door-to-door salesman, so they have largely killed off the old-fashioned party worker. Canvassers still canvass, envelope-stuffers still stuff envelopes, but they do so in smaller numbers than in the past. Why should political elites bother to retail their products when they can sell them—or attempt to sell them—wholesale? As scholars have often pointed out (see, for example, Ware 1996, 296-97), the power of voluntary labor in democratic politics has largely been eclipsed by the power of money: money for television commercials, money for direct-mail shots, money for opinion polling, money for focus groups, money for billboards and poster sites. As a consequence, parties in the form of highly structured organizations with large individual memberships are much less important than they were. Party elites need members less than they did. They need donors more. Actual and potential party members feel, rightly, that their role has been diminished.

The fourth alleged threat to parties comes from the rise of single-issue groups, whether groups promoting "interests" in the old-fashioned sense of the term or groups promoting causes and crusades. Whether or not civic engagement has declined throughout the western world (views on that subject differ), what is clear is that much less of it than in the past is channeled through political parties. People in Great Britain who used to join the Conservative or Labour parties now join Friends of the Earth, Greenpeace, the Royal Society for the Protection of Birds, the Society for the Protection of the Unborn Child, the Countryside Alliance or whatever. In many countries, the membership of such organizations now far outstrips the membership of political parties. Pizzorno, in a paper devoted to developing this point, asserts flatly (1981, 272): "Interest groups asking for specific policies are [now] the main actors on the political scene whereas the political parties, in their effort to represent multiple interests in order to conquer the marginal voter, as well as to have the support of as many interest groups as possible, tend to lose their programmatic and organizational identity."

Finally, it is said that the historic position of the political party in western democracies is threatened by the rise of the think tanks, organizations largely or wholly independent of the parties that conduct political and policy research, generate policy ideas and sometimes propagate not merely specific policy ideas but entire ideologies. Think tanks of this kind proliferate most notably, but not only, in Washington, D.C., and London. In the past, many of the larger political parties, especially in Europe, were important as organized policy generators. They developed ideas "in house," so to speak, and many of the ideas they developed found their way into party manifestos and, ultimately, into public policy. One thinks in this connection of the British Labour party or the Swedish Social Democratic party. Today, however, there are few parties anywhere in the western world that regard in-house policymaking as one of their central functions. Party and policy have, in that sense and to that extent, become disconnected.

So much for a brief catalog of the threats to parties. What is one to make of them? The first thing to be said about them is that they do exist. Most industrial and postindustrial societies are privatized and politically secularized. The mass media do play a large role in many people's lives. It is true that single-interest groups abound. So, at least in some countries, do politically oriented think tanks. Moreover, if these phenomena are indeed threats to parties, they are undoubtedly greater threats than in the past. Privatization and secularization, at least on their present scale, are relatively new phenomena, and the mass media play a far larger role in most people's lives than they did even a generation ago (say, in the 1950s). Single-interest groups, to be sure, are nothing new (consider the pressure groups that lobbied for Prohibition in the United States in the 1920s), and neither are think tanks (the British Fabian Society was founded in 1884); but both kinds of organization have undoubtedly proliferated in recent years.

However, all that said, and before we proceed, two points should be noticed. The first is that there is a slight tendency in some of the decline-of-parties literature to infer effects from causes: in this case to assume that, because a powerful potential threat to the position of political parties exists, the parties must actually be succumbing to that threat (rather as though one were to infer that, because a new virus existed and posed a serious threat to public health, it was bound sooner or later to cause a serious epidemic). The logic is faulty. The second point to notice briefly here—we shall return to it—is that the focus in the discussion above is almost entirely on the size and activism of the membership of political parties. Privatization causes the membership of parties to decline; secularization causes the membership and the members' emotional commitment their party to decline; the mass media, and the fact that the media enable party leaders to communicate directly with voters, make the members of parties essentially redundant; and so on. This focus is undoubtedly narrow. It may well—we shall see later—be too narrow.

To return to the main issue: Have political parties in the western world in fact declined? In order to answer that question, one obviously needs to address two additional questions: Declined compared with when? And declined with respect to what? The late twentieth century and the early twenty-first century are to be compared with when precisely? In what respects, are parties supposed to have declined? The answers to these questions suggest that the decline of parties is a more complicated matter than is sometimes supposed.

PARTY DECLINE: WHEN?

When people say that parties are in decline or may possibly be in decline, they presumably have in mind—they must have in mind—some time in the past, some century, some decade, some era, when the parties were stronger than they are now and loomed larger in the democratic political process. But, strikingly, almost none of the contributors to the party-decline literature, especially the comparative literature, gives a clear indication of when he or she thinks that past century, or decade, or era was. More precisely, almost no one looks at the parties as they are now and compares them, carefully and systematically, with the way they were in some previous and clearly specified historical epoch. In other words, time t_2—the present—is identified, but time t_1 (except in some of the specialist papers on the decline of party membership) is left tantalizingly vague.

Moreover, as soon as one begins to think in these terms, one begins to have grave doubts about the decline-of-parties thesis. For instance: Begin in 1998 and take some slices through time at, say, 20-year intervals over the past century. Were Great Britain's political parties stronger and more robust in 1898 than they are today? Were the French parties stronger in 1918 than they have since become? Were the parties of any democratic country stronger in 1938 than the parties of most democratic countries today? Spool forward to 1958: Were Japan's political parties stronger 40 years ago than they are now? The answers to all these questions are clearly negative. Merely to ask the questions in that form casts serious doubt on whether the implicitly hypothesized "golden age" of democratic parties ever existed. Individual parties have declined, and in some countries whole party systems have been recast; but the idea that parties as institutions have—in some generalized sense and over a wide range of countries—declined seems hard to sustain.

The same issue can be approached from another angle. Anyone reading the party-decline literature is bound to be struck by the fact that a large proportion of the scholars who have contributed to that literature clearly have in mind, when they talk about party decline, a sort of "template," a kind of ideal-type political party that existed in the past and with which the less-than-ideal political party of the present is being compared. But that template is never the French Radical party in the years before the First World War; it is never the various bourgeois parties in Germany under the Weimar Republic; it is never the highly fractured parties that dominated Italian politics both before the rise of Mussolini and after 1945. Parties like these, which dominated much of European politics during most of the twentieth century, simply slide, unnoticed, out of view.

Instead, the template parties, the ideal-type political parties, with which the 1990s parties are compared, mostly to their disadvantage, are chosen from the past on a remarkably selective basis, albeit probably uncon-sciously. The parties chosen, far more often than not, are the German Social Democratic party (SPD) and the Conservative and Labour parties in Great Britain in the 1940s and 1950s. The French and Italian Communist parties are chosen somewhat less often, but still fairly frequently. The Israeli Labour party as it existed during the first 30 years or so of the Israeli state was chosen, uniquely and, in his case, wholly consciously, by Finer (1984).

These parties, however, are far from being a random selection of the political parties that have been important in the twentieth century. On the contrary, along with the social democratic parties of Scandinavia, Australia, and New Zealand, the great majority of them are left-wing, and, more to the point, they are, without exception, exemplars of what Duverger (1954, 63-71) famously called "mass" parties—that is, parties with highly articulated formal structures, networks of local branches and, above all, mass memberships (sometimes, in the larger countries, running into several millions). But, to repeat, parties of this type have never been the dominant type in democracies, and it is simply a fallacy to compare the condition of all political parties in the late twentieth century with the condition of some political parties earlier in the century and to conclude that, because all parties now appear to be weaker than some parties then, the political party as an institution is in decline. Duverger thought the mass party was the most "modern" type of party; he also gave the appearance of believing that in time it would become the most common type. Given that he was wrong on both counts, it is ironic that so many scholars, even if unconsciously, accord the mass party such an exalted status in their analyses.

At the very least, these kinds of considerations, based on comparisons between past and present, should lead one to view the decline-of-parties thesis a trifle quizzically. Perhaps there is not quite as much in it as at first would appear. The past is, after all, another country. Equally important, however, is the second of the two questions posed above: Declined with respect to what? In what specific ways have parties declined?

PARTY DECLINE: WITH RESPECT TO WHAT?

And, once this issue is raised, it becomes immediately clear that the strength or effectiveness of political parties can be assessed according to a wide variety of different criteria. In another context, it would be necessary to make judgments about which criteria are especially important and to consider why some of them might be thought to be more important than others; but for the purposes of this essay a brief summary and discussion should be sufficient. No fewer than 10 criteria for rating the strength of parties suggest themselves. They can be ticked off rapidly.

1. Size of membership ("the body count"). How many members do specific parties have, or do all the parties in a specific country have, or all the parties in a particular part of the world, or indeed in all of the world's democracies? Such membership totals can be expressed either in absolute numbers or, usually more appropriately, as proportions of the total electorate.

2. Activism of the membership. It is not much use to a party if its members, even it has large numbers of them, simply remain names on lists. Party leaders want their members to contribute money. They also want them to contribute time, effort and shoe leather (or, nowadays, a winning way on the phone). It could also be argued that party activism can be taken as an indicator of broader civic engagement.

3. Subculture integration. This criterion has to do with the extent to which parties do or do not constitute, or form part of, their own distinctive subcultures. Do parties have their own bars, their own brass bands, their own football clubs, and their own festivals (like the former Italian Communist party's Feste del'Unita)? In other words, are they—quite apart from their role in fighting democratic elections—forces of social integration and mobilization?

4. Structuring of the vote. With regard to elections, one wants to know how far in a country political parties, rather than factions, interest groups or individual candidates, "structure the vote"—that is, provide the voters with cues to which the voters in turn respond. This is the issue Ranney was referring to in his essay quoted above. (Vote-structuring by parties can take place in American primary elections only if a given American state has reasonably strong party organizations that can indicate to the voters of the state which of the candidates—all usually of the same party—they should support.)

5. Stable mass followings. Another test of party strength is closely related to the vote-structuring test but is considerably more stringent. This is the test of whether parties not only structure the vote, in the limited sense of providing partisan cues, but have, in addition, stable mass followings—that is, large numbers of voters who support their party more or less automatically, through thick and thin ("We've always been Democrats in this family"). Much the same test can be expressed in another way: How widespread, and how strong, are feelings of party identification?

6. Recruitment of political personnel. According to this criterion, the political parties of a country are strong if all or almost all the would-be politicians and aspiring officeholders in that country believe they must build, and do build, their political careers largely within the confines of the party of their choice. The presence in a political system of prominent nonparty or antiparty figures such as Charles de Gaulle and Ross Perot is an indicator of at least some element of party weakness.

7. Control of nominations. A party is strong if it controls its own nominations—that is, controls who will run as its standard-bearers in elections. By the same token, a party is weak if it does not control its nominations. As Ranney points out (1978, 236), a party that no longer controls the nomination of its candidates ceases to act as a "judge"—adjudicating among the claims of competing would-be nominees—and becomes merely a "prize." The candidate who wears the

party label but who has not been chosen by the party is not, in any meaningful sense, the party's candidate.

8. Extent of party government. Parties seek not merely to fight elections but to win them and, as a consequence, to govern. If the government of a country is normally composed of people who have been chosen by their party and elected, in some meaningful sense, as the representatives of their party, then, according to this criterion, the political parties of that country are strong. If, however, those who control a country's government have not been chosen by their party and are not really party representatives, then, on this criterion, the country's parties are weak. For example, in the early years of the Fifth French Republic a sign of the parties' weakness was that the president himself, de Gaulle, did not owe his position to party and many of his ministers were chosen on a deliberately nonparty basis. A sure sign of the French parties' revival since de Gaulle retired is that, for instance, the new government elected in 1997 was a Socialist government under a Socialist prime minister, Lionel Jospin, with mainly Socialists serving under him.

9. Partisan penetration of government. The criterion just cited concerns whether the personnel of government are chosen on a party or a nonparty basis. This further criterion concerns the extent to which those who are chosen on a party basis penetrate the various organs of government. Are party personnel concentrated in the upper echelons of the government, almost entirely among ministers and cabinet officers, or are they more widely spread throughout the administration? The British tradition has limited party personnel to a thin layer of positions at the top of the executive branch; the German tradition, on the contrary, has assumed that heads of department, who are chosen on a partisan basis, should be supported in their departments by professional administrators who are also chosen on partisan grounds.

10. Content of public policy. Finally, anyone seeking to gauge the strength of parties needs to consider the effect of party on the manifest content of public policy. If a party or parties are elected to power, does the content of government policy subsequently reflect their views and priorities? Putting it another way, does it make a significant difference, in policy terms, which party or group of parties is in office? Many would regard this last question as the bottom-line question with regard to party government, the ultimate "So what?" question.

All of these criteria are, of course, much more complicated—both conceptually and in terms of the demands they make on measurement techniques—than has been indicated here. Party activism, for instance, may or may not involve participation in the discussion and creation of party policy. Subculture integration at the partisan level may lead to social disintegration at the national level. Even the strongest party governments may be constrained in their choice of public policies by international economic forces. And so on. All this is conceded. Nevertheless, few would probably deny that the above criteria are appropriate ones—and, further, constitute most of the appropriate ones—for gauging party strength.

But what needs to be noted here, and is very important, is that none of the party-decline literature, voluminous though it is, measures party decline by more than a very small subset of the above criteria. The main focus has tended to be on membership and activism, but political parties that had small and inactive memberships could nevertheless still be the main instruments of political recruitment in a country, could still control the country's government, and could still have a determinative effect on the content of the country's policy. To equate membership and activism with party strength is to fall into the Duverger trap of supposing (or seeming to suppose, since Duverger was often imprecise) that somehow the only "real" parties were mass-membership parties.

Against this background, if one takes into account all of these criteria, and if one looks at a broad range of democratic countries, what sort of overall picture emerges? Are political parties in a state of secular decline or not? And, if they are, with respect to what?

With respect to three of our criteria, parties would appear indubitably to be in decline. Although hard data for most countries are lacking, party activism, and political activism generally, appear to have fallen away almost everywhere. Party newspapers are less often sold on streetcorners. The number of people prepared to canvass on the doorstep during election campaigns is a fraction of what it once was. The number of people prepared to turn up to routine party meetings has, in some countries, shrunk almost to the vanishing point. Moreover, there seems no reason to believe that this trend will be reversed. Political interest is at too low a level in most countries; the counterattractions to party politics are too numerous. Seyd and Whiteley in their studies of the two main British parties in the 1990s (Seyd and Whiteley 1992; Whiteley, Seyd, and Richardson 1994) use a variety of indicators to show that the level of activism in both parties has fallen in recent decades. Only eight percent of rank-and-file Conservative party members, for example, claimed they were now more active than they had been five years before; three times that number, 25 percent, admitted they were less active (Whiteley, Seyd, and Richardson 1994, 68).

The same goes for the parties as creators and carriers of distinctive subcultures. People choose their political party; they choose how and with whom they wish to spend their lives—and the two choices are no longer, if ever they were, the same choice. Again, hard data are lacking, but no one seems to doubt that marriages across party lines are far more frequent than they used to be in some countries, that the incidence of party choirs, party sewing circles and party chess clubs (let alone party militias) has fallen sharply and that parties as instruments of mass political mobilization are everywhere in decline. Even the Netherlands, once famous for its four "pillars" (zuilen), each of them linking one or more political parties with particular social groupings and religious denominations, has seen the pillars crumble rapidly since the 1960s (Andeweg and Irwin 1993).

The third instance of indubitable decline concerns the parties as organizations with large and stable followings in the electorate. In this case, hard data are available, and they show that in almost every democratic country an increase in the willingness to switch from one party to another has taken place in recent years and, even more markedly, a decline in both the incidence of party identification and its strength. Parties once resembled churches at which the faithful regularly worshipped. Now they resemble supermarkets where the voters, individual "consumers," may, or may not, choose to shop. In Dalton's words (1996, 338), "Contemporary electoral politics is now characterized by a greater fluidity in the vote, greater volatility in electoral outcomes, and even a growing turnover in the number and type of parties being represented. The gathering winds of electoral change that first appeared in the 1980s have . . . grown in force."

But, in connection with the other seven criteria listed above, the evidence of party decline is at best patchy, at worst nonexistent. Parties in almost all countries are still the main agencies structuring the vote; only in the United States do large numbers of voters vote on the basis of their judgments of individual candidates. Parties in almost all countries likewise still have a virtual monopoly on the recruitment of political personnel; go-it-alone political careers, like those of Ross Perot, Silvio Berlusconi, and Sir James Goldsmith, are still relatively rare (and none of the three mentioned made more than a temporary impact). Except in the United States, the control of nominations everywhere also remains firmly in the political parties' hands (though, in the U.S., control, at least at the presidential and congressional levels, has of course been almost entirely surrendered). As regards the formation of governments, it is fair to say that the political parties remain overwhelmingly dominant. Except, yet again, in the United States, government in the great majority of democracies is indubitably party government. Heads of government and their ministers are overwhelmingly party figures, and the basic building blocks of governments almost everywhere continue to be parties and coalitions of parties.

That leaves us with three of our 10 criteria still to consider, and in connection with each of these there may be some grounds for dispute or at least for greater uncertainty.

One of the three, rather surprisingly, is party membership. It is widely believed that one sign of party decline in the western world is the decline that has taken place in the mass membership of parties. Yet, as Katz and Mair (1992; 1995; Mair 1994) have shown, the picture at least in Europe, is actually rather mixed. To be sure, political parties in some countries, notably Denmark, the Netherlands, and the United Kingdom, have registered sharp declines in membership—both in absolute numbers and relative to the size of their national electorates—since the 1960s; but others, notably Belgium and Germany, have seen both absolute and proportional increases, and still others, including several of the Scandinavian countries, have seen absolute increases despite some declines relative to the size of their electorates. The overall picture—and not just in Europe—is one of declining party membership, but in only a few countries have the declines been as precipitous as is often supposed.

It is harder to say anything definite about partisan penetration of governments because this aspect of the role of parties in government has never been studied systematically. Nevertheless, almost all of the available evidence (Ware 1996, 359-65) points in the same direction, suggesting that parties have certainly not reduced the scale of their penetration of democratic governments and have, if anything, marginally increased it. Party penetration is, and remains, at high levels in Austria, Belgium, Italy, and the Netherlands and at somewhat lower levels in France and Germany. It is, and remains, at still lower levels in Great Britain and the other "Westminster model" countries. In no country is the existing level, whatever it is, being significantly reduced. In at least one, Great Britain under Tony Blair's post-1997 Labour government, it is being significantly increased

(Chittenden and Austin 1997). Katz and Mair (1995) even speak of the rise of the "cartel party," with the political parties in some European countries effectively colonizing the state and exploiting the state's resources for their own purposes.

The extent of partisan influence on public policy poses the most difficult analytic problems—and also the most difficult problems of evidence—of all. Those who believe that the party or parties in power can have a major impact on public policy point to the radical changes of direction brought about by the Thatcher government in Great Britain between 1979 and 1990 and to the fact that, even in an era of divided government, patterns of federal expenditure in the United States resemble the policy preferences of the president's party more closely than they do those of the opposition (Budge and Hofferbert 1990). Those of a more skeptical disposition point to the failure of the post-1981 Socialist government's economic policies in France and to the substantial continui-ties exhibited by most countries' patterns of public policy irrespective of changes of government and of which party is in power. For the moment, the debate has resulted in something of a stand-off, the most accurate summary probably being that almost all parties in power affect some policy at the margins and that some parties sometimes can effect sweeping changes in the overall direction of policy.

Even that, however, does not address the question of whether, over the past few decades, the parties' capacity to influence policy has remained more or less the same or has declined. Finer (1984, 6) was in no doubt. He referred to "departifying of public policy."

This is so obvious (Finer believed) as to require little elaboration. It is clear that even the most ideologically committed of governments today—and how many are very ideologically committed?—are the prisoners of forces beyond their control. Some of these forces represent external factors: all governments are constrained by the world economy; most of them have entered into associations with other states that curtail their economic independence or their foreign policies. But they are also prisoners of their folie de grandeur, as they preside over vast bureaucratic systems. The day has long since gone when a minister or a president could exert direct control and acquire first-hand information. This is no longer possible and never will be as long as governments operate on such a massive scale. There is clearly much in what Finer says, though it might be added that, to the extent that governments have lost control to market forces and international organizations, the loss represents more a decline in the autonomy of the sovereign state than a decline in the influence of parties as such.

Where does all this leave us? It seems clear that parties have indeed lost a good deal of their capacity to enthuse and mobilize mass electorates. The amount of that sort of capacity that they ever had has probably been exaggerated; but, however much they may once have had, they have undoubtedly lost a good deal of it. Party memberships are down in more places than not. Party activism is in decline. The parties no longer act as forces of social integration. Many fewer of them than in the past have large and stable "followerships." The day of the Duverger-type mass party is done. That said, it is not clear that any of this is the parties' fault. In an age of social privatization and political secularization, there is probably not a great deal that they could have done.

But when it comes to the role of political parties *vis-à-vis* government and the state, the picture is different. Parties have not lost any of their control over political recruitment or nominations for public office. Government in most democracies remains quintessentially party government, and parties are, if anything, advancing further into, rather than retreating from, the administration of the state, at least in some, mostly European, countries. Only in Italy can one speak of full-blown partitocrazia, but parties remain major players in most jurisdictions outside the United States. The only field in which their role remains uncertain—or at least insufficiently assessed—is that of public policy.

So parties rule, OK? Well, almost—but not quite. Readers will long since have noticed that the American parties have appeared in this essay only sporadically and in an unsystematic way. The reason is simple. As many scholars have pointed out (notably Epstein 1986), the American parties remain, as they always have been, *sui generis*. All that can usefully be said in a comparative context is that American parties as organizations, unlike their European and Westminster-model opposite numbers, have undoubtedly declined since the 1960s (even if there has been something of an upswing in recent years). Their capacity to structure the vote is also a pale shadow of what it once was, and, as we remarked earlier, the parties in the U.S. have largely surrendered their control over presidential and congressional nominations. Against that, the spread of two-party competition to the South means that the two main American parties are now more ideologically coherent than for many generations past and can therefore transmit to the voters party signals containing much less "noise" than during the 1930s or in the postwar period. Whether American voters are actually grateful for this benefit seems doubtful.

Political parties, then, have a future, even in the United States. But what kinds of parties will they be?

THE PARTIES OF THE FUTURE

Duverger in his 1950s volume defined and described what he called the mass party, the party of the classic German SPD or British Labour party type; but he also defined and described a different kind of party, which he called the "cadre" party (1954, 64). The cadre party had grown up in the middle and late nineteenth century, before the coming of universal suffrage. Whereas the mass party was concerned with quantity—numbers of members—the cadre party was concerned with quality. It was led by a small number of national-level politicians who had banded together to promote themselves or their views; indeed, for all practical purposes, this small group of politicians was the party. These "notabilities" or "influential persons," as Duverger called them, sought to recruit others like themselves to their party. They hired professional agents to wage political warfare at the local level and to conduct campaigns. They raised money, not from the mass membership, because they did not have one, but from a few wealthy individuals (bankers, industrialists, landowners, or whoever). As Duverger pointed out, these cadre parties were forced to adapt their organization in the light of twentieth-century circumstances—for example, they did begin to recruit members—but they never became parties of mobilization, and their main aim remained the election to office of the leadership cadre.

Clearly, at the turn of the twenty-first century, the old-fashioned cadre party, like the more "modern" mass party, has largely disappeared. The cadre parties were, so to speak, retail parties; their organizational basis, largely informal, lay in individual contacts and leading politicians' personal networks. The utility of such contacts and networks has been substantially reduced by the extension of the franchise, the rise of the mass media, rapid population growth, technological change, and so forth. Retail politics has largely given way to wholesale.

What has taken the place of Duverger's mass and cadre parties? At the risk of some simplification, it seems that there are now two dominant types of party in most western countries, though, of course, many actual parties

294

are hybrids, and traces, sometimes substantial traces, of the old mass and cadre parties remain in evidence. (The German SPD still exists and still has well over half a million members [Poguntke 1994, 203].)

The first type—the more common and more electorally successful type—is what Panebianco calls the "electoral-professional" party (1988, 264). Some electoral-professional parties have evolved from old mass parties, others from old cadre parties. The category includes the Conservative and Labour parties in Great Britain, the CDU/CSU and the SPD in Germany, all the large parties in France save the Communists, several (though not all) of the larger parties in Italy, the Liberal Democratic party in Japan and most of the major parties in countries like Canada, Australia and New Zealand. Even the parties in the United States, in so far as they exist, cleave to this general type.

The electoral-professional party, as its name implies, is concerned with winning elections. Those who lead it and work for it do, of course, have political beliefs, values, and preferences, sometimes strongly held, but the electoral-professional party is not concerned with ideology or with mass mobilization in the nineteenth-century sense. It is not a "movement" in any sense. It tends to campaign in elections on the basis of its claimed superior competence rather than on the basis of its claimed superior ideas. It will often have a large and well-equipped headquarters, but the professionals who man and woman it will bear little resemblance to the mass parties' old-fashioned apparatchiki. Staffs at the mass parties' headquarters were mainly concerned with taking minutes, servicing committees, making sure the party's rules were enforced and maintaining contact with the party branches. The new professionals are mainly concerned with fund raising, opinion polling and the development of effective communications strategies. This shift in emphasis is not merely a matter of new techniques. It reflects a changed conception of what the party is for.

The electoral-professional party finds it useful to have members, but the members are not what the party is about. The members' role is the essentially ancillary one of contributing small amounts of money to party funds, contributing even smaller amounts of time and energy during election campaigns and, not least, providing the party leaders with a modicum of democratic legitimacy (since political parties in democracies are supposed to be internally democratic). In order to keep them happy, the party leaders may even accord the members a considerable say in the making of party policy; but they are able to do so safe in the knowledge that (unlike in the old mass parties) dissident members are unlikely to rebel or to try take the party over: they are more likely simply to allow their membership to lapse.

It goes without saying, however, that such parties—Kirchheimer (1966) called them "catch-all" parties—are bound to leave at least some voters, possibly large numbers of voters, dissatisfied. Seeking to please everybody, they are bound to displease somebody. Old-fashioned socialists, or extreme libertarians, or avid tax cutters, or minority nationalities, or discontented regions or religious groups, will inevitably feel left out; and, feeling left out, they are likely to start a party of their own, possibly under a charismatic leader. Such parties are likely to be short-lived; but, if the electoral-professional parties fail to adapt, and if a new party represents a sufficiently large and cohesive body of sentiment, it may survive.

Examples of such parties abound: the National Front (FN) in France, the Greens and the various extreme-right parties in Germany, the Lega Nord and Forza Italia in Italy, the Progress party in Denmark, Democracy '66 in the Netherlands, the Referendum party in Great Britain, the New Zealand First party in that country, the Reform party in Canada, Ross Perot's party, another Reform party, in the United States—the list could be extended almost indefinitely. There is nothing remotely new about such parties, but they seem almost certain to go on putting in an appearance whenever the dominant electoral-professional parties appear to significant numbers of voters to be failing to address their grievances.

What parties of this type should be called is a more difficult question. Some of them are right-wing, some are left-wing; many are hard to place anywhere on the traditional ideological spectrum. Some of them are avidly nationalist, some are separationist. Some are benign, some are less so. It is not easy to find a term that will embrace them all. "Parties of alienation" is probably as good a term as any. Their leaders, and most of those who support them, are almost invariably alienated, sometimes deeply so, from some aspect of the existing political, social or economic order. Parties of alienation and electoral-professional parties seem certain to be the dominant party forms early in the twenty-first century just as mass and cadre parties were the dominant forms in the earlier part of the twentieth century.

Even if that analysis proves incorrect and new and unexpected party forms emerge, what does seem clear is that the political party, while its role has undoubtedly changed over recent decades, is far from being in terminal decline. As Reiter (1989, 344) says of political parties, "We should be impressed more than ever with their vitality and adaptability." It is clearly much too soon to be calling in the undertakers.

REFERENCES

Andeweg, Rudy B., and Galen A. Irwin. 1993. *Dutch Government and Politics*. Basingstoke, Hants.: Macmillan.

Budge, Ian, and Richard I. Hofferbert. 1990. "Mandates and Policy Outputs: U.S. Party Platforms and Federal Expenditures." *American Political Science Review* 84: 11-31.

Butler, David, and Gareth Butler. 1994. *British Political Facts, 1900-1994*. Basingstoke, Hants.: Macmillan.

Chittenden, Maurice, and Mark Austin. 1997. "Labour's Giant Army of Advisers Branded a Threat to Democracy." *The Sunday Times*, (November 30), 11.

Dalton, Russell J. 1996. "Political Cleavages, Issues and Electoral Change." In *Comparing Democracies: Elections and Voting in Global Perspective*, ed. Lawrence LeDuc, Richard G. Niemi, and Pippa Norris. London: Sage Publications.

Duverger, Maurice. 1954. *Political Parties: Their Organization and Activity in the Modern State*. London: Methuen.

Epstein, Leon D. 1967. *Political Parties in Western Democracies*. New York: Frederick A. Praeger.

Epstein, Leon D. 1986. *Political Parties in the American Mold*. Madison: University of Wisconsin Press.

Finer, S. E. 1984. "The Decline of Party?" In *Parties and Democracy in Britain and America*, ed. Vernon Bogdanor. New York: Praeger.

Katz, Richard S., and Peter Mair, eds. 1992. *Party Organizations: A Data Handbook on Party Organizations in Western Democracies, 1960-90*. London: Sage Publications.

Katz, Richard S., and Peter Mair. 1995. "Changing Models of Party Organization and Party Democracy: The Emergence of the Cartel Party." *Party Politics* 1: 5-27.

Kirchheimer, Otto. 1966. "The Transformation of Western European Party Systems." In *Political Parties and Political Development*, ed. Joseph LaPalombara and Myron Weiner. Princeton, N.J.: Princeton University Press.

Mair, Peter. 1994. "Party Organizations: From Civil Society to the State." In *How Parties Organize: Change and Adaptation in Party Organizations in Western Democracies*, ed. Richard S. Katz and Peter Mair. London: Sage Publications.

Panebianco, Angelo. 1988. *Political Parties: Organization and Power.* Cambridge: Cambridge University Press.

Pizzorno, Alessandro. 1981. "Interests and Parties in Pluralism." In *Organizing Interests in Western Europe: Pluralism, Corporatism, and the Transformation of Politics,* ed. Suzanne Berger. Cambridge: Cambridge University Press.

Poguntke, Thomas. 1994. "Parties in Legalistic Culture: The Case of Germany." In *How Parties Organize: Change and Adaptation in Party Organizations in Western Democracies,* ed. Richard S. Katz and Peter Mair. London: Sage Publications.

Putnam, Robert D. 1995. "Bowling Alone: America's Declining Social Capital." *Journal of Democracy* 5: 65-78.

Ranney, Austin. 1978. "The Political Parties: Reform and Decline." In *The New American Political System,* ed. Anthony King. Washington: American Enterprise Institute.

Reiter, Howard L. 1989. "Party Decline in the West: A Skeptic's View." *Journal of Theoretical Politics* 1: 325-48.

Seyd, Patrick, and Paul Whiteley. 1992. *Labour's Grassroots: The Politics of Party Membership.* Oxford: Clarendon Press.

Ware, Alan. 1996. *Political Parties and Party Systems.* Oxford: Oxford University Press.

Whiteley, Paul, Patrick Seyd, and Jeremy Richardson. 1994. *True Blues: The Politics of Conservative Party Membership.* Oxford: Clarendon Press.

CHAPTER 12

After the Triumph: What Next?

Robert A. Dahl
Yale University

In 1946, soon after I joined the Yale Department of Government and International Relations as an instructor, I became aware of a bright and winning younger colleague who seemed to know more about American politics, parties, and government than anyone I'd ever encountered.

Having spent about half my time since receiving my Ph.D. at Yale in 1940 working at the lower levels of several Washington bureaucracies and the other half engaged at even lower levels in the U.S. Army, I had been completely out of touch with the academic world, and, more important, developments in political science. This young instructor, I realized, could help me fill in the gaps as I plunged into the unfamiliar task of teaching. Fortunately for me he wore his learning lightly, often reinforcing a point—or, for that matter, just providing a moment of hilarity—by a bit of effortless and apt humor drawn from a supply of anecdotes and jokes that was, as best I could tell, endless. Profiting from his knowledge, I learned, was pure gain for me, as, I'm sure, it was for his students. To my astonishment, I learned that this young instructor was also a graduate student who was still pursuing his degree.

So began my lifelong friendship with, and my admiration for, Austin Ranney. It came as no surprise to me when he established himself as a leading scholar on American (and in due time British) parties and politics.

What neither of us could have anticipated in the years following World War II were the enormous changes the future would bring. I want to reflect briefly on two interrelated developments that bore particularly on our mutual interest in democratic theory and institutions: the global expansion of both democracy and market capitalism.[1] I'm dead certain that in 1946 I didn't foresee these changes; neither, I'd guess, did Austin. In fact, I don't know anyone who really did.

BEFORE THEIR TRIUMPH:
DEMOCRACY AND MARKET CAPITALISM ON TRIAL

To put these two epochal changes in perspective, I want to recall an aspect of the postwar years that is familiar to many of us but may be difficult for future generations to understand, much less to believe: Whether either democracy or capitalism was likely to survive in a world of competing alternatives was very much in doubt.

The Great Depression had raised serious questions as to the capacity of democratic governments and market capitalism to deal effectively with mass unemployment. Few people today may know, or even care, that the problem of unemployment in the United States was not solved by New Deal measures. It was solved by war. As late as 1939 more than one out of six persons in the civilian labor force were unemployed. What ended mass unemployment was World War II. In a kind of unintended Keynsianism, by pouring money into the economy on an unprecedented scale, defense expenditures reduced unemployment from over 17 percent in 1939 to about 10 percent in 1941. After the introduction of the draft in 1941, increasing military outlays in combination with a rapid expansion in military personnel virtually wiped out unemployment in the United States. The unemployed fell to a little less than five percent in 1942 and in 1944, when the armed forces numbered over 11 million members, to a microscopic 1.2 percent. Although some people may have mistakenly attributed the ending of unemployment to the New Deal, whether democracies could satisfactorily meet the challenge of unemployment was still not fully resolved in 1946.

---

[1]The usual term is "market economy." However, in principle a market economy might be combined with various systems of ownership and control. By "capitalism" I mean that economic enterprises are predominantly owned "privately" by shareholders who are mainly not workers in the enterprise, and are managed by executives who are nominally and legally responsible to the shareholders.

To be sure, one claim often advanced for authoritarian alternatives in the prewar years had been disproved. Unlike a disciplined dictatorship, the argument ran, a democratic country could not successfully fight a modern war. Either it would lose the war or in the process of trying to win it would become a dictatorship. Either way, democracy would be the loser. Well, by 1946, we knew that this justification for nondemocratic regimes was wrong. By 1946 the Allied victory had demonstrated that at least some democracies could fight a war, introduce a centrally directed economy to mobilize resources, gain the support of their people, win the war, dismantle their war economies, and preserve their democratic institutions intact.

Despite the Allied victory, however, in many parts of the world authoritarian alternatives continued to appeal to political, bureaucratic, technical, intellectual, and military elites—and to many ordinary people as well. Democracies, its critics said, were weak and flabby. They could not achieve social and economic justice or material progress; to attain goals like these required a highly disciplined, centralized, one-party regime. According to some influential critics, democratic politics was a corrupt and ineffectual façade used by the capitalist ruling class, joining perhaps with the military establishment, to conceal its domination. Even bourgeois culture, they contended, was little more than an elaborate ideological rationalization used to shore up ruling class domination. In their view, the whole bourgeois civilization was in inevitable decline. When it vanished, its main constituents—bourgeois (i.e., fake) democracy and bourgeois (i.e., exploitative) capitalism—would vanish with it.

If World War II had resulted in a peaceful world, critical views like these might have had less appeal. But that war was hardly over before the Cold War began. It lasted for almost a half century, interspersed with hot wars in Korea and Vietnam, and the unceasing threat of nuclear war.

Under conditions like these, could democracy survive?

THEIR TRIUMPH: THE GLOBAL EXPANSION OF DEMOCRACY AND MARKET CAPITALISM

Within half a century after the end of World War II the answer was clear. Despite some initial reversals, mainly in Latin America and Africa, democratization took off around the world; and the globalization of market capitalism was even more stunning.

By the time the new century was at hand the idea and practices of democracy had no strong global competitors in the contest for legitimacy. The appeal of the perennial alternative regimes under which most of mankind had lived since antiquity—monarchy, hereditary aristocracy, overt oligarchy—had hugely declined by the end of World War I. The twentieth-century alternatives, Fascism and Nazism, died in the ruins of World War II. Military dictatorships were discredited by their own political, economic, and sometimes (as in Argentina) military ineptitude. The appeal of Communist-led authoritarian regimes and centrally directed economies was fatally weakened by the collapse of the Soviet regime.

To be sure, nondemocratic regimes and ideologies remained, not least in China. Yet authoritarian ideologies and practices stirred little admiration beyond the borders of the countries where they prevailed, and, as with China, they were not even broadly or deeply supported among their own people. The local appeal of antidemocratic beliefs espoused by some Islamic ideologues and nationalists could gain no universal attraction.

Meanwhile, market capitalism in some form had become the dominant economic order throughout most of the globe. Even in China "market socialism" was little more than a politically useful expression for the system of market capitalism that was rapidly evolving.

So: democracy as a political regime and market capitalism as an economic order had not only survived their travails and uncertainties but in half a century they had almost conquered the globe.

AFTER THEIR TRIUMPH: WHAT NEXT?

As long as the Cold War endured we could reasonably look upon democracy as an endangered species—as it had been throughout history. We could always justify its shortcomings by considering the alternatives. The present robust condition of democracy in the world suggests to me that we should remove it from the endangered species list. If nondemocratic alternatives now present only a minimal threat to the continued existence of democracy in countries where it has been established for a half century or more—the older democracies—perhaps we shall commence a new era of vigorous democratic self-criticism and reform. The New Democratic Enlightenment of the twenty-first century would be a period in which existing democratic institutions and practices were more intensely scrutinized for their shortcomings as measured by democratic standards;

and new, well thought-out institutions and practices would significantly decrease the obvious gap between the lofty standards of an ideal democracy and actual democracy as it has been known in the twentieth century.

Perhaps. Alas, I can also imagine less hopeful possibilities.

Given our inability in 1945 to foresee the major changes of the next half-century, I hesitate to predict what may lie ahead. Instead, I would like to offer a sketch of a *possible* future that might result from the complex relation between these two triumphant systems, democracy and market capitalism. The possibility I have in mind can be laid out in three propositions.

1. *Because some features associated with market capitalism provide favorable conditions for democratic institutions, the introduction of market capitalism can be and often has been a powerful force for the democratization of nondemocratic systems.*

Market capitalism helps to create a substantial middle class, and it generates support and demands for the rule of law, subordinating the military and police to civilian control, high levels of literacy and education, a plurality of relatively independent organizations, and free access to relatively reliable information. Conditions like these are favorable for the development and stability of democratic political institutions. Thus the growth of market capitalism in a country with a nondemocratic government will, in the long run, weaken the authoritarian control of the regime and even contribute powerfully to its democratization. The relationship is reciprocal: democracies tend to evolve in countries where these favorable conditions exist, and their existence in turn favors market-capitalism. It is no accident, then, that in the late twentieth century the two systems co-existed in a great many countries.

In summary: a market economy is highly favorable to democratization at least up to the level of polyarchal democracy.[2] If and as market capitalism continues to spread to more countries, its global expansion will further increase the prospects for democratization in countries with nondemocratic regimes.

2. *However, market capitalism also generates some consequences that may have adverse effects on democracy.*

---

[2]See *Polyarchy : Participation and Opposition*, Robert A. Dahl (New Haven: Yale University Press, 1971).

To begin with, the market is a huge sphere of human activities and much of it lies beyond the effective reach of democratic controls. Indeed, if a government were to extend its reach indefinitely, it would destroy a market economy. Some of the limits on democratic controls set by a market economy are by no means entirely undesirable even from a democratic point of view. For in removing a huge area of decision making from direct intervention by the government of the state, a market economy reduces what would otherwise be intolerable burdens on government and voters alike. Moreover, in sharp contrast to a centrally directed economy, this boundary (porous and shifting though it may be) also greatly reduces the capacity of political leaders to use economic resources to strengthen and solidify their power: for example, to punish their opponents and reward their supporters.

A sphere of life that market capitalism places largely outside the zone of democratic control is the *internal* government of business firms. In more extreme forms of neo-classical doctrine and market ideology, no such internal governments exist. The relationships are abstractly interpreted as entirely voluntary and contractual. As with consumers, labor relations are simply extensions of market relations. Yet in reality, most employees of business firms exist in a subordinate relationship of power and influence that might be described as hierarchical, bureaucratic, sometimes oligarchic, even despotic—but surely neither purely voluntary nor, certainly, democratic. Given the importance of work in the lives of most people, the practices of democratic citizenship might, in comparison, appear to them to be of fairly marginal significance.

Finally, a market economy inevitably generates massive inequalities in the distribution of benefits and resources of great variety: incomes, wealth, status, prestige, information, access to influential means of communication, such as advertising, access to political elites, and so on. These are readily converted into *political* resources. Thus a market economy automatically creates an initial distribution of resources that is inimical to political equality among citizens.

From a strictly democratic point of view, an ideal economy would automatically tend to generate a fairly equal distribution of income, wealth, and many other resources that can be converted into political resources. For example, the economic order in Jefferson's ideal republic would consist predominantly of free (white) farmers who owned and mainly worked their own land and were substantially equal in wealth, education, and status. But of course the prospects for that ideal vanished as the agrarian economy was displaced with an urban commercial, financial, and industrial economy.

3. *Market capitalism, then, strongly favors democratization to the level of polyarchal democracy; but it may impose severe limits on democratization beyond that level.*

If the consequences of market capitalism are roughly as I've suggested, we might wonder whether political leaders and citizens in the established democracies will recognize these undesirable effects during the twenty-first century and undertake actions to overcome them.

The likelihood of this happening is greatly reduced, I think, by still another feature of market capitalism: the culture of consumerism that it engenders. However wrong Marx was in so many essentials of his theory—and I believe he was wrong in almost all of them—he was surely right in interpreting capitalism as a *historical* system that was accompanied by its own society and *culture*. What Marx did not foresee, however, was the incredible increase in the incomes of ordinary people—employees, workers, if you like—that market capitalism would engender. By the end of the twentieth century an overwhelming proportion of the population in the advanced capitalist countries were members of a broad and variegated "middle class," neither rich by comparison with the richest nor poor by comparison with the poorest but affluent beyond all Marx's expectations and predictions. Far from living in the misery he predicted, in the rich democratic countries most members of the "working class" lived, by historical standards, in affluence. Throughout all of recorded history only a tiny fraction of human beings had lived at comparable levels of material well being. Indeed, in some crucial respects most citizens in the advanced democratic countries were materially and physically better off than the monarchs and princes of earlier ages.

Widespread affluence helped to create, and in any case was accompanied by, an appropriate culture: the culture of consumerism. Children were socialized into the acquisitive society at ever earlier ages, beginning now in infancy. Efforts to instill them with a passion for democratic practices could scarcely compete with the energetic and skillful efforts made to socialize them into the practices and culture of consumerism. If the symbolic center of a democratic culture was the town hall or the commons, the symbolic center of the consumerist culture was the shopping mall. Where a democratic culture would help to form democratic citizens, a culture of consumerism created consumers. And the resources applied to the task of creating citizens were pitifully small in comparison with the gigantic array of resources poured into the task of creating consumers.

Would a nation of affluent consumers care much about political life? Would they be greatly concerned by the injurious consequences of market capitalism for political equality among citizens? Why should they be concerned? After all, neither in theory nor in practice does a market economy presuppose a "just" distribution of economic resources. Like power, distributive justice is theoretically irrelevant to the functioning of the market economy. From this theoretical perspective, to require an equality of "votes" in the market place would be absurd. Nor does market theory and practice have much place for a "common good" other than the optimal satisfaction of consumers' preferences.

Perhaps, then, as the culture of consumerism gains predominance and citizens are transformed more and more completely into consumers, most persons in democratic countries will come to view *the* (democratic) government (of the state) very much like they view the "government" of a firm. In this perspective, the function of all "governments," whether "public" or "private," is simply to maximize the satisfactions of individual consumers of goods and services.

People in the most economically advanced countries, then, might appreciate and support the values of liberal individualism. But they might care a good deal less about distributive justice and democratic values like political equality among citizens. As long as high levels of affluence allowed most people to satisfy their material wants as consumers in the market and the culture of consumerism prevailed, they might easily tolerate considerable inequality in the distribution of *economic* resources. And as long as their own basic rights were preserved, they might gladly tolerate a good deal of inequality in the distribution of *political* resources.

The ideal society envisioned by citizen-consumers would surely not be harshly autocratic or authoritarian. It would probably be liberal and individualist. But the ideal society of citizen-consumers might not be highly democratic.

OTHER POSSIBLE FUTURES?

Are there other possibilities?

Judged strictly from a democratic perspective, an alternative to market capitalism that would be about as efficient in producing goods and services but more favorable for producing political equality among citizens would clearly be more desirable. But the main alternatives to market capitalism offered by nineteenth- and twentieth-century theory and practice are all but dead. They are not likely to be resuscitated. Will a superior alternative develop in the twenty-first century? None seems to be at hand. If not, then market capitalist economies will continue to prevail in democratic countries, despite any adverse effects they may have on democratic goals.

Yet another possibility is worth considering. A familiar adage has it that money doesn't buy happiness. As it turns out, that assertion is supported by an impressive array of empirical evidence. To be sure, low levels of income tend to produce low levels of well-being by almost any measure, whether health, shelter, comfort, security, life expectancy, infant mortality, or self-assessed happiness. For an individual or a country, an increase beyond low levels ordinarily results in significant gains in well being. Consequently, when market capitalism enables a poor country to develop, the result is a substantial increase in human welfare. Yet once a person or a country has passed beyond a fairly modest threshold, further increments of income are not accompanied by any observable increases in well being. The older democratic countries have long since passed this threshold. Further increases in per capita income redistributed to the most highly disadvantaged persons in a country—à la Rawls' famous principles of justice—might produce a net gain in well-being. But for most persons in an affluent society, higher incomes are not likely to lead to any *lasting* gains in well-being. Like drugs, the effects of consumer indulgence tend to wear off.

Let's imagine, then, that after several more generations of affluence in the twenty-first century a gradually growing number of citizens relearn the ancient wisdom: more money doesn't buy more happiness. Let's imagine further that the number reaches a critical mass at which a fundamental shift in attitudes occurs. Unlikely as it may now appear, having lived through the huge shifts in attitudes that Austin Ranney and I have witnessed during our own lifetimes, I am unwilling to dismiss that possibility as altogether fanciful.

And if it were to occur? What would be its consequences, if any, for the future of democracy?

Well, that's another story.

AUSTIN RANNEY BIBLIOGRAPHY

I. Books

The Doctrine of Responsible Party Government (Urbana: University of Illinois Press, 1954; reprinted in 1962; reprinted by the Greenwood Press in 1982).

Democracy and the American Party System (with Willmoore Kendall) (New York: Harcourt, Brace and Company, 1956; reprinted by the Greenwood Press, 1974).

The Governing of Men (New York: Holt, Rinehart and Winston, 1958; second edition, 1966; third edition, 1971; fourth edition published by the Dryden Press, Hinsdale, Illinois 1975).

Governing: An Introduction to Political Science (New York: Holt, Rinehart and Winston, 1971; second edition, 1975; third edition, 1982; Englewood Cliffs, N.J.: Prentice Hall, Inc.: fourth edition, 1987; fifth edition, 1990; sixth edition, 1993; seventh edition, 1996).

Illinois Politics (New York: New York University Press, 1960).

Politics and Voters (with Hugh A. Bone) (New York: McGraw-Hill Book Company, Inc., 1963; second edition, 1967; third edition, 1971; fourth edition, 1975; fifth edition, 1981).

Pathways to Parliament (Madison, Wis.: University of Wisconsin Press, 1965; and London: Macmillan and Company, 1965).

Curing the Mischiefs of Faction: Party Reform in America (Berkeley, Los Angeles, and London: University of California Press, 1975).

Channels of Power: The Impact of Television on American Politics (New York: Basic Books, Inc., 1983).

Democracy in the Islands: The Micronesian Plebiscites of 1983 (with Howard R. Penniman) (Washington, D.C.: American Enterprise Institute, 1985).

II. Monographs and Short Studies

Participation in American Presidential Nominating, 1976 (Washington, D.C.: American Enterprise Institute, 1977), 37.

The Federalization of Presidential Primaries (Washington, D.C.: American Enterprise Institute, 1978), 40.

III. Books Edited

Essays in the Behavioral Study of Politics (Urbana: University of Illinois Press, 1962).

Political Science and Public Policy (Chicago: Markham Publishing Company, 1968).

The Past and Future of Presidential Debates (Washington, D.C.: American Enterprise Institute, 1978).

Referendums: A Study in Practice and Theory (with David Butler) (Washington, D.C.: American Enterprise Institute, 1978).

Eurocommunism: The Italian Case (with Giovanni Sartori) (Washington, D.C.: American Enterprise Institute, 1978).

Democracy at the Polls (with David Butler and Howard R. Penniman) (Washington, D.C.: American Enterprise Institute, 1981).

The Referendum Device (Washington, D.C.: American Enterprise Institute, 1981).

The American Constitutional System under Strong and Weak Parties (with Patricia Bonomi and James MacGregor Burns) (New York: Praeger Publishers, 1981).

The American Elections of 1980 (Washington, D.C.: American Enterprise Institute, 1981).

The American Elections of 1984 (Durham, N.C.: Duke University Press, 1985).

Britain at the Polls, 1983; A Study of the General Election (Durham, N.C.: Duke University Press, 1985).

The Mass Media in Campaign '84 (with Michael J. Robinson) (Washington, D.C.: American Enterprise Institute, 1985).

Electioneering: A Comparative Study of Continuity and Change (with David Butler) (Oxford and New York: Oxford University Press, 1992).

Referendums Around the World: The Growing Use of Direct Democracy (with David Butler) (Washington, D.C.: The AEI Press, 1994).

Courts and the Political Process: Jack W. Peltason's Contributions to Political Science (Berkeley, Calif.: Institute of Governmental Studies Press, 1996).

IV. Journal Articles and Chapters in Books

"Goodnow's Theory of Politics," *Southwestern Social Science Quarterly* 30 (March 1950): 268-76.

"Toward a More Responsible Two-Party System: A Commentary," *American Political Science Review* 45 (June 1951): 488-99.

"The Reception of Political Parties into American Political Science," *Southwestern Social Science Quarterly* 32 (November 1951): 183-91.

"The Platforms, the Parties, and the Voter," *Yale Review* 42 (September 1952): 10-20.

"'Democracy': Confusion and Agreement" (with Willmoore Kendall), *Western Political Quarterly* 4 (September 1952): 430-39.

"The American Party Systems" (with Willmoore Kendall), *American Political Science Review* 48 (June 1954): 477-85.

"Republicans and Democrats: Principles and Perversities," in Alfred J. Junz (ed.), *Present Trends in American National Government* (New York: Frederick A. Praeger, Publisher, 1960), 48-60.

"Les élections américaines de 1960," *Revue française de science politique* (June 1961): 212-21.

"The Utility and Limitations of Aggregate Data in the Study of Electoral Behavior," in Austin Ranney (ed.), *Essays on the Behavioral Study of Politics* (Urbana: University of Illinois Press, 1962), 91-102.

"Inter-Constituency Movement of British Parliamentary Candidates," *American Political Science Review* 58 (March 1964): 36-45.

"Parties in State Politics," in Herbert Jacob and Kenneth A. Vines (eds.), *Politics in the American States: A Comparative Analysis* (Boston: Little, Brown and Company, 1965; second edition, 1971; third edition, 1976), 82-121.

"The Two Electorates: Voters and Non-Voters in a Wisconsin Primary" (with Leon D. Epstein), *Journal of Politics* 27 (August 1966): 598-616.

"Candidate Selection and Party Cohesion in Britain and the United States," in William J. Crotty (ed.), *Approaches to the Study of Party Organization* (Boston: Allyn and Bacon, 1967), 139-57.

"The Representativeness of Primary Electorates," *Midwest Journal of Political Science* 12 (May 1968): 224-38.

"The Concept of 'Party'," in Oliver Garceau (ed.), *Political Research and Political Theory* (Cambridge, Mass.: Harvard University Press, 1968), 143-62.

"The Study of Policy Content: A Framework for Choice," in Austin Ranney (ed.), *Political Science and Public Policy* (Chicago: Markham Publishing Company, 1968), 3-21.

"Turnout and Representation in Presidential Primary Elections," *American Political Science Review* 66 (March 1972): 21-37.

"Working within the System: Academic Recess and College Student Participation in the 1970 Elections" (with Jack Dennis), *American Politics Quarterly* 1 (January 1973): 93-124.

"Changing the Rules of the Nominating Game," in James David Barber (ed.), *Choosing the President* (Englewood Cliffs, N.J.: Prentice-Hall, Inc., 1974), 71-94.

"Selecting the Candidates," in Howard R. Penniman (ed.), *Britain at the Polls* (Washington, D.C.: American Enterprise Institute, 1975), 33-60.

"'The Divine Science': Political Engineering in American Culture," (APSA presidential address, 1975) *American Political Science Review* 70 (March 1976): 140-48.

"The Impact of Interparty Competition Reconsidered: The Case of Florida" (with Margaret Thompson Echols), *Journal of Politics* 38 (March 1976): 142-52.

"Thirty Years of 'Psephology'," *British Journal of Political Science* 6 (April 1976): 217-30.

"The Democratic Party's Delegate Selection Reforms, 1968-76," in Allan Sindler (ed.), *America in the Seventies* (Boston: Little, Brown and Company, 1977), 160-206.

"The Political Parties: Reform and Decline," in Anthony King (ed.), *The New American Political System* (Washington, D.C.: American Enterprise Institute, 1978), 213-48.

"The United States," in David Butler and Austin Ranney (eds.), *Referendums: A Study in Practice and Theory* (Washington, D.C.: American Enterprise Institute, 1978), 67-86.

"The 1978 Congressional Elections," *Public Opinion* 1 (March/April 1978): 17-21.

"Year of the Referendum," *Public Opinion* 1 (Nov./Dec. 1978): 26-27.

Bibliography

"Candidate Selection," in David Butler, Howard R. Penniman, and Austin Ranney (eds.), *Democracy at the Polls* (Washington, D.C.: American Enterprise Institute, 1981), 75-106.

"Regulating the Referendum," in Austin Ranney (ed.), *The Referendum Device* (Washington, D.C.: American Enterprise Institute, 1981), 89-98.

"Referendums, 1980 Style," *Public Opinion* 4 (Feb./Mar. 1981): 40-41.

"British General Elections: An Introduction," in Howard R. Penniman (ed.), *Britain at the Polls, 1979: A Study of the General Election* (Washington, D.C. : American Enterprise Institute, 1981), 1-29.

"The Working Conditions of Members of Parliament and Congress: Changing the Tolls Changes the Job," in Norman J. Ornstein (ed.), *The Role of the Legislature in Western Democracies* (Washington, D.C.: American Enterprise Institute, 1981), 67-76.

"The Carter Administration," in Austin Ranney (ed.), *The American Elections of 1980* (Washington, D.C.: American Enterprise Institute, 1981), 1-36.

"The Year of the Referendum," *Public Opinion* 5 (Dec./Jan. 1983): 12-14.

"Nonvoting is Not a Social Disease," *Public Opinion* 6 (Oct./Nov. 1983): 16-19.

"The President and His Party," in Anthony King (ed.), *Both Ends of the Avenue: The Presidency, the Executive Branch, and Congress in the 1980s* (Washington, D.C.: American Enterprise Institute, 1983), 131-53.

"Parties and the Media in Britain and the U.S." (with David Butler), in Vernon Bogdanor (ed), *Parties and Democracy in Britain and America* (New York: Praeger Publishers, 1984), 213-39.

"The Micronesian Plebiscites of 1983," *Electoral Studies* 3 (August 1984): 195-99.

"What Constitutional Changes Do Americans Want?," *This Constitution* 5 (Winter 1984): 13-18; *This Constitution: Our Enduring Legacy* (Washington, D.C.: Congressional Quarterly, Inc., 1986), 277-86; reprinted in Allan J. Cigler and Burdett A. Loomis, *American Politics: Classic and Contemporary Readings* (Boston: Houghton Mifflin Company, 1989), 65-73.

"Reagan's First Term," in Austin Ranney (ed.), *The American Elections of 1984* (Washington, D.C.: American Enterprise Institute, 1985).

"Farewell to Reform—Almost," in Kay Lehman Schlozman (ed.), *Elections in America* (Boston: Allen & Unwin, Inc., 1987), 87-111.

"The Politics of Drug Regulation," *Clinical Research Practices and Drug Regulatory Affairs* 5 (Numbers 5 and 6, 1987), 287-93.

"Political Parties and Article VIII of the Constitution," in John Alphin Moore, Jr., and John E. Murphy (eds.), *A Grand Experiment: The Constitution at 200* (Wilmington, Del.: Scholarly Resources, Inc., 1987), 57-68.

"Referendums, 1978-1986" (with John Austen and David Butler), *Electoral Studies* 6 (August 1987): 139-48.

"Referendums 1988," *Public Opinion* 11 (January/February 1989): 15-17.

"Broadcasting, Narrowcasting, and Politics," in Anthony King (ed.), *New American Political System*, second edition (Washington, D.C.: The AEI Press, 1990), 175-201.

"Politics in the United States," in Gabriel A. Almond and G. Bingham Powell, Jr. (eds.), *Comparative Politics Today: A World View*, fifth edition (New York: HarperCollins Publishers, 1992), 563-601. Revised version of "Politics in the United States," in Gabriel A. Almond and G. Bingam Powell, eds., *Comparative Politics Today*, sixth edition (New York: HarperCollins Publishers, 1996), 782-824.

"Divided Party Control in the United States," in Dennis Kavanagh (ed.), *Electoral Politics* (Oxford: The Clarendon Press, 1992), 207-33.

"Nuove Pratiche e Vecchia Teoria" (tr. by Pier Vincenzo Uleri), in Mario Caciagli and Pier Vincenzo Uleri, eds., *Democrazie e Referendum* (Rome: Editori Laterza, 1994), 29-48.

"Référendum et démocratie," *Pouvoirs: Revue françaises d'Études constitutionnelles et politiques* 77 (1996): 7-19.

"The Political Science of Jack W. Peltason," in Austin Ranney (ed.), *Courts and the Political Process: Jack W. Peltason's Contributions to Political Science* (Berkeley, Calif.: Institute of Governmental Studies Press, 1996), 1-17.

CONTRIBUTORS

Lawrence Baum is Professor of Political Science, Ohio State University.

Robert A. Dahl is Sterling Professor *Emeritus* of Political Science, Yale University.

Leon D. Epstein is Bascom Professor *Emeritus* of Political Science, University of Wisconsin, Madison.

Marjorie Randon Hershey is Professor of Political Science, Indiana University.

Robert Jackman is Professor of Political Science, University of California, Davis.

Malcolm Jewell is Professor *Emeritus* of Political Science, University of Kentucky.

William Keech is Chair of Social and Decision Sciences, Carnegie Mellon University.

Anthony King is Professor of Political Science, University of Essex.

Burdett Loomis is Professor of Political Science, University of Kansas.

William Mayer is Assistant Professor of Political Science, Northeastern University.

Jack W. Peltason is President *Emeritus*, University of California, and Professor *Emeritus* of Politics and Society and Chancellor *Emeritus*, University of California, Irvine.

James Pfiffner is Professor of Political Science, George Mason University.

Nelson W. Polsby is Heller Professor of Political Science and Director, Institute of Governmental Studies, University of California, Berkeley.

Douglas Rae is Richard Ely Professor of Management and Political Science, Yale University.

Austin Ranney is Professor *Emeritus* of Political Science, University of California, Berkeley.

Raymond E. Wolfinger is Heller Professor of Political Science, University of California, Berkeley.

INDEX